EAP now!



# English for Academic Purposes

teacher's book

KATHY COX ■ DAVID HILL

PEARSON
Longman

Pearson Education Australia
Unit 4, Level 2
14 Aquatic Drive
Frenchs Forest NSW 2086

www.pearsoned.com.au



Acquisitions Editor: Andrew Brock
Project Editor: Jane Roy/Rebecca Pomponio
Copy Editor: Sonnet Editorial
Proofreader: Editing Solutions
Cover and internal design by DiZign Pty Ltd
Cover illustration by Getty Images
Typeset by DiZign Pty Ltd

Printed by Pearson Australia Demand Print Centre

1 2 3 4 5 08 07 06 05 04

National Library of Australia
Cataloguing-in-Publication Data

Cox, Kathy, 1945-.
EAP Now! : English for academic purposes.

Bibliography.
Includes index.
ISBN 1 74091 074 5.

1. English language - Foreign speakers - Problems, exercises, etc. 2. English language - Study and teaching - Australia - Foreign speakers. I. Hill, David, 1969-.

428.2407094



PEARSON
Longman

An imprint of Pearson Education Australia (a division of Pearson Australia Group Pty Ltd)

# preface—teacher's book

*EAP Now!* was created with the intention of filling what we, the authors, along with many teachers and colleagues, considered to be a world-wide gap within the available English language learning texts designed specifically for English for Academic Purposes (EAP). There are books available based upon the individual skills of academic writing, reading, listening or speaking, and currently, a few based around critical thinking, but there is no single course book that attempts to cover the varied skills necessary for success within tertiary education and offers content and task types that acknowledge the multiple intelligences of students.

We know that most of the time, both students and teachers enjoy having a course book. This is a course book of around 240 hours for teaching EAP to students aiming to study at university or college where the medium is English, and for those wishing to study in an English speaking country where Upper Intermediate and Advanced level English is required. It is also suitable for native English speakers who seek power through usage in English beyond their current understanding.

The book takes a holistic approach to learning in a tertiary environment. To that end, meaningful, varied and relevant tasks are provided which show how grammar creates meaning and how all language is used within a social context and has a social purpose. Largely, our theoretical principles are grounded upon aspects of systemic functional linguistics combined with explicit traditional grammar points. All language is presented as language within context.

As experienced teachers ourselves, we have brought to the writing of the book our understanding of the learning difficulties and cultural challenges that face students when they undertake study in a language other than their first. There are intellectual shifts that may be required as they learn new ways to present their ideas and arguments in writing and speaking contexts; question texts rather than accept them as necessarily correct; make decisions as to the importance of the World Wide Web for their study; increase their ability as independent learners or become independent learners for the first time and strive for cross-cultural understanding as well as critical cultural consciousness.

*EAP Now*! has been designed for use by both experienced and inexperienced EAP teachers. An experienced EAP teacher could supplement it with their own material, expertise and realia. Teachers with little or no experience within the EAP field will 'learn as they go'. There is a guide for teachers that precedes the majority of tasks. It includes explanations of terms and provides the rationale and suggestions for 'set ups' of lessons. Sometimes there are step-by-step guidelines.

Teaching as well as acquiring the academic skills necessary to succeed in a tertiary environment can be an arduous and complex process. Students and teachers who set out on the journey that this course book provides them will work together through that process. The acquisition of these skills is as complicated and difficult as are the various academic environments for which students are heading. We owe it to them to go through these complications, difficulties and complexities of language in order to prepare and empower them for their futures.

We believe this course book breaks new ground for EAP and we sincerely hope you enjoy using it.

**Kathy Cox**
**David Hill**

# to the teacher

## Aims and focus of *EAP Now!*

The aims of the Students' Book include providing students with ways and means to comprehend, question, evaluate and produce a range of discourses which are relevant to academic contexts. The course is designed for students to be able to examine models relevant to the tasks, then relate these models to further realia and, through the exploration of grammar, make their own necessary language choices to write and say what they themselves mean.

Briefly, the aims of the series are:

- to provide a single book which is an EAP course;
- to enable students to become familiar with, and to practise applying, English-medium academic conventions;
- to teach students to consider texts, discourses and issues in a critical light by analysing the power relations that create the purposes behind those texts;
- to provide listening and speaking skills particularly suitable to academic environments;
- to enhance students' abilities to be independent learners and to utilise the World Wide Web for their benefit;
- to facilitate a process for students so that they recognise and appreciate cultural viewpoints that may be different from their own;
- to make as smooth as possible the transition from studying in the students' own countries and languages to studying in English;
- to provide for teachers of English for Academic Purposes a Teacher's Book that will enable them to 'learn as they go', should it be required.

Each unit contains eight skills which are thematically linked. These are:

1. Writing
2. Grammar
3. Speaking
4. Listening
5. Reading
6. Critical thinking
7. English for the Internet Age
8. Learner independence and study skills.

## 1 Writing

As one would expect in EAP, writing is paramount as a skill. A great deal of work is done around essay construction and the types of essays students may be required to produce in tertiary settings. A genre approach is used and this means students will become familiar with and be able to reproduce the schema, outline and stages of essays that are recognisable in English. They will learn to differentiate an explanation from an exposition, and a description from an argument. Many writing tasks are included within the reading sections of each unit so both short and extended writing is practised. A great many models of varying text types are provided. All sources are referenced where the authors have not created them themselves.

There are tasks teaching how to avoid plagiarism and work about referencing and sourcing material. Many university lecturers complain that overseas students do not learn this feature of academia, even though it is a skill emphasised when they arrive on campus.

## 2 Grammar

We have approached the teaching and learning of grammar as language in context. As mentioned above, we have used a genre approach and believe that by providing the social and cultural situations or contexts as well as the texts themselves (outside information), students may understand how to successfully use particular genres. The aim is for students to recognise and participate in discourses by using the grammar which functions to create meaning within those discourses.

Traditional grammar terminology and some traditional grammar points (such as articles) have been included to assist students and teachers who have such a background and because these points have proven to be a recurring difficulty for many students.

## 3 Speaking

Speaking is used as a skill in discussion work in each unit. Often, discussions require critical thinking based upon readings that are provided, as well as thinking about one's own culture.

Additionally, *EAP Now!* assists students to solve problems that they may face on campus. Students learn and practise tutorial participation skills such as learning how to participate actively. Units cover research, preparation and presentation of various oral tasks required at university—oral presentation skills. Students are taught how to make academic requests to individual lecturers and institutions and to consider what an appropriate request comprises. They consider persuasion as a technique in speaking and listening contexts at university.

## 4 Listening

The listening activities are varied. The recordings are designed to motivate students to practise listening in many contexts. They include a number of accents (nine) so that students recognise and attune themselves to the fact that there are many varieties of acceptable spoken English and that they will most certainly encounter these within tertiary institutions.

There are two lengthy lectures of over a quarter of an hour, and, although a 'real' university lecture may go on for as long as three hours, the principles, the lexis, the format and the content are academic and meant to provide authentic practice in listening to a lecture and taking notes.

Unit 4, Literature, includes a listening for pleasure activity which is unconventional for course audio recordings. Students are asked to listen for the non-linguistic cues (sound effects) to complete tasks. We trust you will enjoy it.

## 5 Reading

The reading texts are designed to reflect reality and are placed in real world social contexts. To this end, it is hoped that the teacher will ask students to examine every text they read globally by asking them to consider the following: Where is this text from? When was it written? Who wrote it or might have written it? What could be their purpose for writing it? Who is the audience it is written for? What possible slant or bias is communicated within the text? This global approach prior to every reading links with critical thinking. We have covered what we believe are the most important academic reading skills.

In addition, the texts given in this book should be supplemented with longer texts and, if possible, students should visit a library so that more extensive reading can be carried out. Where possible, students should be given the opportunity to read texts in their own fields. Some tasks direct students to look in journals or other 'real' material supplied by the teacher.

## 6 Critical thinking

In our writing, we have not shied away from controversial issues. We are believers in cultural diversity and would like this book to be easily used in contexts where a wide range of differing views exist.

For students already familiar with a critical approach to texts, the critical thinking tasks provide valuable writing and speaking practice which gives them the opportunity (and sometimes forces (!) them) to explain concepts and justifications for opinions at an academic level. Students from a different academic tradition are introduced to ways of thinking and of approaching texts that they will be expected to use in their further and higher education courses.

Students are asked to consider language in the light of power relationships and to keep in mind that even as they learn the language of academia, they are learning the language of powerful institutions.

The academic culture of the students' own countries is respected and students are treated as cultural informants in discussions and tasks. We hope this book allows and encourages an additive approach—that is, that students using the *EAP Now!* course book will expand their repertoire of ways of thinking.

## 7 English for the Internet Age

Whether students presently have access to the Internet or not, the web is here to stay. We believe the future will only see its importance grow. It is included here as a resource for use in academic research and as a window to the wider world outside of the classroom. Students are provided opportunities to learn navigation around sites and terminology to assist them as they carry out projects. As well, they explore various socio-political issues. Many of the English for the Internet Age tasks may be carried out independently and they link to increasing learner independence.

### 8 Learner independence and study skills

The role of the teacher in this section is one of facilitator. Activities are created to motivate students to consider how best they learn and to work independently. In English-medium tertiary settings, a great deal of learner autonomy is expected of students. Even students who have grown up in the culture often find this a shock, and for others, the degree of independence required may fail them. The teacher could answer any questions students have before they begin and agree to 'check' work from this section.

# Implementing the activities—practical considerations

When writing a teacher's book, there is always a dilemma about where to set the balance between prescription and suggestion. We have placed the balance more towards providing suggestions. But there are clear guidelines and explanations for less experienced teachers or for those teachers who wish to develop their own EAP course using the book as a guide.

## Communicating task purpose to students

If students aren't aware or can't see clearly why they are doing something and how it relates to their future needs, they will be less motivated to do it. Therefore, we have written task headings for each task in the Students' Book. If the teacher reinforces the purpose that these express orally and/or by writing the task headings on the board, it will clarify and reinforce for students both the skill they are practising and the purpose of what they are doing.

Student task types are varied and relevant to EAP purposes. We hope that you find they are fun as well as challenging for your students.

## Evaluation

Students like to know how they are going in terms of their own progress. Tasks may be evaluated against the answers that are provided within the Teacher's Book. Additionally, peer-group evaluation and self-evaluation is included. There are checklists for writing—from paragraphs to essays and for oral presentations, both short and long. Students are encouraged to get used to positive criticism from their peers as well as from you, their teacher.

There are a couple of traditional 'tests' for students after note taking from lectures and readings. Students, in their learner independence sections, should keep records of their own progress as well as noting down their outside of class learning activities.

## Flexibility

Flexibility is important in any course, particularly at higher levels where each student's needs become more differentiated from each other's. So, we would like to emphasise that it's important to use the this book flexibly:

- Miss out activities that practise things your students are already good at or which they are unlikely to need.
- Look at suggestions in this teacher's book and decide which activities to use.
- Add your own activities or teaching points according to the needs of your students. Use other text books and realia as well.
- Jump around the book, if changing topics isn't a problem for your students.
- Focus on a particular skills section if that is the most important area for your students and you don't have the time to teach all the sections.

It is expected that exactly following the teacher's book would be a rare event. However, *EAP Now!* is an English for Academic Purposes *course*, and should you and your students have sufficient time and motivation, you could, indeed, go straight through the book, from Unit 1 through Unit 10—as that is one purpose for which it has been written.

## Timing

Time taken to complete activities will depend on factors that only a teacher who knows the class is in a position to evaluate. Such factors include the:

- level of students;
- motivation of students—generally, and for the particular topic, skill or language point concerned;
- parts of the activity that have been selected by the teacher as being appropriate for the class to do;
- length of time available for lessons—generally, the units have been designed to be covered in a total of about 25 teaching hours.

## A note about terminology

We have used the expression 'English-medium tertiary education' to cover post-high school education in countries such as Australia, Canada, Ireland, New Zealand, the UK and the USA where English is the main medium of instruction and which have many academic traditions in common. These academic traditions include such things as ways of writing and speaking (rhetorical style), methods of assessment (eg assignments, presentations or essay exams) and the concept of plagiarism.

Having said this, we acknowledge that there are variations between the academic culture of each of the traditionally native English speaker countries and also between different disciplines within the same country. Furthermore students from a country with a European academic tradition may be surprised at what they notice by working through this book about differences between their own academic culture and the culture of English-medium tertiary education.

## Exam practice

Many students using this book will be required to take exams such as IELTS, Cambridge CAE or TOEFL. Tasks which enable students to practise language useful for the IELTS test are included in a table. In addition, for other exams, teachers will be able to readily identify appropriate practice tasks. For example, most tasks appropriate for the IELTS Writing Task 2 will also be appropriate for TOEFL writing.

We sincerely wish you success in using this book and hope you enjoy your journey of learning with your students.

**Kathy Cox**
**David Hill**

# About the authors

## Kathy Cox

traces her teaching back through her maternal ancestors. Originally from and educated in the USA, she graduated from the University of Hawaii and taught first in Pago Pago, Samoa, before travelling to New Zealand, Thailand, Malaysia and Singapore, finally settling in Australia. She has taught English for Academic Purposes to many students over the years, and their learning and social experiences form the basis for this book.

Kathy's research interests in Australia have focused on students' listening skills; drama and the part it plays in enhancing language learning; academic writing; and identity. She has a keen interest in teacher professional development and, as a Director of Studies for a decade, implemented successful programs.

## David Hill

grew up in the north west of England. After studying at the University of Durham, his interest in other cultures took him around the world and eventually inspired him to become a teacher of English to speakers of other languages.

After teaching English to adults in the UK, Turkey and Japan, David settled in Australia where he now teaches and coordinates EAP and exam preparation for Australian Pacific College.

# Acknowledgements

Kathy would like to acknowledge the numerous and memorable students and colleagues from whom she has learned so much, particularly those from academic preparation programs at University of Wollongong and APC. Special appreciation goes to Murray for his ongoing love and support during the years this project took to complete.

David would also like to express his appreciation to the students, friends and colleagues with whom he has had the pleasure of working over the years, most recently at APC. He extends his special thanks to Chie, whose help, encouragement and support has been immensely valuable.

# table of contents


Preface—teacher's book iii
To the teacher v
  Aims and focus of *EAP Now!* v
  Implementing the activities—practical considerations viii
  About the authors x
  Acknowledgements x
Contents map xiv
Recording scripts reference xvi

## Unit 1 — Education 1

Speaking 2
  Discussion 2
  Academic requests 1 2
Critical thinking 3
  How do you like to learn language? 3
Listening 1 3
  Register: the new student 3
Writing 7
  Planning essays 8
  Explanations and discourse markers of time sequence 10
  Paragraph formatting 1 12
Reading 16
  Personal learning styles 16
  Identifying theme/skimming 17
  English-medium tertiary education 18
Grammar 19
  Cohesion and avoiding sentence fragments 19
Listening 2 21
  Markers which indicate main ideas: library orientation talk 21
English for the Internet Age 23
Learner independence and study skills 27
  How to use this book in and out of the classroom 27

## Unit 2 — Clan and kinship 29

Speaking 30
  Discussion: orientation to this Unit's topic 30
Reading 31
  Scanning 31
  Finding meaning from context 33
  Collocation 35
English for the Internet Age 36
  Scanning for required information and choosing appropriate links 36
Writing and Reading 37
  Argument essays and staging introductions and conclusions 37
  Essay plans 40
  Cohesion through discourse markers: addition and contrast 42
  Differentiating between main and supporting ideas 43
Critical thinking and Writing 44
  Differentiating between weak and strong evidence 44
  Providing concrete supporting evidence 45
Listening 46
  Note taking 46
  Predicting focus and listening for supporting ideas 46
Grammar 51
  Definite articles 51
Learner independence and study skills 53
  Self-correction marking code 53
Speaking and Writing 53
  Discussion and essay questions 53

## Unit 3 — Science and technology 55

Speaking 1 56
  Orientation: some issues in science and technology 56
Listening 57
  Listening for reasons: interview with a scientist 57
Writing 1 60
  Discussion essays 60
Reading and Writing 62
  Avoiding the repetition of words 62
Grammar 63
  Cohesion through discourse markers: contrast, deduction, example, addition and summation 63
English for the Internet Age 66
  Searching the World Wide Web 66
Speaking 2 67
  Interrupting, suggesting, accepting and rejecting ideas 67
Critical thinking 68

Analysis of positive and negative aspects of technology 68
Writing 2 68
Writing a discussion essay 68
Learner independence and study skills 69
How to remember for longer 69
Writing 3 69
Issues in science and technology 69

## Unit 4—Literature 71

Writing 72
Paragraph formatting 2: topic sentences 72
Methods of paragraph development: providing concrete supporting evidence 73
Creative writing 74
Grammar 75
Cause and effect: discourse markers or signals 75
Ellipsis and substitution 76
Reading 77
Writers talk about writing 77
Text types 78
Note taking from whole books 81
Listening 82
Listening for pleasure and listening for non-linguistic cues 82
Critical thinking 87
Considering writing styles 87
Speaking 88
Tutorial participation skills 1 88
Learner independence and study skills 89
Time management 89
English for the Internet Age and Critical thinking 90
Evaluating academic credibility of information on the Internet 90

## Unit 5—The news 93

Speaking 94
Oral presentation skills and oral discourse markers 94
Oral presentation assignment 96
Writing 97
Compiling bibliographies 97
Grammar 99
Pronominal referencing and participant tracking 99
Tense review: perfect tenses 100
Register revisited 104
Listening 105
Distinguishing between fact and opinion 105
Reading 109
Newspaper editorial 109
Purpose or intention of writer: indentifying bias, connotations and attempts to influence 110
Critical thinking 112
Language as power: becoming a critical reader 112
English for the Internet Age 113
Refugees: Internet research project 113
Learner independence and study skills 114
Assignment research skills 114
Vocabulary for tertiary purposes: university word lists 114

## Unit 6—A global connection: the environment 115

Speaking 1 116
What do you know about environmental issues? 116
Writing 116
Research reports 116
Writing and Speaking 118
Mini-research project 118
Learner independence and study skills 120
Reading outside class 120
Listening and Speaking 121
Listening for main purpose: tutorial questions about business and the environment 121
Tutorial participation skills 2: asking questions in tutorials 125
English for the Internet Age 126
Using university library catalogues on the net 126
Speaking 2 127
Using visual aids in presentation 127
Critical thinking 130
Distinguishing between fact and opinion 130
Grammar 1 131
Reporting verbs in citation and paraphrasing 131
Reading 132
Skimming and scanning 132
Grammar 2 133
Future predictions 133

## Unit 7—On campus 135

Speaking 1 136
Campus vocabulary 136
Listening and Speaking 1 137
Academic requests and replies 2 137
Speaking 2 142
Further oral presentation skills 142
English for the Internet Age 144
Referencing from Internet sources 144
Reading 145
Examining texts from different points of view 145
Using texts to assist in making and supporting judgments 146
Speaking and Listening 148
Giving constructive criticism 148
Critical listening and peer marking of presentations 149
Critical thinking 150
What is the purpose of education? 150

Listening and Speaking 2 151
Tutorial participation skills 3: various discussion techniques 151
Grammar 154
Hypothesising and speculating 154
Conditionals 155
Learner independence and study skills 156
Speaking outside class 156
Writing 157
Extended essay assignment 157
Writing and Speaking 158
Issues in education 158

## Unit 8—A global connection: economics 159

Reading and Writing 160
Compare and contrast essays 160
Cause and effect 165
Writing 166
Exposition schema: discussion and argument 166
Grammar 169
Nominalisation: moving towards more academic writing 169
Speaking and Listening 174
Orientation discussion about global trade 174
Listening to predict main focus, understand key points and take notes 174
Reading and Critical thinking 176
Vocabulary and scanning 176
Skimming for main ideas 182
English for the Internet Age 183
Internet research project 183
Learner independence and study skills 184
Faculty requirements within different disciplines 184

## Unit 9—Language 185

Speaking 1 186
Languages quiz and introductory discussion 186
Listening, Speaking and Critical thinking 187
Language of persuasion 187
Critical thinking: reflecting on cultural aspects of persuasion 191
Speaking: persuasion 191
Grammar 192
Articles 2 192
English for the Internet Age 193
Internet directories 193
Writing 1 194
Dissecting essay questions for meaning 194
Expositions revisited and expanded 196
Reading 199
Finding implied meaning 199
Listening 200
Listening skills: interview with a student 200
Learner independence and study skills 202
Listening outside class 202
Poster session about language learning experiences 203
Speaking 2 203
Explaining grammar features of languages other than English 203
Writing 2 205
Short answer questions 205
Writing and Speaking 205
Discussion and essay questions 205

## Unit 10—A global connection: cross-cultural communication 207

Writing 208
Genre overview 208
Grammar 210
Reviewing academic writing 210
Register 210
Nominalisation 212
Referencing 213
Modality 213
Speaking 215
Cross-cultural discussion of common beliefs and practices 215
Listening 216
Note taking from a lecture: cross-cultural communication 216
Critical thinking 223
Critical cultural consciousness: political protest 223
Reading 224
Peer review of extended essays 224
Reading and Writing 225
Precis, abstracts and introductions: reading to discover the usefulness of texts for assignments 225
Extended introductions 228
Conclusions and summaries 229
Writing and Reading 230
Interpreting and describing information from charts and graphs 230
English for the Internet Age 233
How does and will the Internet affect you, as a student? 233
Learner independence and study skills 233
End of course: friendship compliments! 233

**Appendix A—Correction Codes** 235
**Appendix B—Information gap activities** 236
**Appendix C—Assessment sheets: Oral presentations and essay** 239
**Appendix D—IELTS Grid: Preparation tasks for IELTS Academic module: Answers and Explanations** 245
**References** 252
**Index** 255

# Contents map


| Unit Number and Theme | Speaking | Writing | Grammar | Listening | Reading (skills, texts) | Critical Thinking | English for the Internet age | Learner Independence & Study Skills |
|---|---|---|---|---|---|---|---|---|
| 1 *Education* | Exploration of previous education system 2<br>Academic requests 1 2 | Planning essays 8<br>Explanations 10<br>Paragraph formatting 1 12 | Register: spoken v. written 3<br>Cohesion through discourse markers: time sequence, evidence 19<br>Avoiding sentence fragments 19 | Register: the new student 3<br>Listening for markers which indicate main ideas: library orientation talk 21 | Differentiating register/style 3<br>Personal learning styles 16<br>Identifying theme/ skimming 17<br>English-medium tertiary education 18 | How do you like to learn language: quiz 3 | Introduction to using the WWW and internet vocabulary 23 | How to use this book outside the classroom 27 |
| 2 *Clan and Kinship* | Types of families 30, 53 | Arguments 37<br>Staging introductions and conclusions 37<br>Essay plans 40<br>Providing concrete supporting evidence 45 | Cohesion through discourse markers: addition and contrast 42<br>Definite articles 51 | Listening and note taking 46<br>Predicting focus of a lecture: families 46<br>Listening for supporting evidence 46 | Scanning 31<br>Differentiating between main and supporting ideas 43<br>Finding meaning from context 33<br>Collocations 35 | Differentiating between weak and strong evidence 44 | Scanning for required information and choosing appropriate links 36 | Two stage self-correction marking code 53 |
| 3 *Science and Technology* | Issues in science and technology 56<br>Interrupting, suggesting, accepting and rejecting ideas 67 | Discussions 60, 68<br>Analysing questions: which genre? 70 | Cohesion through discourse makers: contrast, deduction, example, addition and summation 63 | Listening for reasons: interview with a scientist 57 | Avoiding repetition 62 | Analysis of positive and negative aspects of technology 68 | Searching the Internet 66 | How to remember for longer 69 |
| 4 *Literature* | Tutorial participation skills 1 88 | Paragraph formatting 2: topic sentences 72<br>Methods of development: providing concrete supporting evidence 73<br>Creative writing 74 | Cause and effect discourse markers 75<br>Ellipsis and substitution 76<br>Language features of a variety of text types 79 | Listening for pleasure and listening for non-linguistic cues: Ned Kelly 82 | Writers talk about writing 77<br>Note taking from whole books 81 | Consider writing styles of own countries 87 | Evaluating academic credibility of information on the Internet 90 | Time management 89 |

| Unit Number and Theme | Speaking | Writing | Grammar | Listening | Reading (skills, texts) | Critical Thinking | English for the Internet age | Learner Independence & Study Skills |
|---|---|---|---|---|---|---|---|---|
| **5** *The News* | Oral presentation skills and oral discourse markers 94<br>Oral presentation assignment 96 | Compiling bibliographies and avoiding plagiarism 97 | Pronominal referencing and participant tracking 99<br>Tense review: perfect tense 100<br>Register revisited 104 | Distinguishing fact and opinion: talkback radio program about fast food 105 | Newspaper editorial 109<br>Purpose or intention of writer: identifying bias 110 | Language as power: becoming a critical reader 112 | Internet research project: refugees 113 | Assignment research skills 114<br>Vocabulary for tertiary purposes: university word lists 114 |
| **6** *A Global Connection: The Environment* | Environmental issues 116<br>Tutorial Participation Skills 2: Asking questions 125<br>Using visual aids in presentations 127 | Research reports 116<br>Mini-research project 118 | Reporting verbs in citation and paraphrasing 131<br>Future predictions 133 | Listening for main purpose 121<br>Tutorial questions: business and the environment 121 | Skimming and scanning 132 | Distinguishing between fact and opinion 130 | Using library catalogues on the Internet 126 | Reading outside class 120 |
| **7** *On Campus* | Academic requests and replies 2 137<br>Further oral presentation skills 142<br>Constructive criticism 148<br>Giving an oral presentation 149<br>Tutorial participation skills 3: discussion techniques 151 | Extended essay assignment 157<br>Issues in education 158 | Hypothesising and speculating 154<br>Conditionals 155 | Academic requests and replies 2 137<br>Critical listening and peer marking of oral presentations 149 | Examining texts from different points of view 145<br>Using a text to assist in making and supporting judgments 146 | What is the purpose of education? 150 | Referencing from electronic sources 144 | Speaking outside class 156 |
| **8** *A Global Connection: Economics* | Effects of global trade 174 | Compare and contrast essays 160<br>Cause and effect 165<br>Exposition schema (argument and discussion) 166 | Nominalisation 169 | Predicting main focus: university lecture on deregulated global trade 174 | Vocabulary and scanning 176<br>Skimming for main ideas 182 | Issues around globalisation 174 | Internet research project 183 | Faculty requirements within different disciplines 184 |
| **9** *Language* | Languages quiz and discussion 186<br>Persuasion 187<br>Explaining grammar features of your own language 203 | Dissecting essay questions for meaning 194<br>Exposition revisited and expanded 196<br>Answering short answer questions 205 | Articles 192<br>Language of persuasion 137 | Language of persuasion 187<br>Interview with a student about listening skills 200 | Finding implied meaning 199 | Reflecting on cultural aspects of persuasion 191 | Internet directories 193 | Listening outside class 202<br>Language learning experiences: poster session 203 |
| **10** *A Global Connection: Cross-Cultural Communication* | Cross-cultural discussion of common beliefs and practices 215 | Genre overview 208<br>Precis, abstracts and introductions 225<br>Extended introductions 228<br>Conclusions and summaries 229<br>Describing charts and graphs 230 | Review: register 210 nominalisation 212 referencing 213<br>Modality 213 | Note taking from a lecture: cross-cultural communication 216 | Peer review of extended essays 203<br>Precis and abstract 203<br>Interpreting information from charts and graphs 230 | Critical cultural consciousness: political protest 223 | How does and will the Internet affect you, as a student? 233 | End of course friendship compliments! 233 |

# recording scripts reference

| Rec no. | Unit | Title | **Page** SB=Students' Book, TB=Teacher Book |
|---|---|---|---|
| 1 | Unit 1 | The new student | SB p.7 |
| 2 | Unit 1 | Library orientation talk | TB p.22 |
| 3 | Unit 2 | Lecture 1: Family | TB p.49 |
| 4 | Unit 2 | Lecture (intro): Cosmology | TB p.50 |
| 5 | Unit 2 | Lecture: (intro) East Asian Art | TB p.50 |
| 6 | Unit 3 | Interview with a scientist: Genetically modified food | TB p.58 |
| 7 | Unit 4 | Goin' down fighting | TB p.83 |
| 8 | Unit 5 | Talkback radio program: Fast food around the world | TB p.105 |
| 9 | Unit 6 | Tutorial: Business and the environment | TB p.123 |
| 10 | Unit 7 | Academic requests | TB p.138 |
| 11 | Unit 7 | Tutorial: Funding for education | TB p.152 |
| 12 | Unit 8 | Lecture: Economics | SB p.193 TB p.178 |
| 13 | Unit 9 | Discussion: Saving languages | TB p.187 |
| 14 | Unit 9 | Interview with a student: Listening skills | SB p.218 |
| 15 | Unit 10 | Lecture: Cross-cultural communication | TB p.219 |

unit 1

# education

Education sows
not seeds in you,
but makes your
seeds grow.

**KAHLIL GIBRAN**

**Skills focus: In this Unit, students will learn and use the following skills:**


**Speaking:** discussion; academic requests 1 2

**Critical thinking:** how do you like to learn language? 3

**Listening 1:** register—the new student 3

**Writing:** planning essays; explanations and discourse markers of time sequence; paragraph formatting 1 7

**Reading:** personal learning styles; identifying theme/skimming; English-medium tertiary education 16

**Grammar:** cohesion and avoiding sentence fragments 19

**Listening 2:** markers which indicate main ideas—library orientation talk 21

**English for the Internet Age** 23

**Learner independence and study skills:** how to use this book in and out of the classroom 27

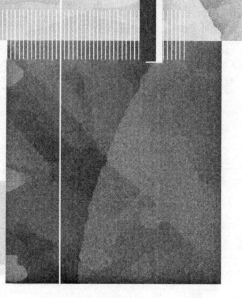

In this Unit, students will gain an overview of education as conducted in English. English-medium tertiary education is explained through the reading texts and students will be asked to consider what type of learners they themselves are and how they may adapt to a perhaps different methodology than the one to which they are accustomed. They will begin to understand a little about essays and, in particular, explanation essays, and work from paragraph level to whole texts in writing and reading. Initial concepts of cohesion and register are introduced. Additionally, they will be introduced to Internet research and net vocabulary in as amusing a way as is possible within the topic.

Students will also consider outline approaches in essay planning and discover what comprises a tutorial in Western university systems. The overall purpose of the Unit is to begin 'making seeds grow'!

# Speaking

✓ *Discussion*
✓ *Academic requests 1*

## Discussion

### Task A: Exploration of previous education system

SB P.2

Will (or Has) learning in my new educational setting be (or been) the same as learning in my home country?

Students may use this discussion to begin thinking about their own language and study methods compared with what will be expected of them in English.

The teacher may draw parallels, and contrast findings from different countries and the students' differing experiences.

## Academic requests 1

Tasks A, B and C serve the purpose of providing students with an opportunity to practise speaking in a role play where they wish to request an extension to an essay.

### Task A: Thinking about academic requests

SB P.2

- allows the students to actually think up questions in groups

### Task B: Creating a model

SB P.3

- provides a tighter model so that students may use it for both spoken and written requests

### Task C: Role play

SB P.3

- asks students to carry out the actual speaking

*The role of the teacher here is one of facilitator. Depending on your class level, you may need to provide sample sentence structures using polite forms.*

# Critical thinking

## How do you like to learn language?

SB P.4

### Task A: Quiz

In this section, students take a quiz and answer according to their own feelings.

The *purpose* of this section is to:

- acquaint students with their own style of learning, especially if they have not considered it much before;
- assist students to broaden their possible methods of learning and encourage them to diversify or experiment;
- reassure them that there is not only one way to learn successfully.

# Listening 1

## Register: the new student

The goal of this lesson is to understand register and to illustrate the importance of dialect being appropriate to register. Also, the objectives for this lesson around register are for students to:

- gain an understanding of some of the differences in speaking as opposed to writing that are one of the keys to understanding register;
- appreciate and recognise humour as a result of language;
- increase socio-cultural understanding;
- practise speaking using personal recount;
- write dialect in personal recount.

SB▷

Register involves the particular situation of a social activity with its particular participants (where, with whom, about what, how). Register occurs in all discourse (both talking and writing are discourses). Register must be appropriate. If you write to your mother, it will be a different register than if you write to an important politician in your country to complain about an injustice. (I'm assuming here, that your mother does not happen to be an important politician, but of course she could be!)

1 **RECORDING NUMBER 1 (10 MINUTES, 20 SECONDS)**

### Task A: Listening for register–appropriate speech or writing in appropriate situations

SB P.6

1 Listen to (and follow along with) the extract titled *The New Student*.

2 Answer the questions which follow.

## TEACHING idea!

It's important to teach the following informal vocabulary in order for the students to understand the humour:

stunned mullet: slow person who does not understand
tool: useless person, stupid
vegies: shortened word for vegetables
bloody: swear word
you'll know what for: you will be punished in some way
cut it out: stop doing something

In order to understand the differences in speech between the two participants, the following points should be noted:

- There are more verbs and shorter utterances by the 'chef' in the story and he uses colloquialisms.
- This is to be compared with the more formal speech of the 'student' who uses more nouns, higher vocabulary and longer sentences (quite unnecessarily, and this provides the humour in the situation as well as the misunderstanding).

### Answers

1 Did you think anything about the text was amusing?

Hopefully, the students will answer that they found the situation amusing and some of the swear words and colloquialisms silly and amusing.

2 What was amusing?

The misunderstanding between the supposed English teacher and the student. Also, the chef's anger and swear words.

3 Why do you think it was amusing?

Partly because the student is speaking in a more proper English than the 'teacher', who is really a chef.

4 What was the actual misunderstanding between the two participants in the story?

The student thought he was in an English class when he had accidentally walked into a cooking class with a nasty chef.

5 How does the language make it funny?

The register is inappropriate and that is where the humour comes from. The student is speaking far too formally for the situation and the chef, who the student thinks is an English teacher, is using colloquial language.

6 What words did you notice the student used that were very formal or very high lexis?

Obstacles, my lateness, having encountered, regretfully request, locate, receptionist, administrator, instruction room.

7 What do you think makes the student's speech inappropriate, in other words, how do you recognise that the student is using the wrong register for the situation?

The vocabulary is too high for the situation and he uses too many words to say simple things, ie there are too many 'big words' for the situation and sentences – taxis don't encounter obstacles in travelling, they run into traffic, or simply go slowly.

The student also uses phrasing like 'I am informed' and 'location of' rather than 'She told me' or 'The room was here'.

8 What words did you notice the chef using that were colloquial or simple?

The chef uses informal language and colloquialisms such as 'stunned mullet', 'tool', 'vegies', 'bloody', 'you'll know what for', 'cut it out'.

9 When people are talking at 'cross purposes', ie they don't understand one another and are not communicating, is it always funny?

No, it is not. Students should be able to relate a similar story (often about catching the wrong train or trying to order something that they cannot get the right vocabulary for).

10 Provide examples. In your group, tell one another about any incident that has occurred where you did not understand someone or where they did not understand you. Tell about any incident where you could not communicate or where a misunderstanding led you to not understanding someone else or not being understood yourself.

Students may write this story if you wish, before relating it to each other in groups. They should explain their personal misunderstanding and communication problem.

## Task B: Listening—differences between spoken and written register

SB P.9

On completion of Task A, and after discussion, use Task B to illustrate a few of the fundamental differences between spoken register and written register. If students actually write each noun and noun group and each verb and verb group from two texts, they will see the differences easily. We have used a short text (text two) found later in this Unit to demonstrate academic written as opposed to spoken register. The two texts are about the same topic, which is survey research.

***Point one***: They have almost exactly the same number of words, but the academic text has more nouns than verbs and the spoken text has more verbs than nouns. This is one feature of academic register which is easy for students to observe. When attempting academic register, they should check their own work and make sure that there are not a lot of verb groups at the expense of nouns.

***Point two***: Personals—words like I, you, we, my, people and all the personal pronouns—are features of spoken register. Academic texts have far fewer personals.

## Task C: Analysing evidence between spoken and written register

SB P.10

1 Ask students to fill in the grid in their books using Text 1 and Text 2.

2 Write each noun and noun group.

3 Write each verb and verb group.

4 Count all the words in each text.

5 Count how many nouns and verbs in each text.

SB▷

**Text 1** (61 words)

I used survey sampling when I did my first research project. It was about how many people lived in my neighbourhood and who those people were. I needed statistics in order to discover the demographics around where I lived. You can use survey sampling in a lot of disciplines and I used it because I knew it was an accepted method.

**Text 2** (58 words)

Survey sampling is a quantitative method of research which is a 20th century phenomenon with most of its growth since the 1930s. Today, it is a widely accepted method for providing statistical data on an extensive range of subjects. Disciplines such as sociology, social psychology, demography, political science, economics, education and public health all rely on sample surveys.

| | Nouns/noun groups | Verbs/verb groups |
|---|---|---|
| **Text 1**<br>61 words<br>around 9 nouns/noun groups (or participants)<br>around 12 verb groups (or processes) | survey sampling<br>first research project<br>my neighbourhood<br>how many people<br>statistics<br>the demographics<br>survey sampling<br>a lot of disciplines<br>an accepted method | used<br>did<br>was<br>lived<br>were<br>needed<br>lived<br>can use<br>used<br>knew<br>was |
| **Text 2**<br>58 words<br>around 17 nouns/noun groups (or participants)<br>around 5 verb groups (processes) | Survey sampling<br>a quantitative method of research<br>a 20th century phenomenon<br>most of its growth<br>Today<br>a widely accepted method<br>statistical data<br>an extensive range of subjects<br>Disciplines such as sociology, social psychology, demography, political science, economics, education and public health<br>sample surveys | is<br>is<br>is<br>Rely |

**2** Students could observe that although the text lengths are the same, Text 2, (the more academic text) has **double the nouns and fewer than half the verbs** of Text 1 (the non-academic text).

# Writing

SB P.11

✓ *Planning essays*
✓ *Explanations*
✓ *Paragraph formatting 1*

Students are to analyse essay questions and understand that they will have to use their own opinions (judgment) when answering essay questions.

- Students are to consider the structure and variations concerning essays in each of their own languages.
- Students will examine an explanation as a text and as a form of essay.
- The most important overview here is for students to begin to consider what essays are and what various types of essay possibilities exist in English.

## Overview for the teacher

Included in the section on planning essays are:

- explanations;
- types of essays;
- methods of development for paragraphs.

Below is a textual overview of three types of essays: explanation, argument, and exposition, to assist you.

### Explanation essay

Explanations have the schema:

**1** *General statement.*
**2** A series of *sequenced explanations.*

### Argument

Arguments must persuade the reader and have the schema:

**1** *A thesis statement* within the introduction (introduces the main idea and tells the reader what the writer's position is in regard to the topic).
**2** *Present arguments* which back up the writer's position or opinion.
**3** *Conclusion* which sums up and restates the writer's opinion.

### Exposition

An exposition is an argument—it must persuade the reader and has the schema:

**1** *A thesis statement* within the introduction (introduces the main idea and tells the reader what the writer's position is in regard to the topic).

2 *Present arguments* which back up the writer's position or opinion.

3 *Conclusion* which sums up and restates the writer's opinion and gives recommendations or judgments concerning the topic.

*Note that exposition and argument overlap and are almost the same.*

The students begin with an explanation essay schema.
*You may use this as an overhead when you get to Explanations Task D* (see Students' Book, page 16 and Teacher's Book, page 12).

**Explanation essay schema**

There are four ways to write an explanation essay. In other words, there are four ways to develop an explanation. The development methods refer to the body of the essay, as there is no variation in the introductions or conclusions. Depending upon the level of your students, you may wish to point out these different methods of development.

All essays have the obligatory introduction, body and conclusion. In an explanation, the **body** may consist of the following:

1 Steps in a linear process a → b → c → d → e.

2 Steps in a cyclical process.

3 Explanation of steps due to factors and conditions, reasons and/or effects which link all the phenomena together.

4 Two phenomena which link together and are mutually influencing a↔b.

# Planning essays

## Task A: Discussion

SB P.11

Students discuss what they think an essay is in their own country. From this discussion, they should begin to think about the structure they use in order to explain something. For example, do they have an introduction which sets out exactly what the explanation will include (as English requires)? Does it contain definitions in the introduction stage? Does it offer the explanation in a sequenced order?

## Task B: Definition of an essay

SB P.11

What is the definition of an essay in your country? Does it exist?

Number 3 is the correct answer.

Next, the students are told that the structures of various essays in English are learnable and that to learn the structures (schema) is a second strategy for essay writing.

## Task C: Three different types of essay questions

SB P.12

Students read the three essay questions:

SB▷

**1** Explain the life cycle of a butterfly.

**2** One very important issue surrounding families today is the issue of the working mother. Women should not be allowed to work until their children are at least 12 years old. Discuss.

**3** China in the 21st century is committed to strengthening exchange and cooperation with countries around the world. What are the historical and political factors which have led to this policy shift and what will be the possible economic consequences?

*The rationale for introducing three <u>different</u> types of essay questions here is one of familiarisation. Later in the book, each type will be dealt with thoroughly. At this point, they are simply introduced to differentiate an explanation from the others.*

SB▷

Students consider the definition of judgment:

What is judgment? According to the *Macquarie Dictionary* definition 4, it is 'the forming of an opinion, estimate, notion, or conclusion, as from circumstances presented to the mind'.

In other words, based upon the reading you have done when researching your essay topic, you must make a decision and form an opinion.

## Task D: Understanding key phrases

SB P.12

The words

- explain
- what are
- what will
- discuss

are important; however, the following answers should be included for the three essay questions. Some *key phrases are italicised* and what <u>students must do is underlined.</u>

SB▷

Write a brief explanation of what you think you must answer in each question:

### Answers

1 I must <u>tell about</u> *the life cycle of a butterfly.*

2 <u>I must think about</u> the question around working mothers <u>and make a decision</u> whether <u>I agree or disagree</u> with the premise: *Women should not be allowed to work until their children are at least 12 years old.* <u>I must argue</u> one way or the other. In the beginning of the body, <u>I must define</u> '*the working mother*' and tell why it is an issue.

3 There are two questions here. <u>I must research and discover others' opinions</u> as to *what political factors have led to China being committed to strengthening exchange and cooperation with countries around the world.* And what are *the historical factors* which have led to the same? Also, <u>I must explain</u> why it is *a policy shift* by explaining the previous policy. <u>I also must speculate</u> on the *possible economic consequences* for the future.

## Task E: Creating an outline

SB P.13

Student outlines or maps will vary. The Students' Book explains briefly that there are:

1 map type essay plans;

2 sequenced and numbered outlines; and

3 circles connected with arrows.

There are more plan types than this; however, these are the three most common.

**Suggestion:** After the students have completed the writing section up to the practice essay, they make a plan based upon each of the three essay questions provided in **Task C**. Students can compare their essay plans and the teacher may wish to use one or two of them as models on an overhead for the rest of the class.

# Explanations and discourse markers of time sequence

## Task A: Structure of an explanation

SB P.14

What is an explanation? What is an explanation essay?

SB▷

All language is situational. It has a social function. Explanations in writing are usually found in science or social science. They often use the simple present tense and explain things or processes in an order or sequence.

The structure for the *explanation essay* titled *What is a tutorial?* is as follows:

1 Introductory statement which lets the reader know something general about the subject.

2 A sequenced explanation. Sequencing can be temporal (time markers are used = time sequence) or participatory (the same participant is used as the theme). The steps are linear ie a → b → c → d.

***Teacher please note: You will recall that there are three other structures possible in the body of explanations*:**

- Structure two: steps in a cyclical process.
- Structure three: explanation of step due to factors and conditions, reasons and or effects which link all the phenomena together.
- Structure four: mutually influencing factors and conditions.

- Students read the *explanation of an explanation* and then they read the explanation essay titled *What is a tutorial?*
- The entire text of *What is a tutorial?* is found after Task C, on the next page of this book.
- The schema is shown beside the text *What is a tutorial?* in the Students' Book.

## Task B: Staging in introductions

SB P.15

SB▷

**1** Underline the *introductory* general statement.

**2** Double underline the *definition* found in the introduction.

**3** Triple underline the sentence that reveals the *purpose* of the writer's explanation.

### Answers

1 The initial sentence is the *introductory* sentence.
Tutorials occur in all Western university systems.

2 The second sentence is the *definition* found in the first paragraph.
The term *tutorial* derives from *tutor* which means instructor. A tutorial comprises an instructor and a group of students. It used to mean a small group of students, but today, there may be as many as 60 or 70 in a group or as few as eight or ten.

3 The *purpose* is: to explain to the reader/student what a tutorial is and how it affects the student.
So, what is a tutorial and what does it have to do with you, the student?

## Task C: Time discourse markers

SB P.15

Name as many time markers as you can think of, for example, *secondly* or *next*.

### Answers

Some examples of time markers are: before, since, as, until, meanwhile, at the moment, when, whenever, as soon as, just as.

Sequence markers are: first(ly), initially, second(ly) etc, to begin with, then, next, earlier/later, after this/that, following, afterwards, finally, lastly.

Time markers (temporal sequencers) are **bolded** in the text that follows—**first, after, while, during, following.**

**Note** that the main participants in this text are: tutorials, students and tutors.

## TITLE: What is a tutorial?

1 Tutorials occur in all Western university systems. The term *tutorial* derives from *tutor* which means instructor. A tutorial comprises an instructor and a group of students. It used to mean a small group of students, but today, there may be as many as 60 or 70 in a group or as few as eight or ten. So, what is a tutorial and what does it have to do with you, the student?

2 **First,** students attend lectures within their chosen fields of study. These lectures take place in large halls with seating for up to 300 or even a 1000 students. Students must listen carefully and take notes while the lecturer is speaking. Students do not usually interrupt the lecturer in order to clarify something they do not understand or did not hear.

3 **After** the lecture, students should review their notes and prepare for their tutorial. The tutorial will be held in the same week as the lecture, but with fewer students. The tutor or instructor will not usually be the same person who gave the lecture in the hall.

4 **While** students attend their tutorials, the tutor will point out important, relevant issues or points that were made at the lecture. They may also ask for students' input in the form of a discussion or prepared paper.

5 **During** the tutorial, a student is allowed to ask questions, to speak and indeed, at times, they are required to speak whether they are prepared or unprepared.

6 **Following** the tutorial, students will have time to prepare assignments that may have to be submitted to their lecturer and/or their tutor. You will learn more about this later in this book.

### Task D: Understanding the structure (schema) of explanation essays

SB P.16

Students could be taught the three structures for development of the body of an explanation by using the model provided in the introductory section of this Unit.

**Answers**

A Linear—6.

B Cyclical—1, 5.

C Factors and conditions, reasons and effects— 2, 3, 4.

### Task E: Writing an explanation

SB P.16

You may wish your students to work in a more structured way and give them a title for their explanation essay. You could choose that they explain the education system in their own country from primary school to university. This would follow the model of *steps in a linear process* as described in the essay *What is a Tutorial?*, pages 14–15.

## Paragraph formatting 1

There are many ways to show students how paragraphs evolve in English. Oshima and Hogue (1991) in their *Writing Academic English* books have particularly good examples with funnel diagrams to visually illustrate the nature of paragraphs.

A lot of information is given in this introduction to paragraph formatting but *EAP Now!* comes back to the topic more than once. (If there is any confusion about the *stages* turn to Unit 2, page 43 of the Students' Book for a thorough examination of introductory paragraphs and their stages in writing.) Students need to begin to understand metalanguage that you will use during the course such as 'staging'. Each paragraph in English has *staging*. This means that it follows an organised pattern of *stages*.

### TEACHING idea!

Use any paragraphs you can find or photocopy the ones from this lesson and cut them into three parts, which will be the three stages. Each topic sentence should be separate from the supporting sentences and from the concluding sentence. Get students to work in groups or pairs and place the cut up pieces in their correct order. Depending on the level of students, you could mix up the paragraphs so that they are working on content as well as form, but this would be a fairly advanced thing to do. It is often a good idea to focus on one skill at a time—in this case gaining an understanding of the format of paragraphs in terms of sequencing and function in terms of their staging.

Paper clip the sentences from each cut up paragraph together and give to groups to reassemble.

## Task A: Understanding what makes a paragraph

SB P.16

Students read the two texts—one concerning being a good learner and the other which consists of three different paragraphs. They study the table in their book.

SB

A paragraph in English is like a little essay all on its own. It has an introduction, a body and a conclusion. The introduction is the topic or initial sentence, the body is made up of sentences which provide concrete, supporting evidence of the topic or about the topic and the conclusion is the last sentence of the paragraph. Other terminology that may be clearer is **theme** for sentence 1, **support** for other sentences and **rheme** for the last. The theme is all the information up to the first verb, the support is just what it says—support (props up, verifies, holds up, gives meaning to the first sentence), and the rheme is where new information is allowed to be introduced.

So:

**1** Theme/topic sentence

**2** Support sentences

**3** Rheme/concluding sentence.

Here's a model paragraph which is at the *beginning* of an essay (thus it is the *introductory paragraph*) where a student who is studying to become an English teacher has been asked the following essay question:

**ESSAY QUESTION: Consider and evaluate Rubin and Thompson's description of the 'good language learner'.**

In the past ten or fifteen years a great deal of research has been carried out in the field of Linguistics. A significant portion of this research has held as its focus the learner and how learners actually acquire or set about to acquire language. More specifically, much of the research has been concerned with learning strategies and cognitive styles and in particular with the '... identification of learning strategy preferences with a view to isolating those characteristics of the 'good language learner' (Nunan, 1991:78).

SB▷ Examine the following table:

| | |
|---|---|
| **THEME or TOPIC SENTENCE**<br>Sentence 1<br>Also:<br>STAGE 1—A general statement (Linguistics is general) | In the past ten or fifteen years a great deal of research has been carried out in the field of Linguistics. |
| **CONCRETE SUPPORTING EVIDENCE**<br>Sentence 2<br>Also:<br>STAGE 2—More information, sometimes a definition | A significant portion of this research has held as its focus the learner and how learners actually acquire or set about to acquire language. |
| **RHEME or CONCLUDING SENTENCE**<br>Sentence 3<br>Also:<br>STAGE 3—Scope and focus of the entire essay signalling what will come next | More specifically, much of the research has been concerned with learning strategies and cognitive styles and in particular with the '... identification of learning strategy preferences with a view to isolating those characteristics of the 'good language learner' (Nunan 1991:78). |

This paragraph follows certain other rules because it is the *first or introductory paragraph* of the essay. It has stages. All introductions in English have stages. There are at least three stages to an introduction. Look at the stages outlined above.

## Task B: Identifying paragraph requirements

SB P.18

In the following three paragraphs, underline and identify:

1 the topic sentence;

2 concrete supporting sentence/s;

3 concluding sentence;

4 find stages 1, 2, and 3 if you think the paragraph is an ***introduction***;

5 if a paragraph is not an introduction, then do not identify the three stages outlined above.

### Paragraph 1

**ESSAY QUESTION: Define survey research and discuss the method.**

*Sentence 1*—the theme is *survey sampling* and it is introductory so this sentence is Stage 1, a general statement:

> Survey sampling is a quantitative method of research which is a $20^{th}$ century phenomenon with most of its growth since the 1930s.

*Sentence 2*—more information or support or definition is provided:

> Today, it is a widely accepted method for providing statistical data on an extensive range of subjects.

*Sentence 3*—the rheme is *sample surveys*, new information is the fact that the various disicplines use survey samples, but no new topic is introduced in this example:

> Disciplines such as sociology, social psychology, demography, political science, economics, education and public health all rely on sample surveys.

**Paragraph 2**

*Sentence 1*—the theme or topic sentence:

> Guling, with its curious English-style villas, has a number of beauty spots.

*Sentence 2, etc*—provides concrete evidence of the 'beauty spots' found in Guling and names what is possibly 'the best known' one:

> Perhaps the best known is the Cave of the Immortal, where the Daoist monk Lu Dongbin is said to have mastered the secret of everlasting life. The Botanical Garden is the only sub-alpine one of its kind in China.

*Sentence 3*—concludes and adds more information concerning the sights at this location. Does not have a rheme unless the general Chiang Kai-shek is talked about in the topic sentence of the next paragraph.

> Visitors can also see the former residence of Generalissimo Chiang Kai-shek.

**Paragraph 3**

**ESSAY QUESTION: Refugees seeking safe havens around the world are becoming a global issue. Discuss.**

*Sentence 1*—theme or topic is 'the biggest problem on earth'—refugees. Also, Stage 1—the sentence is a general statement to introduce the topic:

> Some twenty years ago, this writer read that in the new millenium, the biggest problem on earth would be homeless people seeking refuge.

*Sentence 2 onwards*—support for the topic that refugees constitute a problem and further explanation of what the topic means. Also, Stage 2—as a stage it is close to a definition of the problem:

> These people, it was said, would sail from port to port because their own countries were ruined as a result of pollution, war or famine. Other homeless peoples would be living in their own countries, but would have to live on the streets without shelter or employment.

*Sentence 3*—concluding sentence. Also Stage 3—it sets the focus, scope or preview of the coming essay which will have to discuss 'solutions to the growing number of refugees' and explain something about which 'growing number of countries' who are 'members of the United Nations':

Sadly, it appears that this prophecy has begun to come true as countries that are United Nations members seek solutions to the growing number of refugees from a growing number of countries.

## Task C: Writing paragraphs

SB P.19

1 Students should write at least one paragraph based on the models and compare them with each other. Criteria they have just studied should be applied when they examine the paragraphs. You can use the checklist for the students with regard to this criteria for a correct paragraph.

| Does my paragraph contain: | Yes | No |
|---|---|---|
| ■ A topic sentence? | ☐ | ☐ |
| ■ Concrete supporting sentences? | ☐ | ☐ |
| ■ A concluding sentence or sentences? | ☐ | ☐ |
| ■ Theme, support, rheme (where new ideas are presented that lead into the topic sentence of the next paragraph)? | ☐ | ☐ |

2 Students exchange paragraphs and, using their checklists, peer mark each other's writing.

# Reading

✓ *Personal learning styles*
✓ *Identifying theme/skimming*
✓ *English-medium tertiary education*

## Personal learning styles

SB P.19

There are two reading tasks.

1 Students skim the text, following instructions not to read every word and to note each topic sentence at the beginning of each of the four paragraphs.

2 Students should not be given more than two minutes.

**TITLE: Personal learning styles and learning strategies**

1 **The 5th century Greek philosopher, reformer and teacher, Socrates, used a method of questioning students as a method of teaching.** Socrates believed that 'no one is wiser than you' (Apololgy 21A). The main idea was that learners should be active participants in their learning and not trust that knowledge is learned by being a passive recipient.

2 **This ties into current theories of language learning and studies of language.** These theories maintain that users construct reality through the use of the language. Language learning is characterised by certain strategies and research has analysed the strategies of good language learners over the years.

3 **Good language learners are known to carry out a number of tasks.** They are supposed to be willing to make guesses, take risks, have a strong desire to communicate, listen to themselves speaking and monitor it, transfer one thing they have learned to new situations, and work cooperatively with teachers and other students in order to develop their language learning.

4 **One researcher, Howard Gardner (1983), suggests that individuals have at least seven different intelligences.**

# Identifying theme/skimming

## Task A: Ask a partner

SB P.20

**1** Two minutes should have been enough time if they were reading topic sentences only.

**2** Should be answered 'yes'.

**3** Two themes were:

- Socrates as a teacher
- (This) = methods of teaching language learners.

Also, what good language learners *do*.

## Task B: Write

SB P.20

**1** Make a list of the four topic sentences.

### Answers to Task B: Write 1, 2 and 3.

1 The 5th century Greek philosopher, reformer and teacher, Socrates, || used …

2 This || ties into current theories of language learning and studies of language.

3 Good language learners || are known to carry out a number of tasks.

4 One researcher, Howard Gardner (1983), || suggests that individuals have at least seven different intelligences.

## Task C: Understand what you have read

SB P.20

### Answers

Answers to the questions about the text *Personal learning styles and learning strategies.*

A: 1 True
2 False
3 True
4 True

B: All the tasks that good language learners are known to carry out:

a willing to make guesses;

b take risks;

c have a strong desire to communicate;

d listen to themselves speaking and monitor it;

e transfer one thing they have learned to new situations;

f work cooperatively with teachers and other students in order to develop their language learning.

## English-medium tertiary education

Ask the students to highlight anything that they know to be different in their own education systems, and explain the difference to their partner. You may have to do some vocabulary work which expands on the vocabulary in the text, by giving opposites and synonyms.

### Task A: Orientation to the field using prediction and skimming

SB P.21

Students are to complete Questions 1–4, in which they predict and discuss, in their groups or in pairs, similarities to and differences between their own previous experiences of education, and skim the text to find the main points.

### Task B: Writing, recognising stages

SB P.21, P.24

**Answers**

1 Underline the introductory general statement.

*Mainstream education systems in most English-speaking countries are broadly similar to each other.*

2 Underline the definition found in the introduction.

*Education in general refers to a result and is produced by instruction, training or study. It is also the process involved to obtain this result.*

3 Underline the sentence that reveals the purpose of the writer's explanation.

*This essay will explain some of the common features of typical systems in the United Kingdom, Australia and the United States and give a brief overview of the organisation of education in these countries.*

4 Highlight or underline markers of time—temporal sequencers. These are words like next, after that, finally, before, after.

Questions 5, 6 and 7 are for discussion; Students are to discuss similarities and differences between their own system and the one described in the reading and to guess (if they do not have a clear understanding) what the bibliographic entries are about. Bibliographies and referencing are tackled thoroughly in subsequent Units.

### Task C: Writing an explanation essay using your own knowledge

SB P.24

Students are to write an explanation essay outlining the education system of their own country. This could be an assessment task; the marking would include the checklist of staging, explanations and paragraph formatting.

# Grammar

## Cohesion and avoiding sentence fragments

SB P.25

Cohesion in texts comes about either through organisation of texts, grammar or lexis. An obvious way to help students create a unified or cohesive text is to begin teaching them the language signals or discourse markers which native English speakers use. Time sequencing in texts, especially in explanations and recounts, is a good place to start.

Cohesive devices or sentence connectives or discourse signals or markers – all these terms are used to describe the same thing. You need to choose what makes best sense to you and your students.

Some *temporal sequencers* (the term used in the Students' Book) are:

- *Time markers* – before, since, as, until, meanwhile, when, at the moment, as soon as, just as, when.
- *Sequence markers* – firstly, initially, secondly etc, to begin with, then, next, earlier/later, lastly, finally, afterwards, this/that, following, after this/that.
- *Sentence markers* (or discourse cues as they are sometimes referred to) serve to signal the reader or listener about new information or refer to previous information within a text. In this section, we examine time and sequence.

**TEACHING** idea!

Students may search for and circle these temporal sequencers in texts and place them in columns under the headings Time or Sequence. They need to make sense of where to use them by examining some texts.

### Task A: Examining cohesion in texts—sense or no sense

SB P.25

Task A begins by asking students to read a text which is not cohesive. It does not make sense. It concerns a boy who died from suicide.

SB

Tim's story and a couple of TV shows I have watched recently got me thinking about just what we ate. More importantly, just what are all these chemicals going to do to us? Piperohal – extensively used as a substitute for vanilla. Benzyl acetate – used to give ice cream its strawberry flavour. It is used as a nitrate solvent. Chemical additives are much less expensive than the real thing.

***Work with the students, explaining the following (as per Students' Book).***

You might almost have been fooled into thinking this paragraph makes sense because it is about the same thing which is something to do with chemicals in foods. However, it is *nonsense* because:

SB

1 Who is Tim? A writer cannot simply begin with such a specific idea (Tim's story), because the reader does not know who Tim is, nor what the story is.

2 What is Tim's story?

**3** The next sentence begins with the sentence connector, *More importantly* – more importantly than what? Than Tim's story that the reader knows nothing about? What is the reference to something important? The first important thing needs to be stated **previously** for the words *more importantly* to be used.

**4** Sentence 2 begins *more importantly* and then goes on to use *these*. What does *these* refer to? It must **refer back** and there is nothing earlier in the writing to which *these* may refer.

**5** *Piperohal – extensively used as a substitute for vanilla* is not a sentence. It needs the verb 'is' after the theme or main idea which is the chemical name, Piperohal.

**6** *Benzyl acetate* – is not a sentence. It needs the verb 'is' after the chemical name.

**7** The last sentence – *chemical additives are much less expensive than the real thing* is a statement of fact but it does not relate to the information above. It has nothing to do with Tim, and it does not explain.

## Task B: How can we make the paragraph cohesive?

SB P.26

Read the rewritten paragraph below. Underlining indicates parts that have been added.

**1** Underline all differences you find in the rewritten text.

**2** Make a list of the additional information that was needed to make it make sense.

**3** What is the topic of the paragraph now?

**4** What is Tim's story?

I recently read a story about a 13-year-old boy, named Tim, who committed suicide. Some doctors believed it was due to chemical imbalances brought about by food additives that Tim could have been allergic to. (All this information has been added so that there is an introduction with background information for the reader.)

Tim's story and a couple of TV shows I have watched recently got me thinking about just what we ate. Many foods, particularly ice cream, use chemicals. Piperohal is used extensively as a substitute for vanilla and benzyl acetate is used to give ice cream its strawberry flavour (it is used as a nitrate solvent). We eat these foods and enjoy them, but, more importantly just what are all these chemicals going to do to us? Chemical additives are much less expensive than the real thing, so I think companies are tempted to use them and will continue to do so, perhaps at the expense of our health. (By including an opinion, there is a reason for the beginning of the story which states that the writer 'has been thinking about just what we ate'.)

# Listening 2

## Markers which indicate main ideas: library orientation talk

② **RECORDING NUMBER 2: LIBRARY ORIENTATION TALK (2 MINUTES, 47 SECONDS)**

Listen to the following *University library orientation talk.*

**Task A:** Listening for signals or cues (discourse markers) which signal (point to) important ideas and features of a listening

**SB P.27**

Students use the grid provided in their books in order to listen for the different signals which indicate:

- order (sequence or time within talk)
- importance
- definitions
- conclusion.

| **Lecturer signals order/using the following phrases** | | **Lecturer signals importance (main ideas)** | | **Lecturer signals definitions** | | **Lecturer signals conclusion or end of part or whole** | |
|---|---|---|---|---|---|---|---|
| I'm here to tell you ... | ✓ | The most important thing ... | ✓ | What I mean by that is ... | ✓ | Finally... | ☐ |
| First ... | ☐ | You also need to know ... | ✓ | There are several ways to look at ... | ☐ | To sum up ... | ☐ |
| Next ... | ☐ | It's essential that ... | ✓ | For example ... | ☐ | In conclusion ... | ☐ |
| | | You certainly need to know | ✓ | | | | |
| Now ... | ✓ | There is/ there are a couple of important ... | ✓ | | | So ... | ✓ |

## Recording script

(2) RECORDING NUMBER 2 (2 MINUTES, 47 SECONDS)

**TITLE: University library orientation talk**

**Listening for markers which indicate main ideas**

Good morning students. I'm here to tell you all about our university library. Of course, everything cannot be covered today, but I will be able to tell you the main things you need to know to get started.

**The most important thing** to remember is that there are two libraries—your department library and the university library.

The university library has more general texts, and the individual department is better for older or more obscure journals.

**It is essential that** you bring your student card to both – at the main library you won't get past the turnstiles without your card. And at a department library, spot checks may be carried out at any time.

**You also need to know** how long you can borrow books for. Three weeks loan for most books, but only seven days for the popular books, for example, those books which are on a course reading list. Our university library also has a reserve collection—you may only borrow and use these resources for three hours.

**Now, about fines–you'll certainly need to know about the fining system**. It is very simple, for each day you have a book out overtime, you will pay $2.00. Yes, that's $2.00 per day and it adds up quickly. Please be sure to keep an accurate track of the books you borrow. Marks, degrees, and end of year results are not given if you have library fines.

**There are several things and people** to help you find information. There is the computer catalogue—it is also online. There are several CD ROM databases—for example, ERIC.

If you need something that isn't available in the library, **what can you do?** You can ask the librarian to arrange an inter-library loan for you. This means that the library borrows the book from another library. It costs $2.00 per book, and you can wait up to two weeks. But the library does do its best to get them quicker. Inter-library loans are only available to postgraduates and final year undergraduate students.

So, to conclude. I hope I've helped you to orientate yourself to our library system. Just ask and of our staff for assistance and good luck with your studies.

## Task B: Listening for specific information

SB P.27

**Answers**

1 How much does it cost to get an inter-library loan? $2.00.

2 What does she say is the 'most important thing to remember'? There are two libraries.

3 Why is it 'essential that' you bring your student card to the library? You will not get past the turnstiles.

4 How much is a library fine for a day? $2.00.

5 For how long can you borrow popular books? Seven days.

6 For how long can you borrow books from the reserve collection? Three hours.

7 What happens to you at the end of the year if you have library fines which are outstanding? You will not get your marks or graduate.

8 What is one of 'several things' that can help you find information? CD Rom Catalogues such as ERIC.

9 What are the names of the two libraries discussed in her talk? The university library and your department library.

10 May anyone request an inter-library book loan? No, postgraduate and final year students.

# English for the Internet Age

The *purpose* of this section is to:

- ensure that all students have the basic vocabulary necessary for work in later units on Internet research;
- provide a further example of a written explanation;
- add to awareness of register difference as taught earlier in this Unit;
- provide further practice of skimming to identify topic.

If some of your students already know the Internet vocabulary in this text, the others can be set Task B as homework.

Before students read the text, explain that there are some popular series of books known as 'Idiot's Guide to …' or '… for Dummies'. These are written for people who feel they have no knowledge of the subject they are written about. 'Dummy' and 'Mug' are both humorous, colloquial words for idiot.

A more detailed and technical explanation of the Internet than the text here can be found at http://library.albany.edu/internet/www.html

## Task A: Identifying stages in an explanation essay and skimming—further practice

SB P.28

The *purpose* of this task is to:

- provide a further example of a written explanation;
- provide further practice of skimming to identify topic.

Even though this text has a completely different register and style from the other explanation essay in this Unit, its structure is still that of an explanation.

**Answers**

1 General statement: 'The Internet is a wonderful research tool, and using it can really help you find the information you want.'

Preview/scope: 'But first, you should get to grips with the basics.'

2 i: using websites—para 6 and 7
ii: speeding things up—para 9
iii: web addresses—para 3
iv: starting—para 2
v: organisation of home pages—para 8
vi: domain names—para 4 and 5

## Task B: Reading—scanning; identifying methods of defining; Internet vocabulary

SB P.31

The *purpose* of this task is for students to:

- become familiar with some Internet vocabulary that will be useful later in the book;
- learn to identify when a word or expression is defined or explained;
- identify methods of explaining meaning or defining;
- practise scanning (this will be developed in more detail in the next Unit).

**Note:** The first purpose will be achieved almost without the students noticing, while they are focusing on the second purpose, but will be consolidated later (Question 4 of this task).

The second purpose is very useful to help students in their reading – a common cause of frustration is not recognising that a 'new' word is actually defined in the text. Also, even though the text is quite informal, some of the techniques for defining could be employed by the students in their own writing, although it's important to realise that the definition section of the introduction, dealt with in more detail in Unit 2, may use quite different language.

**1** Students may have to be shown what 'circle' and 'highlight' mean. Emphasise that during the race, words must be marked not just for the purposes of the game but also to prepare for the next task.

If students are finding it difficult, you could point out to them that the words are given in the table in roughly the same order as they occur in the text, reading across the table.

Early finishers could be asked to move on to the next task.

**2 and 3** Students can do this individually or in pairs. When finished, they should compare their answers with other students or pairs. Answers can be checked as you monitor, with any common difficulties being covered in open class. Putting the text on OHT may help with this.

**4** When giving the instructions, explain the meaning of 'technical term' – it's a useful expression!

Direct students to look at the table first, because this will assist them in completing it more quickly.

**Answers**

The middle column gives paragraph numbers.

| Grammar/expression | Para number | Example from the text |
|---|---|---|
| **word + relative pronoun + meaning** | 2 | … your web browser, which is a program that lets you view Internet pages …. |
| | 3 | … URLs, which stands for 'Uniform Resource Locaters'. |
| | 6 | hyperlinks, which are the underlined words such as the one |
| **word** … … they are **meaning** | 2 | … Internet pages … basically they are documents on the Internet |
| **word (meaning)** | 2 | icon (… it's a little picture) |
| | 5 | slash ('/') |
| **abbreviation**. This/which/that stands for **full expression** | 2 | … 'www'. This stands for World Wide Web, … |
| | 3 | … URLs, which stands for 'Uniform Resource Locaters'. |
| **word** … … It is **meaning** | 2 | … 'www'… they call it the 'web'. It is a vast collection of … |
| for example | 3 | … a web address (for example, www.bbc.co.uk) |
| **meaning** … is/are … called (a) **word** | 5 | … this name, … is often called a 'domain name', … |
| | 6 | Clicking on a link is called 'following a link' |
| **meaning** … is/are … known as **word** | 3 | … web addresses are technically known as URLs, … |
| | 8 | … use the right mouse button. Doing this is known as 'right clicking' |
| **word**, that is, **meaning** | 6 | … the 'home page', that is, main document, … |
| **full expression** … shorten(ed) to **abbreviation** | 6 | … hyperlink … shorten this to 'link' |
| **meaning** means … **word** | 6 | … 'following a link', … doing this several times means you're 'navigating' the web |
| **meaning**, or (a) **word**, | 7 | … a separate side panel, or a frame, … |

**Note:** Brackets can often be replaced by hyphens in this context.

**5** This task can be done by earlier finishers of other parts of this task, and as homework by other students, but if set for homework, make it clear to the students when they can ask you about vocabulary they don't understand. If several students have problems and there are computers available, asking them to follow the instructions in the text on a computer should help. Otherwise, a print-out of a web page could be used, and students could annotate it with the Internet vocabulary.

## Task C: Language features of informal writing

SB P.32

The *purpose* of this task is to:

- increase students' awareness of register differences;
- highlight some of the features of informal writing.

Focusing on informal writing may not only give some relief from academic work, but also enable students to know what to avoid in their formal writing.

A good way to introduce this task is before students look at it, to ask them in open class or small groups to identify features of the text that they feel are informal. Be prepared to give hints to any groups that have trouble with this.

'Register' is useful meta-language to teach at this point, unless already covered at Students' Book, page 9. It is useful to think of it as referring to the tone of the language, as well as of the situation in which the language is used. It covers such things as degree of formality and politeness. We can talk about 'an informal register', or advise students that 'removing the personal pronouns will alter the register (and it should make it more academic when combined with other features of academic writing)'.

**1** In the gaps can be put:

- 'really' and 'gibberish' (examples of informal vocabulary);
- 'bags of money' (example of an idiom);
- 'file names and folder names' instead of 'file and folder names' (example of ellipsis). There are probably more examples of these, as well as other features of informal texts.

Point out to students that formal texts may contain some of these features, but are unlikely to contain a lot, though this does depend on such things as the style of the writer and how much informality is tolerated in the institution or discipline. A useful analogy is with clothes – some organisations tolerate more informal attire than others, and different individuals have a different style, just like writing.

**2** Some suggestions are emails, informal letters, some kinds of advertising or information pamphlets where a friendly, informal impression is important, personal websites and diaries, and some fiction.

## Task D: Writing—giving meanings

SB P.33

The *purpose* of this task is for students to:

- practise writing an explanation;
- practise using some of the methods of defining and explaining found in Task B;
- depending on student need, to practise some of the features of informal writing identified in Task C.

This task could be started in class and finished for homework, or done completely for homework.

# Learner independence & study skills

## How to use this book in and out of the classroom

SB P.33

The *purpose* of this section is to:

- increase students' awareness of what is in the book
- encourage students to use the book as a reference
- encourage students to look elsewhere in the book, according to any purpose they have
- draw students' attention to other features of the book that may help them.

### TEACHING idea!

Depending on the cultures in your classroom, it's a good idea at this point to introduce a discussion about differences and similarities in approaches to study in different cultures, and to give students an insight into why learner autonomy is generally valued in English-speaking countries at the tertiary level. Some questions that may bring out this kind of discussion include:

**1** In your country, are students encouraged to make their own decisions about:

**a** how to study, and to try different methods of study?

**b** to study beyond what the teacher covers in class?

**c** to use resources such as libraries and the Internet on their own initiative?

**2** For the country in which you intend to study, what do you know about the answers to Question 1? (Feel free to ask your teacher for lots of information here!)

**3** What similarities and differences should you expect between education in your country and the country in which you intend to study? With the help of the other students in your group, make a list.

The importance of learner autonomy was mentioned in the essay earlier in this Unit (Students' Book, pages 21–24) about some Western education systems.

### Task A: What's in this book?

SB P.33

While looking for the answers to Question 2, students are likely to notice other things that appear in the table of contents, and thereby gain some idea of what they might come across later in their course.

#### Answers and comments

1 a] What sections come before Unit 1?

Preface, 'To the student', Table of contents, Contents map.

b] Read these sections. How do you think they can help you? Many books have similar sections, so it's useful to know their purpose.

Preface: gives the main points and purposes of the book.

To the students: gives more detail about each section and explains it.

2 Look at the Contents map on pages x and xi. Where will you look?

a] if you're going to write an argument essay, and aren't sure you remember all the features of one? Unit 2, page 42

b] if you've heard that Internet directories are useful, but aren't sure how exactly to use them or how to find them? Unit 9, page 208

c] if you want to listen to some tutorials to find out more about them? Unit 6, page 142

d] In this unit, you've already done some work on academic requests. In which unit will you find further practice on this? Unit 7, page 156

## Task B: Using the cross-references

SB P.34

This task helps students to use the cross-references. The bullet points at the end draw students' attention to other features of the book that they may find useful.

### Answers

a] Look at Unit 3, page 61. A cross-reference appears which says 'See Unit 2, page 43'. How can this help you?

It helps students to find similarities between what is being introduced now (in this case, discussion essays), and what they have seen previously (argument essays in this case).

b] Look at Unit 4, page 78. The cross-reference says 'See Unit 1, page 16'. How can this help you?

The section on Unit 4, page 78 is entitled *Paragraph formatting 2*. The cross-reference takes students to Paragraph formatting 1, if they need to review it.

c] Look at Unit 4, page 86. The cross-reference says 'See Unit 1, page 15; Unit 2, page 48; Unit 3, page 66'. How can this help you?

At Unit 4, page 86, discourse markers of cause and effect are introduced. The cross-reference takes them back to places where other types of discourse marker were introduced.

unit 2

# clan and kinship

Show me your mother's face;
I will tell you
who you are.

KAHLIL GIBRAN

**Skills focus: In this Unit, students will learn and use the following skills:**


**Speaking:** discussion—orientation to this Unit's topic 30

**Reading:** scanning; finding meaning from context; collocation 31

**English for the Internet Age:** scanning for required information and choosing appropriate links 36

**Writing and Reading:** argument essays and staging introductions and conclusions; essay plans; cohesion through discourse markers—addition and contrast; differentiating between main and supporting ideas 37

**Critical thinking and Writing:** differentiating between weak and strong evidence; providing concrete supporting evidence 44

**Listening:** note taking; predicting focus and listening for supporting ideas 46

**Grammar:** definite articles 51

**Learner independence and study skills:** self-correction marking code 53

**Speaking and Writing:** discussion and essay questions 53

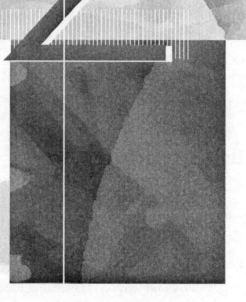

This Unit is based upon the theme of clan and kinship – that is, families and other forms of social organisation. Skills for reading are extended from the previous unit and practised in useful contexts, and new ways of dealing with vocabulary are introduced. Building on work in Unit 1, a detailed overview of argument essays, focusing first on introductions and conclusions, is included.

The work on providing supporting evidence extends the last unit's work about the structure of body paragraphs. Writing and reading skills are then transferred to lecture listening, to help students follow the main ideas and arguments presented in spoken form. The definite article becomes the grammar focus, and students are also encouraged to correct their own written mistakes, with teacher assistance, using a two-stage marking code.

# Speaking

## Discussion: orientation to this Unit's topic

The *purpose* of this section is for students to:

- relate to the theme in a personalised way;
- find out more about each other and thus further develop rapport;
- develop their knowledge of each other's cultures;
- have opportunities to learn vocabulary and ways of expressing ideas associated with the theme of this unit, from other students;
- practise giving and listening to spoken explanations.

### Task A: Orientation discussion

SB P.36

Students discuss the questions. In case some students aren't comfortable talking about their family, it's useful to pre-teach expressions such as 'I'd rather not say' or other techniques to avoid answering.

If you are teaching a monolingual class, students could still answer the questions, but try to give more reasons and to discuss any points of disagreement. Alternatively, students could do the *Variation 2* activity provided on the next page.

The commonly taught lexical item 'nuclear family' has been deliberately avoided here to reduce over-use—it is not a common word in ordinary conversation.

**Variation 1:** Other questions that can be used include the following, though the teacher should exercise judgment about which, if any, to introduce the class to, especially the latter two.

- Are there any stereotypes about family roles (for example, that mothers-in-law try to control their son's wife and that this leads to a bad relationship with her)?
- Is it normal for men and women to live together before getting married, or to live together without getting married at all? If people want to do this, are there social and legal obstacles that they have to overcome?

- Can gay and lesbian couples live together openly in your country? If so, for how long has this been possible? Do they have the same legal rights as heterosexual couples who are living together? Or as heterosexual married couples?

**Variation 2:** Write several different types of family on the board and ask students to put them in order of popularity and social acceptability for their society. Then ask the students to compare each other's lists and discuss the differences.

Some example family types are:

- grandparents, mother + father, children
- mother + father, children only
- one parent + children only
- two married adults who never have children
- grandparents + children, with the children's parents absent, perhaps working elsewhere
- parents + children + one parent's sibling + spouse + children
- adult brothers and sisters with their children, and grandparents as well
- two unmarried adults with their children
- married couple with adopted children
- a same-sex couple
- a same-sex couple with children.

# Reading

✓ *Scanning*
✓ *Finding meaning from context*
✓ *Collocation*

## Scanning

The *purpose* of this section is for students to:

- increase awareness of scanning as a reading technique;
- increase awareness of when to scan and when to skim;
- practise scanning in realistic contexts, including locating information in a book and on Internet sites.

### Task A: What is scanning and when is it useful?

SB P.37

*The purpose* of this task is for students to:

- develop their concept of scanning, first briefly introduced in Unit 1;
- contrast scanning with skimming in order to clarify the two concepts;
- practise deciding in which situations skimming is more appropriate and when scanning is more appropriate.

1 Find out if any students know about scanning already. If so, they can explain it to the other students. Otherwise you can use the explanation in the book. The task itself isn't difficult, but does serve to quickly build awareness.

**Answers**

| | skimming | scanning |
|---|---|---|
| Aim to read quickly | yes | yes |
| Know the particular word or idea you're looking for before you begin reading | no | yes |
| Read every word of the text | no | no |
| Look for main ideas | yes | no* |
| Look for specific information, such as numbers, dates or specific facts | no* | yes |
| Focus on topic sentences, summary sentences, introductions, abstracts and conclusions | yes | no |

*Although doing this may help, it is not the main thing to concentrate on when using this skill.

2 Get students to choose whether skimming or scanning is the most useful strategy in the situations given, but first highlight the difference between a table of contents and an index, ideally by showing examples.

**Answers**

| | | |
|---|---|---|
| a] | Reading the TV times pages of a newspaper to find when a particular program is on. | scanning |
| b] | Reading the contents page of a book to decide whether it covers the area you're looking for. | scanning |
| c] | Reading a book review to decide whether it's generally good, OK or bad. | skimming |
| d] | Reading a journal article to find the percentage of people who said that they believe TV violence affects children negatively. | scanning |
| e] | Reading an index to find the pages on which something called Heisenberg's uncertainty principle is mentioned. | scanning |
| f] | Reading a chapter of a book to find out whether it mentions M A K Halliday. | scanning |
| g] | Reading an article to decide whether it might contain information useful to your research project. | skimming |
| h] | Reading the blurb on the back cover of a book to find out whether it is useful for beginning students in a particular field. | skimming |

**Note**, however, that each situation could involve a little of the other skill. For example, in (a), if the TV times page has headings for morning, afternoon and evening, and you knew the program you're looking for is in the afternoon, you would skim before scanning.

## Task B: Scanning quiz

SB P.38

The *purpose* of this task is for students to:

- practise scanning in a fun way;
- gain a little more familiarity with this book;
- use competition as an incentive not to read every word.

The second purpose is useful because many students find it difficult not to use strategies that they feel safer with, such as reading every word consecutively.

Students will scan various parts of this course book to find the answers to the questions. By doing this as a race, students are forced to scan. Don't let them start until you say 'go'. It's best not to direct them to the table of contents – they'll remember much better how useful this is if they work it out for themselves!

**Answers**

1 If you want to focus on skills for dealing with vocabulary, which section of this Unit will be particularly relevant? The reading section.

2 Imagine your teacher has just given you back some homework with symbols written on it. He tells the class that this is a 'self-correction marking code'. In which section of this unit is a self-correction marking code explained? *The Learner independence and study skills* section.

3 Where in the book (near the back) is this code given? Appendix A.

4 If you enjoy fiction, which Unit of this book will be especially interesting for you? Unit 4—*Literature.*

5 In which Unit is Tutorial Participation Skills I covered? Unit 4.

6 Which other units also cover tutorial participation skills? Units 6 and 7.

7 In Unit 3, what kind of essays are covered? Discussion.

8 In Unit 3, which essay is about genetically modified food? The first.

9 In the essay starting on page 39, which paragraph mentions the proportion of older people in the population? The fourth.

10 Which paragraph of the same essay mentions social interaction? The third.

# Finding meaning from context

The *purpose* of this section is for students to:

- improve their ability to deal with unknown vocabulary when reading by using context to find meaning;
- provide further practice in scanning.

## Task A: Scanning race

SB P.38

The *purpose* of this task is for students to:

- practise finding meaning from context;
- improve confidence in their ability to find meaning from context.

**1** The opportunity is taken here for more scanning practice in which students find the words that they will work on later in the task. After you say 'go', the first students to find in the text (Students' Book, page 39, *Social benefits of extended families*) the words from the table are the winners.

It's essential that students, including early finishers, do not look up the words in their dictionaries, because the next task focuses on finding their meaning from context. If you have a heavily dictionary-dependent class, you may need to make them bring their dictionaries to the front of the class.

Early finishers can read the text again more carefully, thinking about its structure.

## Task B: Finding meaning from context

SB P.40

The *purpose* of this task is for students to:

- develop new insights into techniques for finding meaning from context;
- develop their awareness of the benefits of finding meaning from context.

**1** Put the sentence in the Students' Book on the board and elicit the meaning of 'putongsway'. 'Putongsway' is a nonsense word, but its intended meaning (a kind of winter hat) is clear from this context.

Before referring to the table, emphasise to the students that the technique they have just used is to find meaning from context. It should also be emphasised that **the point of this technique is not to learn the vocabulary but to help understand meaning.**

If your class has a particularly high level of vocabulary knowledge and would know most of the words in Task A, choose a more difficult text.

**2 and 3** Put students in pairs of similar level. Ask them to explain the meanings of any words in the list that they know, and then find the meaning of the other words using the context of the text.

### Answers

| | | |
|---|---|---|
| 1 | albeit | though (introduces an opposite idea) |
| 2 | trend | a general change in a number over time – up or down |
| 3 | a burden | a problem, hard work |
| 4 | supplemented | added |
| 5 | demography / -ic | sizes populations of different age groups etc. |
| 6 | attuned to | familiar with |
| 7 | gain | get, obtain, receive |
| 8 | rather than | instead of (separates two alternative ideas) |
| 9 | sustained | kept over time |
| 10 | numerous | a large number of; many |
| 11 | mutual | shared, affecting both |
| 12 | prevent | stop |

Ideally, students should practise working out their own meanings from context rather than choosing the best meaning given to them, as in this task. One way to encourage this is as follows:

In any future reading, when a student asks the meaning of a word, don't give the meaning straight away. Instead, direct them first to contextual clues that may help to show the meaning. The meaning can be given later to confirm the finding and to help improve confidence in the technique.

It's important that students practise this technique constantly!

**4** Here, students analyse how they found the meanings from the context. This conscious thinking process should make it clearer to the students how to go about finding meaning from context, and give confidence that this technique works and isn't 'just guessing'.

Some suggestions:

- Comparing the unknown word with words with similar pronunciation or spelling sometimes helps—for example, 'numerous'.
- Words like 'demographic' in para 1 and 'mutual' are best understood after reading the whole text.
- Sometimes the meaning is better expressed by the relationship it shows between other ideas (eg 'albeit' and 'rather than').

## Collocation

The *purpose* of this section is to:

- introduce the concept of collocation for students who haven't come across it previously;
- develop an awareness of and sensitivity to collocation;
- give practice of using new vocabulary in speaking;
- encourage students to practise new vocabulary in the future.

### Task A: Vocabulary—collocation

SB P.41

Ask the students whether 'attuned' in the first essay can be replaced with 'familiar'. The answer is explained in the Students' Book.

Definitions of collocation include: 'Collocations are those combinations of words which occur with more than random frequency' (Lewis, 1997: 25) and 'it is a marriage contract between words' (McCarthy, 1990: 12). McCarthy in the same work cites a good illustrative example: It's possible to say 'blond hair' ... but could you imagine someone saying 'blond car'? Likewise, 'beige car' is possible, but 'beige hair' would sound very strange to a native English speaker. Both books, together with Lewis (1993), provide excellent explanations of the importance of collocation for language learning.

Once students understand what collocation is, ask them to cross out the expressions from the table that don't collocate.

#### Answers

1 considerable advantages
~~considerable good points~~
considerable benefits

2 members of the family
~~members of the company~~
members of the group

3 high quality
top quality
~~large quality~~

4 have contact with
~~do contact with~~
make contact with

5 birth rates
~~marriage rates~~
divorce rates

6 ~~friend support~~
government support
family support

### Task B: Vocabulary extension and discussion

SB P.41

The *purpose* of this task is for students to:

- extend vocabulary knowledge by applying it to other situations;
- do this in a personalised way in order to increase retention and keep it relevant to them;
- consider using these techniques on future texts (learner independence);
- have the opportunity to react to the ideas in the essay.

Students discuss answers to the questions. Before they start, put some useful collocations on the board to help your students. For example, 'upward/downward trend' and 'a significant trend'. Answers will vary.

To check whether something collocates, students could ask almost any native speaker whether an expression sounds natural.

# English for the Internet Age

## Scanning for required information and choosing appropriate links

### Task A: Choosing links by scanning

SB P.42

The *purpose* of this task is:

- for students to practise finding information quickly on English-medium Internet sites;
- to provide further practice of scanning in a realistic context;
- to increase awareness of the kind of tertiary study-related information available on the Internet;
- for students to practise spoken negotiation.

This activity has to be done in a computer room. Students must race to navigate web pages to locate the information given. Using the computers in pairs encourages spoken interaction in English and is an integral part of this activity as students will then have the opportunity to negotiate about what action to take. The winning pair is the first to obtain answers to all questions.

**Answers**

Answers will vary.

**Variation:** If possible, it's a good idea to replace these questions with some for the cities in which your students are going to study in future.

# Writing and Reading

✓ *Argument essays and staging introductions and conclusions*
✓ *Essay plans*
✓ *Cohesion through discourse markers: addition and contrast*
✓ *Differentiating between main and supporting ideas*

## Argument essays and staging introductions and conclusions

The *purpose* of this section is for students to:

- find out the purpose and use of argument essays;
- learn to identify and write the stages in an argument essay;
- practise writing argument essays, with a focus on staging the introductions and conclusions.

### Task A: Prediction to help comprehension

SB P.42

The *purpose* of this task is for students to practise *prediction* as an aid to comprehension.

In Task B, students will read an essay expressing the opposite opinion to that in the *Social benefits of extended families* essay (Students' Book, page 39). To prepare for this, they are given a chance to re-read the *Social benefits of extended families* essay, to focus on the ideas in it, and then predict the content of the next essay based upon the title.

Predictions should made in small groups or pairs.

### Task B: Stages of an argument essay

SB P.43

The *purpose* of this task is for students to:

- find out the purpose of argument essays;
- find out how argument essays are generally organised, and the names and purposes of each stage;
- to practise identifying the stages in an argument essay, thereby:
  - to increase their understanding of these stages in preparation for their own writing.

This section includes all stages of an argument essay, but gives more detail about introductions and conclusions. Stages of paragraphs are covered in Unit 1.

1 Students examine a chart giving the stages in an argument.

2 They read an essay (the one they made predictions about in Task A), looking at the marked stages.

3 They go back to the essay on page 39 of the Students' Book and mark the argument essay stages.

### Suggested answer for step 3 of this task

## TITLE: Social benefits of extended families

*General statement* · *Thesis statement* · *Preview/ Scope* · *(introduction)*

1 A major social trend in many countries has been for elderly people to live increasingly by themselves rather than with their children. Often they have pride in remaining independent and don't want to feel a burden on their families. However, there would be considerable advantages for society if more elderly people lived with their adult children rather than alone or in nursing homes. Clearly this wouldn't work in every case, but reasons include mutual benefit for all members of the family, and the fact that this can help society cope with the massive demographic changes predicted for the future.

*(body)*

*Argument 1's topic sentence* · *Concrete supporting evidence for Argument 1* · *Further concrete supporting evidence for Argument 1*

2 All generations gain benefit from living in extended families. Most grandparents and great-grandparents enjoy spending time with their grandchildren – it is common to hear them say that having children around makes them feel younger. In addition, for parents, it is cheaper when children are looked after by their older relatives than in child care centres.

*Second topic sentence also supporting Argument 1* · *Links to thesis and further information to topic sentence* · *Four items of concrete supporting evidence for Topic Statement (Argument 1)* · *Optional demonstration that opposite viewpoint to topic sentence has also been considered*

3 Benefits for the children are numerous, and clearly what is good for them is good for the whole family. Family care is likely to be of higher quality than at a child care centre for many reasons. It will be better attuned to the children's needs because the family members know them better and because there are fewer children to look after in a family home than in a child care centre. Further, families generally have greater emotional involvement in the child's development than people looking after the child as a job. It's also an advantage that this kind of care can strengthen family bonds due to the increased contact that family members have with each other. The experience that grandparents and great-grandparents bring to child-rearing, from the years of raising their own children, is an additional reason. However, it must be remembered that care centres have staff with professional training which family members rarely get the opportunity to gain, and they also provide opportunities for social interaction with other children beyond those available in the family home. Child care facilities thus do have a place in children's upbringing, but their use must be balanced against the advantages of home care.

*Argument 2's topic sentence* · *Concrete supporting evidence (step-by-step explanation) for Argument 2*

4 A further benefit to society results from expected changes in the demography of almost every country. As health care improves, people are living longer lives. Also, in most developed countries, birth rates are decreasing. Both these trends serve to increase the proportion of older people in the population, and decrease the future proportion of working age people. The result is that government services, such as subsidised health care and nursing homes, cannot be sustained at the same level into the future. Therefore, other ways of looking after

the elderly must be considered, for example, families looking after their own elderly parents. This must be supplemented, however, with some government support, albeit reduced from the present level, to prevent people having to leave jobs or reduce their working hours to look after elderly relatives.

conclusion

Summary → 5 In summary, the benefits of encouraging more elderly people to live with their children or grandchildren are considerable and, overall, provide advantages for all members of the family and offer a way to deal with demographic shifts. However, some level of support services would still be necessary in many cases. Therefore, the elderly should be encouraged, where reasonable, to move in with their children while welfare services should be tailored to support this. ← Recommendation

## Task C: Useful expressions for preview/scope (in introductions) and summary stages of essays

SB P.45

The *purpose* of this task is to:

- expose students to real materials;
- relate their recent learning to these materials;
- practise identifying stages in introductions and conclusions.

These stages have been chosen because they have quite specific language, and because they appear in a variety of genres that may be found in journals. This task provides a great opportunity for students to be exposed to authentic materials. Often students are unfamiliar with the concept of academic journals, so this task provides a good opportunity for an introduction to these.

Students should be given real journals (if you don't have access to subject-specific journals, then English teaching journals, kept in most institutions for teachers' reference, can be used). They should look at articles, find the preview/scope and summary and note the expressions used. These stages will not always be clear (or present!) in all articles (but they are in most) but discovering this is part of their learning experience.

**Variation:** This would be a good activity to do on a trip to a library, either as a class trip or as a homework assignment. Be careful though if setting this as a homework assignment – students who aren't familiar with academic journals would not be able to find them by themselves.

If journals can't be found, here are some expressions that may be useful.

| Preview/scope expressions | Expressions to begin conclusions |
|---|---|
| ■ This essay will look at/examine/ advocate/consider/discuss/suggest/... | ■ In summary/conclusion |
| ■ Here, ... will be examined/considered/ discussed/suggested/ | ■ To sum up/summarise/conclude |
| ■ Evidence for ... includes ... | |
| ■ In order to demonstrate this [=the thesis], ... and ... will be examined | ■ Overall, |
| ■ This essay will limit itself to (consideration of) .../concentrate on/focus on/. | ■ From these points, it is clear that ... |

## Task D: Speaking—brainstorming as preparation for writing

SB P.46

The *purpose* of this task is:

- for students to prepare and share their ideas before writing argument essays;
- to emphasise the usefulness of brainstorming.
- to provide a break from reading and writing!

Refer students to the learning tip. Then ask them to look at the essay questions, decide their own opinions and then discuss their opinions with other students. Be prepared for this discussion to continue for a while—a chance for a good chat will probably be appreciated after the hard work they've done so far!

## Task E: Writing an argument essay

SB P.46

The *purpose* of this task is for students to practise writing argument essays, with a focus on introductions and conclusions.

Depending on your teaching context, controversial questions such as the following may be more motivational:

- Same-sex marriage should/shouldn't be allowed.
- Adoption by same-sex couples should/shouldn't be allowed.

Students should begin writing in class the answers to the questions they discussed in Task D, while you monitor carefully. When it is clear that everyone's writing is heading in the right direction, they could be asked to finish the task for homework.

# Essay plans

The *purpose* of this section is for students to:

- expand their repertoire of, and practise using, discourse markers of addition and contrast;
- practise differentiating in reading between main and supporting ideas, and between different items of support, using discourse markers to help;
- learn how to write one form of essay plan;

- critically evaluate supporting evidence;
- write body paragraphs that include the ideas focused on in this section.

## Task A: Writing essay plans

SB P.46

The *purpose* of this task is for students to:

- learn one way to write an essay plan;
- perceive the usefulness of essay plans;
- discover that discourse markers show the relationship between the ideas in a paragraph.

1 Put the essay plan diagram from the Students' Book on the board or OHT, and see if the students can work out the significance of the indenting. Ask students to read the gapped essay plan in conjunction with the *Social benefits* essay to see the connection between the ideas in the text and the plan. When they can all see this connection, ask them for their opinions about the usefulness of essay plans, and refer them to the *Learning Tip* in the Students' Book on page 47. Then tell them to put the expressions from below the plan into the gaps.

**Answer**

- Thesis: extended families – beneficial
  - benefits all generations
    - g/parents enjoy g/kids
    - cheaper child care for parents
    - children benefit: ↑ quality care
      - better attuned:
        - family knows child well
        - fewer children
      - ↑ emotional involvement
      - strengthen family bonds
      - experience of g/parents
      - but advs of care centres
        - professional training
        - social interaction
        - ⇒ use them sometimes
  - demographic change
    - longer lives + birth rate ↓: ⇒ proportion of old people ↑ & working age people ↓
    - ⇒ services for old people: future problems
    - ⇒ extended families: solve this problem
    - but: some government support: keep people employed

2 Ask students what kind of words they can see between the main and supporting ideas, and between each supporting idea. The answer is *discourse markers*, introduced in Unit 1, page 15, Students' Book.

There are also other discourse markers in the essay which haven't been mentioned. They have different purposes, for example, to show consequence, or to indicate examples (these will be covered later in the book), but again, they mostly follow the pattern of separating ideas.

## Cohesion through discourse markers: addition and contrast

### Task A: Cohesion through discourse markers

SB P.48

The *purpose* of this task is for students to:

- practise identifying and differentiating between discourse markers of addition and contrast;
- learn new discourse markers of addition and contrast.

The boxed comment in the Students' Book is the conclusion that students drew from the previous task. After focusing on this, students should look for discourse markers in the two essays they have read in this Unit and insert them in the table. They can then add others to the table, perhaps from each other. If they can't think of many, put the ones from below randomly on the board. Seeing them may jog their minds to remembering their function.

**Variation:** If time is short, instead of having the students read the essays again, you could write all the markers from the answers randomly on the board. The students, in pairs or groups, would then place them in the correct column in the table in their books.

**Answers**

| Addition | Contrast |
|---|---|
| *Social benefits* essay<br>■ … and …<br>■ In addition, …<br>■ Further, …<br>■ Also, … / … also …<br>■ … additional …<br>■ Both … | ■ However, …<br>■ … but …<br>■ …, albeit … |
| *Dangerous policy* essay<br>■ … not only … but also …<br>■ The first …<br>■ (When …)<br>■ Secondly …<br>■ (In other cases …) | ■ Though …, … |
| *Not in the two essays*<br>■ Furthermore, …<br>■ Moreover, …<br>■ … as well as …<br>■ Besides …, … | ■ On the other hand, …<br>■ In contrast, …<br>■ On the contrary, …<br>■ Conversely, …<br>■ …, although…<br>■ …, though …<br>■ While ….., ……<br>■ …, whereas …<br>■ In spite of …,<br>■ Despite …, |

**Notes**

- Capital letters are used in the table to indicate words that can begin sentences.
- 'When' is an interesting case – it isn't normally used as a discourse marker of addition.
- 'In other cases ...' could be used to introduce a contrasting idea if it is followed by a contrast marker such as 'however'.
- The way that 'Though' is used here is a little different from the other words. The other discourse markers relate an idea before the word with the idea after it. 'Though' in this essay shows the relationship between the two ideas after it.

# Differentiating between main and supporting ideas

## Task A: Differentiating between main and supporting ideas

SB P.48

The *purpose* of this task is to practise differentiating between main and supporting ideas by writing an essay plan.

Students write an essay plan from the second essay they read, *Family Responsibility*, using the discourse markers to help them.

### Suggested answer

- Thesis: Encouraging extended family households: problems
  - elderly people reluctant
    - want independence
      - freedom
      - don't want to fit lives around others
      - in family, lose control of their lives
    - proud to look after themselves/shame otherwise
    - leave parents & friends? Other town?
  - takes time to look after them ⟹ take time out from work
    - lose income + self respect
    - career gap ⟹ loss of opportunity
  - younger generation also lose independence
    - stifling
    - against nature
    - may learn from g/parents' experience, but personal growth ↓
  - some can't live in extended family
    - eg children overseas, argument, no children
    - government must support

# Critical thinking and Writing

✓ *Differentiating between weak and strong evidence*
✓ *Providing concrete supporting evidence*

## Differentiating between weak and strong evidence

### Task A: Critical thinking—what constitutes strong/weak evidence?

SB P.49

The *purpose* of this task is for students to:

- critically analyse whether evidence is weak or strong;
- discover some traps to avoid when writing their own supporting evidence.

Students look at the text extracts, and underline the evidence in each. When answers have been checked, they decide how strong they feel the evidence is, then discuss the reasons for their decisions in pairs or small groups. In the last part, they try to articulate some of the traps that students commonly fall into.

If students have difficulty with the second and third points, hints that could help are:

- Is the main point general or specific? How about the support?
- Where did the evidence come from? Do we know?
- Could there be bias? That is, does the writer of the evidence have a special reason, perhaps financial, in persuading people to a particular opinion?

#### Answers

1 Another reason that women are better than men at raising children is that they are kinder. My mother was a good example. She did many kind things not only for me but also for many other people she met, including strangers.

2 Living costs are also increasing in the area of housing affordability. In a recent survey, 68% of people said that they found it more difficult to pay their rent or housing loan than last year.

3 The decline in the fertility rate is a further reason that immigration will become more and more important. According to Weston (2001), the fertility rate in this country has fallen from 3.5 live births per woman in 1961 to its lowest level ever, 1.8 babies per woman, in 1999 and 2000. This trend looks set to continue into the future. Weston (Ibid.) also states that the minimum fertility rate necessary to sustain a population at a constant level is 2.1 births per female. Therefore, unless this trend reverses, immigration is necessary to sustain the population.

4 No evidence has yet been found of a direct link between this particular product and heart disease or other illnesses. Therefore, we would conclude that it is perfectly safe for people of all ages to take it.

5 It appears for the moment that there is unlikely to be a connection between eating this product and ability to concentrate. Despite extensive research focused on investigating this link, such as Crumlin (1996), Detford (2000) and Gandiger-Hertzog (2002), no evidence has yet been found.

6 People from Govindia can no longer be trusted. This conclusion stems from the fact that two tourists from that country were recently convicted of murder while visiting this country. Also, the Prime Minister of Govindia has declared that he will search any fishing boats from our country if his police suspect them of carrying illegal drugs, which is obviously a ridiculous accusation. Any country that does that clearly does not respect our national sovereignty.

7 Despite popular myths, chocolate contains little that is bad for the skin. The Confederation of Chocolate Product Manufacturers report of 2002 states that 'Our research demonstrates there is no direct link between chocolate consumption and teenage acne' (page 35).

Comments about whether the evidence is weak or strong will vary. The important thing is that they are clearly thought out and logical. Following is a brief commentary on each extract.

### Answers

1 Very weak. An individual case does not provide strong evidence for a general situation.

2 Weak. The lack of reference for the survey is suspicious. The survey could have been made up, or organised by a biased political pressure group, etc.

3 Stronger. It is well-referenced, and logical. The weak point would be 'This trend looks set to continue into the future'—where is the evidence for that?

4 Weak. Stating that no evidence exists is not proof. It's quite possible that if research is done, it would support the opposite opinion. However, compare with number 5!

5 Much stronger than 4. It indicates that plenty of research has been done, that it was recent, and that it was focused on the issue concerned—all good signs. Also, instead of giving a definite statement (such as 'is perfectly safe' in example 4), the use of the word 'unlikely' in the statement of opinion allows for the possibility that further research may reach a different conclusion. Further study of this language point can be found in Unit 10, page 231.

6 Weak. It contains two examples of over-generalisation, that is, reaching a conclusion that applies to everyone from just a small number of specific examples. Even an elected Prime Minister does not represent the views of all people from a country.

7 Weak. Who paid for the research? What kind of companies do they represent? This looks like an example of bias and vested interest. Even though a reference is given, this source must be treated with suspicion.

Traps to avoid include:

- trying to show a point from too little evidence, eg a single example;
- over-generalisation;
- demonstrating bias;
- missing out referencing when it's necessary.

## Providing concrete supporting evidence

### Task A: Writing body paragraphs

SB P.50

The *purpose* of this task is for students to:

- practise providing strong supporting evidence in writing;
- practise using discourse markers.

Students revise the body paragraphs of the essays they wrote earlier (see page 46, Task E of the Students' Book). They may need to revise the introduction and conclusion to maintain coherence, that is, to ensure all parts fit together well.

# Listening

✓ *Note taking*

✓ *Predicting focus and listening for supporting ideas*

## Note taking

### Task A: Note taking

SB P.50

The *purpose* of this task is for students to:

- consider why note taking is useful to them;
- extend note taking skills they already have;
- be exposed to potentially useful note taking techniques.

Students discuss the questions in pairs or small groups. Common symbols and abbreviations that lecturers may write on the board or that may be found in texts are given. Ask students if they have seen them before, perhaps in their own language. Encourage students to invent symbols and abbreviations for themselves.

The information in the notes was taken from Powers, J (1997). *Ancient Greek Marriage* MA thesis, Tufts University. Available: http://www.pogodesigns.com/JP/weddings/greekwed.html (15 July 2002).

## Predicting focus and listening for supporting ideas

### Task A: Predicting the focus of a lecture; stages in introductions of lectures

SB P.52

The *purpose* of this task is for students to:

- realise that the focus or main idea of a lecture is usually given at or near the beginning of the introduction;
- realise a clear lecture will be structured in distinct stages, each of which has a particular rhetorical purpose and which assists in helping the listener to understand;
- perceive similarities in the rhetorical or generic structure of lectures and essays.

Discuss with the class how they would predict the focus of a lecture. If some immediately see parallels with essay structure, looked at in earlier in this Unit as well as in Unit 1, this is good. If not, there's no need to tell them—they will discover this in Question 1 of this task. This way of discovery may help the idea to stay in their minds better than if they are simply told the information.

3 Ask students to read instruction one. Then play the introduction to the lecture (see page 49 of this book, Recording number 3). Stop the recording after 'pretty much what everyone else does is considered not normal'.

- Students compare their answers in pairs.
- Students write their reason for choosing their answer.

Here, or after the next stage, may be an appropriate time to emphasise the point in the box below—perhaps by asking 'How important do you think stages are in lectures—When you're listening? When you're giving a talk?'

- Students match the other quotes to their function.

Draw students' attention to the fact that even in speaking, every idea that comes from other people, unless it is common knowledge, must be referenced.

### Answers

1 (c) is the best choice.

2 It can be seen that quotation (c) shows the main idea of the focus of the lecture because of the sentence that comes before it. In other words, it's because the lecturer states, *'From a naturalist sociological perspective, this talk today would like to pose more questions than it answers'*. The key words—'*... this talk ... would like to ...'* signal to the listener that this will be the main focus or purpose of the talk.

3
| | | |
|---|---|---|
| Thesis | [d] | Part of the general statement [a] |
| A supporting idea | [ ] | Definition [b] |

## Task B: Listening for supporting ideas

SB P.53

The *purpose* of this task is for students to:

- develop familiarity with the kind of supporting ideas which are used in academic talks in English-medium tertiary education;
- practise listening for supporting ideas.

1 Ask your students what methods of support they might find in this lecture, based on what they've heard so far (if they have very little experience of this style of academic expression, this stage may have to be skipped).

- Students read the list of support methods in the book.
- Play the rest of the lecture. Students indicate which methods of support they hear.

2 **Variation:** This activity has been constructed as a gap fill because it is near the beginning of the course. However, for students with a high level of listening ability or who have wider experience of EAP, you could:

- ask students to close their text books;
- draw on the board a version of the table with the 'supporting ideas' columns completely blank;
- ask students to copy these tables into their notebooks while you are drawing them, with plenty of space to write in their supporting ideas;
- play the recording.

## Answers

1 *(c) research* is the main point, but *(d) references from the literature* is also included. It could be argued that *(a) logical argument* is used, as all research involves logical argument in order to draw conclusions.

2 **Perspective 1**

| Main idea | Supporting idea |
|---|---|
| research procedure | ■ US students, similar backgrounds<br>■ swapped families<br>■ weren't allowed to ask how to act<br>■ tried to participate naturally at mealtime<br>■ discussed and wrote about the experience afterwards |
| results | ■ their new family did everything differently from their own family<br>■ they didn't know how to react<br>■ they considered their new family's habits to be 'wrong' or 'not normal'<br>■ they considered their own family's practices to be the 'right' or 'normal' ones |
| conclusions | ■ even families in the same culture and socio-economic group have different ideas of normal family behaviour |

**Perspective 2**

| Main idea | Supporting idea |
|---|---|
| Each family has a different view of what is 'normal' behaviour | Students who swapped families found:<br>■ their new family did everything differently from their own family<br>■ they didn't know how to react<br>■ they considered their new family's habits to be 'wrong' or 'not normal'<br>■ they considered their own family's practices to be the 'right' or 'normal' ones<br>■ this was despite the students having the same culture, socio-economic status etc. |

## Task C: Listening to identify focus of lectures—further practice

SB P.54

The *purpose* of this task is for students to:

- gain further familiarity with introductions to lectures;
- have further practice in identifying the focus or main idea of lectures;
- give the context of the next lecture.

Teachers should: ask students to listen and mark the best answer; get students to compare in pairs before moving to instruction two, which is a little harder because students have to take notes instead of choosing an answer already given; repeat the recording as many times as appropriate for their class.

## Answers

1 c] applications of the anthropic cosmological principle.

2 Theories about who painted Korean folk art.

# Recording scripts

(3) **RECORDING NUMBER 3 (4 MINUTES, 46 SECONDS)**

## LECTURE 1: From the beginning of a course entitled 'Families', given by the Department of Sociology, Faculty of Social Science

1 Of all our social institutions, the family is probably the one about which the most contradictory issues abound. The family has been found to be a major institutional component in every known social system. In other words, it is a universal institution.

2 A family may be defined as a group, related by marriage, blood or adoption residing in a common household, communicating with each other according to their respective roles and maintaining a common culture.

3 From a naturalist sociological perspective, this talk today would like to pose more questions than it answers. For example, what is a 'normal' family? And, is there such a thing as a 'normal' family?

4 Now there has been some very interesting research carried out around the idea of normality within families. What has been discovered for example, by Garfinkel in his 1967 study, is that whatever any family does within its own structure is considered 'normal' by that family and pretty much what anyone else does is considered not normal.

5 Now let me explain that ... Jules Henry in 1989 carried out some research with students from a North American university. In this study, he asked his students to swap families and have a dinner at their house one night. The students were matched for age, gender, nationality and ethnicity wherever possible. They also were from similar economic backgrounds. The idea was for each person to be a sort of stand-in and to participate naturally in the 'preparation and serving, the eating and the aftermath of the family meal, relying on their familiarity with normal mealtime routines in their own families.' They weren't allowed to ask questions about 'how things were done' or 'what am I supposed to do?' After the dinner, each student met later with their double for a conference to discuss how it went and to write up a description of what happened.

6 Now the interesting conclusion was that even around something as seemingly safe and simple as the evening meal, there were huge differences in the way families behaved. The subjects (students) were sitting in on other people's family dinner found they did not know how to act, how to behave, how to do or ask for anything. Now, remember that they were not from differing cultures, only different families with the rule imposed that they could not ask questions about how to do things. They were to try to fit in naturally with the family dinner.

7 It is such a simple experiment, this one. And yet the results were fascinating, I think. The students were absolutely miserable and thought that all the habits and customs around any family other than their own were strange and wrong. They considered them not normal. They considered their own family practices the only way to do things right and the other families' practices wrong.

8 The typical way things were done centred around questions like 'How do you know when and if you have been called to the dinner table? Do you help with serving? Do you clear the table or only your own dish? Do you wash up before sitting down or go right to the table? Do you use the kitchen sink to wash up or must you use the bathroom? Do you drink wine before, during or after the meal? Do you help yourself, wait to be served or do you serve each other? Do you speak one at a time, do you all speak together' and so on and so on.

9 There are so many customs around a simple meal in any family that there is not really a typical, normal way to do it. Every family is unique, even within the same country, the same culture or the same socio-economic group.

(4) **RECORDING NUMBER 4 (1 MINUTE, 43 SECONDS)**

## LECTURE 2: From a course on cosmology, within the Department of Physics, Faculty of Science

1 *Lecturer*: Good afternoon. Does everyone remember last week's lecture? We had a look at how various cosmological constants such as the speed of light and the gravitational constant have been determined, didn't we? Does anyone remember generally why such things are important? ... Yes, Ayako.

2 *Ayako*: Well, they're essential for working out all kinds of things—for example, you need the speed of light to get an idea how big the universe is, and to find out how much energy is released from an atomic nucleus when mass gets converted to energy.

3 *Lecturer*: Yes, good, that's it. We're going to extend this now to move in a fascinating new way—towards looking at what physics can tell us about why life exists. Specifically, we'll consider the anthropic cosmological principle, which demonstrates that life could not possibly exist if some of those cosmological constants were just a little different, and then apply the principle to some theories of how the universe was formed, to show that, actually, it seems that despite this theory, life isn't such a stroke of luck after all.

(5) **RECORDING NUMBER 5 (1 MINUTE, 11 SECONDS)**

## LECTURE 3: From a course on East Asian Art, in the Department of Art History, Faculty of Arts

Good morning. Last week, if you remember, we looked at representations of people in pre-modern Korean art. This week, we'll look at the difference between the art of the higher classes and art painted and used by more ordinary people. In particular, we'll look at Korean folk art and the various theories about who actually painted it. Was it really ordinary people, or could it have been court painters doing work during periods when they couldn't work for the upper classes? And if so, could this mean that, after all, even the folk art was actually painted by the upper class?

# Grammar

## Definite articles

The *purpose* of this task is for students to:

- improve their use and understanding of articles;
- use teacher-aided self-correction as a tool to improve lexicogrammatical accuracy.

### Task A: What does 'the' actually mean?

SB P.54

The *purpose* of this section is for students to:

- improve their instinct for what 'the' indicates and when to use it.

Ask students if they can say what *the* means. If not, going through the examples and explanation in the Students' Book should provide a deeper insight into the use of this article. Matching the example sentences to the explanations of why speaker and listener, or writer and reader, both know which one or ones are being mentioned, should clarify things if students are a bit confused. This is set up as a hypothesis-testing activity in the Students' Book, but the teacher can choose not to do it this way. The hypothesis isn't actually proven here, but it does seem to stand up to testing so far!

**Variation:** Instead of the examples in Task A, expressions taken from the texts of this Unit can be used. This would perhaps be more methodologically 'sound' in that by now students should be fully aware of the context of these expressions, but some will find the language in the expressions too abstract to relate to easily. It's up to you which you choose! Suggested expressions are:

- 'A major social trend' (*Social benefits* essay, para 1, line 1, page 39, Students' Book)—this idea is introduced here, so the reader doesn't previously know which trend.
- '... the current trend towards increasingly smaller families' (*Family responsibility* essay, para 1, lines 3–4, page 44, Students' Book)—the reader knows which trend here because the text specifies it exactly within the same noun group.

or

- 'A further benefit' (*Social benefits* essay, para 4, line 1, page 39)—introducing a new benefit, so the reader doesn't know which benefit it is yet.
- 'The benefits of encouraging more elderly people to live with their children or grandchildren' (*Social benefits* essay, final para, line 1, page 39)—the reader knows which benefit because it is given in the same noun group.

**Answers**

SB

**Possible reasons**

a] Only one exists in the context.

b] The idea has already been introduced in the text/conversation.

c] The noun is in a noun group which defines it or makes it more specific.

d] Using a superlative automatically specifies which one(s) you mean.

e] It is referring to all that exist in the context.

| | |
|---|---|
| 1 The moon's looking beautiful tonight. | a] there is only one moon, at least from the context of looking from the Earth! |
| 2 The dangers of overeating shouldn't be ignored. | c] 'of overeating' tells the listener or reader which dangers the speaker or writer intended |
| 3 The first prize went to Simona. | a] There is only one first prize! |
| 4 I hope I can meet the girl we spoke to in the restaurant again—she's stunning! | c] the relative clause (with 'that' or 'who' removed) after 'the girl' specifies which girl |
| 5 That's the best restaurant I've eaten at since I came here! | d] – there can only be one 'best' restaurant |
| Last week, if you remember, we looked at representations of people in pre-modern Korean art. This week, we'll look at [6] the difference between the art of the higher classes and art painted and used by more ordinary people. | c] most of this noun group specifies which difference |
| In particular, we'll look at Korean folk art and [7] the various theories about who actually painted it | c] 'about who actually painted it' explains which theories |
| Was it really ordinary people, or could it have been court painters doing work during periods when they couldn't work for [8] the upper classes? | e] it means all upper classes |
| And if so, could this mean that, after all, even [9] the folk art was actually painted by the upper class? | b] this means 'Korean folk art', mentioned already |

## Task B: Using articles

SB P.55

The *purpose* of this task is for students to practise choosing when to use 'the'. Students choose whether 'the' or nothing (=Ø) is the best choice for each gap.

### Answers

Marriages in ancient Greece involved young brides. Girls were thought more likely to be [1] Ø virgins if they got married early, and 14 appears to be [2] the most common age (Powers, 1997). However, for [3] Ø men, it was a completely different story. Due to [4] the fact that they had to perform military service, [5] the age at which they got married was around twice that for women.

Choice of [6] Ø husband was something that women had no control over. Instead, their *kyrios* (male guardian) chose for them. Factors involved were [7] Ø money and [8] Ø family politics. [9] Ø Alliances between [10] Ø families were more important than [11] the feelings of [12] the people who were actually getting married (ibid). It seems that it was only in [13] the myths of [14] the period that [15] Ø love marriages occurred.

Numbers 1, 3, 6, 7, 8, 9, 10, 15: general. Not specific enough for us to know which one, so 'the' isn't used.

Number 2: superlative.

Numbers 4, 5, 11, 12, 13: specified by the rest of the noun group.

Number 14: mentioned before ('ancient Greece' in the first line specifies the period).

# Learner independence & study skills

## Self-correction marking code

### Task A: How to use the code

SB P.56

The *purpose* of this task is:

- to encourage students to self-correct;
- for students to learn a system to help them do this.

Ask students if they remember better how to do something if someone does it for them or if they do it themselves. Most will feel that doing something themselves helps them learn. Then the self-correction marking codes can be introduced as a way to help them do this with their grammar and vocabulary choice.

**To use the system, the teacher:**

1. Reads the student's work.
2. Writes the codes next to and above mistakes (or at the beginning of a line containing a mistake).
3. Returns work to students.

**The students:**

4. Refer to the table of codes in Appendix A to see what kinds of mistakes they made.
5. In class, make corrections to their own work based on the codes the teacher has written.

**The teacher:**

6. Circulates around the classroom and is a resource for students to draw upon while they make their corrections.

Students enjoy self-correcting with the input of the teacher. It is important that the teacher gives each student individual attention for the correction stage in class.

Early finishers can begin a new writing activity.

# Speaking and Writing

## Discussion and essay questions

SB P.56

The questions in the Students' Book are intended as a resource to help provide extra speaking or writing practice. For example, students who want to practise writing could produce essays in answer to these questions for homework—making sure they know whether to write explanation or argument first. If the class needs extra speaking practice, a discussion could be organised around one of these issues.

unit 3

# science and technology

There is no convenience in our present day civilisation that does not cause discomfort.

KAHLIL GIBRAN

**Skills focus: In this Unit, students will learn and use the following skills:**


**Speaking 1:** orientation—some issues in science and technology 56

**Listening:** listening for reasons—interview with a scientist 57

**Writing 1:** discussion essays 60

**Reading and Writing:** avoiding the repetition of words 62

**Grammar:** cohesion through discourse markers—contrast, deduction, example, addition and summation 63

**English for the Internet Age:** searching the World Wide Web 66

**Speaking 2:** interrupting, suggesting, accepting and rejecting ideas 67

**Critical thinking:** analysis of positive and negative aspects of technology 68

**Writing 2:** writing a discussion essay 68

**Learner independence and study skills:** how to remember for longer 69

**Writing 3:** issues in science and technology 69

The theme of science and technology has been with us since antiquity. In modern life, new developments in both areas seem to alter the way we do everything and create new social paradigms. In this Unit, students will be asked to critically consider some of the issues around science and technology, to understand discussion as a discourse skill in writing and speaking, continue to improve their skills in reading as well as listening, and learn how to retain and recall knowledge better and for longer.

# Speaking 1

## Orientation: some issues in science and technology

The *purpose* of this section is to:

- orient students to the field of this unit;
- activate any knowledge that students already have about the topics covered;
- give practice at using an English-to-English learner's dictionary.

### Task A: Discussion

SB P.58

In **Task A**, students discuss the statements in groups or pairs. While monitoring this, focus on supplying subject-related vocabulary for any concepts they are struggling to find the words for. In **Task B**, ask students to form groups and match the words to their meanings, using an English–English learner's dictionary to help them.

**Note:** Students can switch between **Task A** and **Task B,** using the context of each Task A text to assist in vocabulary comprehension.

### Task B: Vocabulary for this Unit

SB P.58

**Answers**

| Words | Meanings |
|---|---|
| diesel (n) | a kind of fuel, usually for heavy vehicles |
| the (general) public (n) | ordinary people |
| rural (adj) | countryside where farmers work |
| radically (adj) | surprisingly big, or dramatic |
| legislation (n) | laws |
| determine (vb) | find out |
| consumers (n) | people who buy and use things |
| the environment | natural things around us (air, plants, etc) |
| mechanisation (n) | replacing older ways of doing things with machines |
| environmentalist (n) | person opposed to damage to natural things around us |
| processed food | food that has been highly cooked and packaged |

| Words | Meanings |
|---|---|
| breed (vb) | to choose carefully which animals or plants to allow to reproduce, in order to produce a better version. This commonly happens, for instance, with race horses. |
| pests (n) | insects or other animals that damage crops or property |
| reproduce (vb) | produce more of the same kind (usually for animals and plants) |
| gene (n) | part of animal and plant cells which controls the characteristics of the whole animal or plant—it's made up of DNA |
| genetically modified (GM) | living things with altered genes |
| yield (n, vb) | amounts produced—in this Unit, crops |
| resistant to (adj) | not damaged or affected by something |
| produce (n) | the food grown on a farm |
| genetic (adj)/ genetically (adv) | associated with the genes |
| assert (vb) | say strongly |
| urban (adj) | related to cities |

# Listening

## Listening for reasons: interview with a scientist

The *purpose* of this section is for students to:

- practise listening for markers that indicate reasons, which will help them to
- listen for reasons.

### Task A: Orientation discussion

SB P.59

Students discuss the questions in order to activate and share background knowledge around the topic of the listening.

6

### Task B: Listening for markers that indicate reasons

SB P.60

Tell the students to tick the words in the box as they hear them. All these words indicate there is a reason either before or after them. Play the recording only once, as the purpose is to sensitise the students to these markers in preparation for the next task.

**Answers**

| | | | | | |
|---|---|---|---|---|---|
| in order to | ✓ | because | ✓ | so | ✓✓✓ |
| reasons | ✓✓ | mean | ✓ | why? | ✓ |
| infinitive with 'to' | ✓ | thus | ✓ | as a consequence | ✓ |

## Recording script

⑥ **RECORDING NUMBER 6 (5 MINUTES, 11 SECONDS)**

**TITLE: Interview with a scientist about genetically modified food**

1 **Simon Bennet:** Good morning, Doctor Reynolds, and welcome to the studio. To begin with, can you tell us a little about the history of genetic modification of food?

2 **Dr Reynolds:** Well, I er, yes, of course. Briefly humans have been deliberately altering the genes of food crops for hundreds if not thousands of years, though for most of the time not even realising quite what they were doing. Well, from the earliest times, humans have been breeding new plants, and seeking to produce better varieties of existing plants, in order to do things like increase yields and, umm, well, reduce the amount lost because of disease. However, before this, this could only be done slowly and on a small scale, whereas over the last decade or so, genetic engineering techniques have been developed which have enabled scientists to directly introduce genes from one organism into another, even from animals into plants, would you believe!

3 **Simon Bennet:** Well, er, what are the differences, then, between genetically modified, or GM, crops and old fashioned plant breeding?

4 **Dr Reynolds:** Well, errr, mmm, well, it's sort of like this. Plant breeding techniques are slow and they only allow for small changes to happen at any stage. With breeding, development of a new species can only be done over the time it takes for, oh, at least, several generations of the plant to grow, usually many years. And besides this, because living things which are, well, obviously genetically very different, for example, plants and bacteria, they can't naturally reproduce with each other, so it's impossible to introduce big changes in a species. Genetically engineering overcomes both of these problems by allowing for very significant changes to be made within a short timeframe.

5 **Simon Bennet:** Yes, I can see how bacteria can't be bred with a vegetable! Could you elaborate as to why it's desirable for radically different genes to be introduced into a particular species?

6 **Dr Reynolds:** Well, put simply, it's like this. The population of the world is growing at a tremendous rate, as we all know. For example, when I was in primary school, some twenty years ago, I remember being taught that the population of the world was, er, about three billion. Now, the figure's more like six billion and by the time we get to the year 2020, it'll be around about eight billion people. Now, we're running out of space for any further farming land, and without rises in food production, there simply won't be enough food to go round. I mean, it's bad enough as it is. Genetic engineering aims to increase yields, and thus go some way to solving this enormous problem. And apart from that, many food companies want to increase profits, and the use of GM food provides a very powerful means of doing this.

7 **Simon Bennet:** Many consumers are very concerned about GM foods, but could you explain to us some of the reasons?

8 **Dr Reynolds**: Ahh, sure, certainly, I mean, there are plenty of them. Many people are concerned that there are hidden dangers in GM foods and that food companies don't want to tell us about it for fear of losing business. And they would like food containing GM ingredients to be clearly labelled as such. I mean, there's a bit of debate about it in the country at the moment. And furthermore, environmentalists are concerned about the effect that GM foods will have on the ecosystem. And one of the main reasons for the use of GM foods in the first place is to make the crops that are resistant to pests – but, many ordinary animals feed on these pests. So, planting large areas of crops which are resistant to a particular insect which normally eats that crop, well, it'll mean that the insect cannot live in that area any more. So, as a consequence, the animals which eat that insect will also not be able to live there, and so on. And so the variety of life, in fact the whole ecosystem in that area, will be affected considerably.

9 **Simon Bennet**: I see, so to reduce the fear amongst consumers about GM foods, the food companies are talking a lot about the testing that is being carried out on GM food before it's sold to the public. What sort of testing is actually carried out before a GM crop can be grown?

10 **Dr Reynolds**: Well, mmm, a lot actually. Now, before any new food can be grown commercially, it has to be grown under test conditions and they have to do that in several different places, under a variety of circumstances, over a period of several years. And, then, before it can be sold to the general public, it has to undergo even further assessment.

11 **Simon Bennet**: Well, I think that sums up the main issues around this controversial subject. Thank you very much for your time, Doctor Reynolds. I'm sure we'll hear lots more on this topic over the coming years.

12 **Dr Reynolds**: Simon, it's been a pleasure.

## 6 Task C: Listening for reasons

SB P.60

Students listen again and answer the questions, all of which ask for reasons.

### Answers

| | |
|---|---|
| 1 Why have humans been breeding plants? | ▪ increase yields<br>▪ reduce loss to disease |
| 2 Why is it impossible to quickly make big changes in a species by breeding? | ▪ different species can't reproduce with each other |
| 3 Why is genetic engineering considered a good thing by some people? | ▪ increases crop yields to keep up with expanding population<br>▪ increases profit |
| 4 Why are some consumers concerned about GM foods? | ▪ food companies afraid to give information about dangers |
| 5 Why are environmentalists concerned about GM foods? | ▪ effect on ecosystem |
| 6 Why are the food companies publicising the testing they have done on GM foods? | ▪ reduce fear amongst consumers |

# Writing 1

## Discussion essays

SB P.60

**Teacher:** please use Students' Book for texts.

The *purpose* of this section is for students to:

- find out the purpose and use of discussion essays;
- learn to recognise amd write the stages (schema) of a discussion essay;
- practice writing discussion essays.

### Task A: Stages in a discussion essay

SB P.61

The *purpose* of this task is to:

- introduce the stages of a discussion essay;
- highlight the distinction between argument and discussion essays.

Students examine the chart giving stages of discussion essays, then find the differences between argument essays and discussion essays (Students' Book, page 43).

### Task B: Reading—example discussion essay

SB P.61

Students read and study the essay *Genetically modified foods* and its various stages.

### Task C: Recognising stages in a discussion essay

SB P.63

Students apply their knowledge of staging from the model to another essay.

**Answer**

**TITLE: The mechanisation of agriculture and its effect on quality of life**

introduction

General Statement → Major developments have taken place in the field of agriculture during the last century, one of the most important of which has been the introduction and extensive use of machinery.

Position → This has had great effects on the environment and on the lives of millions of people around the world.

Definition → For the purposes of this essay, we will take the mechanisation of agriculture to mean the use of any device that is powered by anything other than humans or animals, on a farm.

Preview/Scope → Careful consideration of some of the effects of agricultural mechanisation, both positive and negative, is essential for any country currently experiencing an increase in the use of such machines.

body

Positive statement 1 → The vast increase in output that has been made possible by more use of mechanisation is probably the most important positive effect of this process.

Supporting, concrete evidence for Positive statement 1 → The speed of planting crops, spreading fertilisers and pesticides, and harvesting, is phenomenal. All three of these processes contribute to equally enormous increases in production.

Positive statement 2 → Mechanisation has improved food production during this century and has helped to feed the larger world population.

Positive statement 3

Concrete supporting evidence for Positive statement 3

3 Increased use of farm machinery has also generally led to a decrease in costs. This may seem surprising when the considerable cost of initial purchase of equipment is considered (this may be tens of thousands of dollars for a tractor, or hundreds of thousands of dollars for a large piece of equipment like a combine harvester). However, a tractor enables one person to perform so much more work that the extra profit, made from having more crop to sell, more than covers the purchase and running costs of the tractor. Through similar savings using other pieces of equipment, costs per hectare of food production have fallen significantly.

Transition sentence, linking positive to negative ideas

Negative statement 1

Concrete supporting evidence for Negative statement 1

4 Despite these highly positive results of mechanisation, there are also several negative factors that aren't always considered by the proponents of this process. One of the most important of these is employment. As in all other fields of life, the increasing use of machines inevitably results in the same job being done by fewer people. It can be argued that some jobs are created in designing and maintaining the machines, but almost always more jobs are lost than created, and in addition the people whose jobs are lost often do not have the skills to undertake the newly created jobs. Therefore many jobs have to go, leading to a variety of social problems in rural communities.

body

Negative statement 2

Concrete supporting evidence for Negative statement 2

5 One of these problems is that the unemployed of the countryside have to go elsewhere to find work—the obvious places to look are the larger cities, where further problems occur. Thus the increasing use of machinery leads to an explosion in urban population. Because the people moving to the cities are usually poor, this causes problems of sub-standard housing (resulting in slums), transport problems and urban poverty, as there are not necessarily more jobs available in the city than there were in the countryside. Also, the movement of people to the cities often means that families are spilt up, and villages which were once strong communities become too small to support essential services such as post offices and public transport. This leads to the irreversible break-up of these communities as people move to the cities.

Negative statement 3

Concrete supporting evidence for Negative statement 3

6 In addition, the use of machinery on farms contributes to environmental destruction. Machines allow larger areas to be cultivated, thus leading to loss of the habitat in which wildlife lives. For example, in England, the increasing use of machines has made it easy for farmers to remove the hedges that used to separate fields. Thus many species of butterfly are now facing extinction because they have nowhere to live and breed. In Australia, over-use of the land by machines has resulted in many farms becoming like deserts.

Further evidence for Negative statement 3

7 Furthermore, the energy that agricultural machines use is mostly produced from the burning of diesel, which causes pollution as well as adding to global warming. Electricity that is sometimes used to

power farm machinery is also usually produced in environmentally unsound ways.

Summary within the conclusion

In summary, there are many disadvantages to the mechanisation of agriculture as well as advantages. With the increasing population of the world, most governments consider that expanding mechanisation is the only way to feed the additional hungry mouths. However, it would be sensible for governments to take steps to minimise the disadvantages of this process.

Recommendations within the conclusion

Developed countries experienced these disadvantages some time ago, and while many of them have been overcome, a significant number of mistakes were made. It would be wise for countries currently undergoing mechanisation to carefully study these mistakes and to avoid making the same ones themselves.

conclusion

# Reading and Writing

## Avoiding the repetition of words

SB▷

Repeated words in essays make an essay boring to read. To produce a good style in writing, it is important to repeat as few words as possible. To do this, you need to use synonyms. Synonyms are words that have the same meaning.

### Task A: Identifying synonyms; vocabulary development; understanding lexical cohesion

▶ SB P.65

The *purpose* of this task is for students to:

- practise searching for words within a text with a purpose;
- identify synonyms within the text;
- increase their vocabulary range;
- increase their awareness of lexical cohesion.

**Answers**

| Word | Paragraph number | Synonym |
|---|---|---|
| large | 1<br>3<br>9 | great<br>*considerable (cost)<br>*significant (number) |
| very big | 2<br>2<br>2 | *vast (increase)<br>*enormous<br>*larger (world population) |
| agricultural mechanisation | 1<br>3 | mechanisation of agriculture<br>increased use of farm machinery |

* means that the word that goes in this space belongs in front of other words.

# Grammar

## Cohesion through discourse markers: contrast, deduction, example, addition and summation

SB▷ Cohesion within a text means that the text makes sense. A text with good cohesion is sensible, not nonsense. Cohesion comes about in a text through lexis (words) or grammar. One way of providing cohesion is to refer to the same idea using different words (see previous section). Another way is to use discourse markers. We looked at time sequence discourse markers in Unit 1, page 15 of the Students' Book and discourse markers of addition and contrast in Unit 2, page 48. You'll look at cause and effect markers on page 86 and another way of providing cohesion, using pronouns, in Unit 4, page 87.

### Task A: Discourse markers and their function

▶ SB P.66

The *purpose* of this section is for students to:

- extend their knowledge of discourse markers and recognise how they function.

**Answers (including Task B answers)**

| Add information | Contrast | Summarise/ conclude | Reason/ result/ cause/effect | Give examples |
|---|---|---|---|---|
| and | but | to summarise | therefore | for example |
| in addition | whereas | in summary | thus | such as |
| additionally | on the contrary | in conclusion | though | for instance |
| moreover | on the other hand | | because | |
| also | however | | as | |
| furthermore<br>as well as | despite | | if<br>so | |
| … not only<br>… but also | | | | |

### Task B: Identifying discourse markers

▶ SB P.67

The *purpose* of this task is for students to:

- identify more discourse markers and identify their functions;
- read with an awareness of discourse markers and their functions.

**Answers**

See Task A.

### Task C: Grammar of discourse markers

▶ SB P.67

The *purpose* of this task is for students to:

- increase their awareness of how discourse markers are used (grammar);
- increase their ability to notice for themselves how words are used;

See Students' Book for explanation.

### Noun groups

If students aren't sure what noun groups are, explain that they are groups of words that can be treated as a single noun. For example:

- cars
- your friend's car
- a big car with a broken window
- the car that my father bought last year.

In contrast, a **clause** always has a subject and a verb.

### Answers

The commas and capital letters in the table below represent typical punctuation. This list isn't comprehensive—students may find more!

| Connect ideas in different sentences (followed by a clause) | Connect ideas in the same sentence (followed by a clause) | Connect ideas in the same sentence (followed by a noun group) |
|---|---|---|
| addition<br>In addition, …<br>Additionally, …<br>Further, …<br>Also, …<br>The first …<br>Secondly …<br>Furthermore, …<br>Moreover, … | … and …<br>… not only … but also … | … and …<br>…, as well as …<br>Besides …, …<br>… not only … but also …<br>… additional … |
| contrast<br>However, …<br>On the other hand, …<br>In contrast, …<br>On the contrary, …<br>Conversely, … | … but …<br>Though …, …<br>…, though …<br>Although …, …<br>…, although …<br>While …, …<br>…, while …<br>Whereas …, …<br>…, whereas … | … albeit …<br>In spite of …, …<br>Despite …, …<br>In contrast to …, … |
| summary<br>In summary, …<br>To summarise, …<br>In conclusion, …<br>To conclude, … | | |

| Connect ideas in different sentences (followed by a clause) | Connect ideas in the same sentence (followed by a clause) | Connect ideas in the same sentence (followed by a noun group) |
|---|---|---|
| reason/result/cause effect | | |
| Consequently, ... | ..., so ... | The reason is ... |
| As a consequence, ... | ..., as ... | ... because of ... |
| This is because ... | ... because ... | ..., due to ... |
| Because of this, ... | Because ..., ... | |
| As a result, ... | ..., hence ... | |
| Therefore, ... | | |
| Thus ... | | |
| example | | |
| For example, ... | | ..., for example, ... |
| For instance, ... | | ..., such as ... |
| | | ..., exemplified by ... |

**Note**

- There are other ways of expressing reasons and effects, such as using infinitives, verbs like 'means' and 'leads to', as we saw in Task B, page 60, Students' Book.
- The following words can also be put between the auxiliary verb and main verb (or after the main verb if the tense is present simple or past simple): in addition, also, on the other hand, however, in contrast, on the contrary, conversely, though, in summary, in conclusion, consequently, as a result, therefore, thus, for example.

## Task D: Using discourse markers

SB P.69

The *purpose* of this task is for students to practise choosing appropriate discourse markers, paying attention to meaning and grammar.

This activity requires students to read the passage, understand the relationships between the ideas, and then choose discourse markers which show these relationships.

**Answers**

1 There are two reasons for supporting pure scientific research. First, it satisfies humans' natural curiosity about the universe in which they live. ... ... ... ... ... ... ... ... ... ... ... ... ... ... ... ... ... ... ... ... ... ... ... ... ... ... ... ... ... ... Secondly, technological advances that followed on from pure scientific research have led to improvements in our lives. For example/For instance, the non-stick coating on saucepans has made washing the dishes so much easier. Also/Further/In addition/Furthermore/Moreover, improved aeroplane materials have made flying faster, quieter and cheaper. Therefore/Thus/ Consequently, we should be grateful for pure scientific research.

2 Exploration of space has led to improved understanding about weather systems on other planets and moons in our solar system. Consequently/As a consequence. As a result, we have an improved understanding of the Earth's weather systems as well as the consequences of future changes such as global warming.

3 It is so easy for scientific advances to cause problems. For example/For instance, nuclear energy sounded wonderful when it was first developed, because of its expected low cost and/as well as lack of pollution. Safety was a concern and was taken seriously so careful precautions were usually taken, and in most cases these did actually result in a low chance of an accident. However, nothing is perfect, including safety systems, and when problems do happen, the consequences are extremely serious. In addition/Further/Furthermore/Additionally/Moreover, although actual operation of a nuclear reactor produces little visible pollution, disposal of the radioactive materials that are produced is extremely difficult and expensive, and consequently nuclear power is now considered too expensive in many countries. As a result/Therefore/As a consequence/Because of this/Thus, many governments have stopped planning to build more nuclear reactors. This example clearly shows that the miracle of yesterday may become the disaster of tomorrow. Not every scientific advance has the expected result.

# English for the Internet Age

## Searching the World Wide Web

The *purpose* of this section is:

- to increase student's familiarity with search engines on the World Wide Web;
- to provide practice in searching for sites;
- to provide practice in skimming and scanning;
- to provide practice in spoken negotiation.

### Task A: How to use a search engine

SB P.69

Students follow the instructions in the Students' Book on a computer that is already connected to the Internet.

If they do this in pairs, they will have to negotiate with each other about which links to choose. They will also be able to practise skimming and scanning when they do this.

### Task B: Looking at the effect of key words on searches

SB P.70

Again, students follow the instructions in the Students' Book. As in Task A, the purpose for students to work in pairs is to allow opportunity for spoken negotiation over each decision made about which link to follow etc.

#### Answers

1 The last one, + television + 'effect on children', is specific but also covers the whole topic, so it is the most likely to be effective.

2–4 Tell students that there is no perfect answer—the only way to know for certain that a site is useful is to visit it and read the information. However, if they can eliminate many of the sites from their list, they will be able to find what they are looking for more quickly. To do this, the ideas from Step 1 (using specific search words which cover the topic) will help. This requires reading and critical thinking skills. Step 4 should allow students to evaluate their own answers.

## Task C: Internet research

SB P.71

Students are asked to choose an issue around technology and search the Internet for information. You could put a list of issues on the board, or students could be referred to the table on page 73 of the Students' Book, which gives a list of issues in science and technology.

# Speaking 2

## Interrupting, suggesting, accepting and rejecting ideas

The *purpose* of this section is for students to:

- learn new expressions for the functions of interrupting, suggesting, accepting and rejecting ideas;
- practise using these expressions in the context of a discussion around current, relevant issues;
- practise culturally appropriate turn taking.

## Task A: Expressions for interrupting, suggesting, accepting and rejecting ideas

SB P.71

Listen and check that students speak with appropriate intonation. Tell them, in pairs, to choose the best column in the table for each expression. They should also add their own ideas, which you can check while monitoring.

**Answers**

| Interrupting to make a relevant point | Suggesting an idea | Rejecting an idea | Accepting an idea, but putting your own view forward |
|---|---|---|---|
| Hang on …<br>Yes, but on the other hand … | Could I just say …<br>What about the fact that … | No, I don't agree …<br>That's what you've read, but I've read …<br>I think …<br>My view is that<br>I'm afraid I disagree with that idea … | That may be so, but …<br>Well yes, however …<br>I agree with you to some extent, but …<br>Well, you may have a point, but … |

## Task B: Discussion

SB P.72

- As a class, choose some recent science or technology related issues that the students find interesting. Examples at the time of writing include genetically modified research, mobile phone safety, cloning and stem cell research.
- Search on the WWW prior to a discussion (see previous section—*English for the Internet Age*).
- Students prepare for the discussion by making notes about their opinions.

- A good group size for discussions of this kind is four.

**Game idea**

- In groups of four, all students' names are written down. One person is the writer. As they discuss different sides of an issue, the writer listens for the expressions just learned for turn taking and places a tick next to the name of any person who uses any of them.
- The person with the most ticks is the winner.

It's important that students know why they are counting the expressions. The reason is that at this level, they are often able to express themselves in discussions without actually using the language they are supposed to be focusing on, and as a result they lose the opportunity to extend the range of language they use. Doing this as a game gives the students a strong incentive to use all the expressions.

**Variations**

1. If you have a very talkative class, you could choose just one issue, and order counting to stop after certain time intervals, say five minutes.
2. Each discussion could stop when one person from the group has used all the expressions.

**Extension:** Students can write an essay about the topic they have researched. First, they have to decide on a question, and then plan their essay. The steps in the writing section, Task A on pages 75–76 of the Students' Book, could be introduced here—there will be no problem following them again later in the Unit, because they apply to most essays.

# Critical thinking

## Analysis of positive and negative aspects of technology

The *purpose* of this section is for students to:

- develop their critical thinking skills around the theme of the Unit.
- further practise language useful for discussing, from earlier in this Unit.

### Task A: Discussion about technological advances

SB P.72

- Ideas are provided from both essays in this Unit in table form in the Students' Book.

# Writing 2

## Writing a discussion essay

The *purpose* of this section is for students to bring together several of the points they learnt in this unit and write a discussion essay.

### Task A: Writing a discussion essay

SB P.73

This can be an in class assignment or given for homework. The teacher could refer students to the list of stages in writing a discussion essay on page 61 (Students' Book) of this Unit. Use the two-stage correction marking code from the Appendix taught in Unit 1 for corrections. Students will make multiple drafts before a final essay is accomplished.

# Learner independence & study skills

## How to remember for longer

The *purpose* of this section is to:

- illustrate to students the fact that memory is enhanced when notes are reviewed soon after taking them;
- encourage students to review.

### Task A: How good is your memory?

SB P.74

As per Students' Book. Most students draw very different graphs from the one they are referred to.

### Task B: Discussion—how important is review?

SB P.74

As per Students' Book.

### Task C: Planning your reviewing—writing your own review timetable

SB P.75

As per Students' Book.

# Writing 3

## Issues in science and technology

The *purpose* of this section is for students to:

- apply the knowledge of genre they have gained so far;
- analyse essay questions in order to know how to plan their answer;
- critically consider contemporary issues around the topic of science and technology.

## Task A: Analysing questions—which genre?

SB P.75

### Answers

| Question | Comment |
|---|---|
| 1 It is too early to know the long-term effects of growing genetically modified (GM) food. Therefore, GM food should not be grown outside well protected laboratories. To what extent do you agree with this point of view? | **Argument or discussion**. 'To what extent' questions can be answered in three ways: i] express agreement or disagreement with the stated opinion: argument ii] discuss different aspects of the issue and come to a conclusion about which side is the stronger: discussion iii] express an opinion that's somewhere between complete agreement or complete disagreement, and support only this opinion: argument |
| 2 Mobile phones have brought new rules of etiquette to society. What are the rules about the use of mobile phones in your society? For example, should you switch off mobile phones before going into a cinema? What is the rationale behind these rules? | **Explanation.** The question doesn't ask for an opinion about mobile phone etiquette, just to give the current situation as the writer understands it is. |
| 3 Explain your opinion about the following statement: 'The use of animals in scientific research should be restricted to the areas of medical research which could potentially result in human life being saved.' | Even though the question contains the word 'explain', the focus is on an opinion, not facts. Therefore, it can't be explanation. **Argument or discussion** are both possible. |
| 4 Money spent on sending people into space should be diverted to other more worthwhile causes such as reducing world hunger. Discuss. | The instruction 'discuss' indicates that more than one side of the issue should be included. **Discussion.** |
| 5 Scientific research is an expression of humanity's natural curiosity about the universe around us. Give your reasons for your point of view about this statement. | **Argument,** because a single point of view is asked for. |

## Task B: Speaking and writing—discussion

SB P.75

The stages given in the Students' Book provide a useful checklist for the essay writing process. While students are going through this process, the teacher should monitor carefully. It is a good idea for students to submit an early draft for comment, and two stage correction, by the teacher (see Students' Book, Unit 2, page 56).

unit 4

# literature

The pen is a sceptre, but how scarce kings are among the writers!

**KAHLIL GIBRAN**

## Skills focus: In this Unit, students will learn and use the following skills:


**Writing:** paragraph formatting 2—topic sentences; methods of development—providing concrete supporting evidence; creative writing 72

**Grammar:** cause and effect—discourse markers or signals; ellipsis and substitution 75

**Reading:** writers talk about writing; text types; note taking from whole books 77

**Listening:** listening for pleasure and listening for non-linguistic clues 82

**Critical thinking:** considering writing styles 87

**Speaking:** tutorial participation skills 1 88

**Learner independence and study skills:** time management 89

**English for the Internet Age and Critical thinking:** evaluating academic credibility of information on the Internet 90

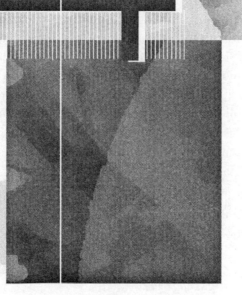

# Writing

✓ *Paragraph formatting 2: topic sentences*
✓ *Methods of development: providing concrete supporting evidence*
✓ *Creative writing*

## Paragraph formatting 2: topic sentences

The following information concerning theme/rheme and the topic sentences in the Students' Book require further explanation around the idea of *context*. De-contextualised examples are difficult to grasp and have little merit. The students should be made to understand that if 'last night, I' (from the example) is the most important idea, the reason for that is found in the context of the conversation that the people are having around the main participant going somewhere or doing something last night. The movie the person saw will come into the discourse, but the language choice of theme must be taken from the context of the discussion and the purpose/s of the speaker/s in terms of the meaning they are wanting to convey.

SB▷

When expressing ideas in English, the main thought or important point generally comes first. For example, if I want to tell you *what I did last night* (and what I did was go to a movie) ... and, in the context of the conversation the words *last night* indicate the **time** of the action, and time of action is the most important point ...

I **don't** say:

1 *The movie I went to last night was very good.*

I **don't** say:

2 *I saw a very good movie last night.*

I **do** say:

3 Last night, I went to a very good movie.

Why don't I say (1) or (2)? What is wrong with those sentences? Nothing is grammatically wrong with them in terms of clause construction. But the answer is the *order* is wrong. Number (3) is the only way to express the importance of 'last night, I'. Remember I said I wanted to tell you **what I did last night,** *therefore*, **Last night, I** becomes the theme of the sentence—**Last night, I ...** is most important and it comes first in the sentence. It is the theme, it is the main idea, it is the beginning of the topic sentence; and it is the topic of the conversation until the conversation shifts (probably to discuss the movie seen last night). 'It' (the topic, the theme, the main idea) consists of all the words up to the first verb.

The end of the sentence—*very good movie*—is the rheme or the other important idea/participant in the sentence.

### Task A: Theme/topic in English

SB P.78

Student's answers will, of course, vary. However, the important point is that each student recognises that the sentences must begin with the theme (all the words up to the first verb) and thus become the topic sentence for expansion to a paragraph.

**1** The kitchen in my apartment | *looks* ____________________ or *is* ____________________.

**2** The blue shirt | *will look* better for Aaron's party than the black one. I know it will!

**3** If you | *need to find* a word that is better than the one you are thinking of, use a thesaurus.

*Reinforce the concept of cohesion with your students:*

SB▷

How can you make certain your paragraphs are cohesive? In other words, how can you make sure your paragraph makes sense to the reader?

Some common problems in student writing:

- too many ideas are introduced in one paragraph;
- sentences are not related closely enough to each other;
- methods of development are not clear.

# Methods of paragraph development: providing concrete supporting evidence

## Task A: Developing paragraphs using different methods

SB P.79

Students may use the sentences they have created (you will need to make sure their main ideas represent what is to become the topic of the paragraph) in order to develop their sentences into the topic sentences of paragraphs. There are three ways they can develop the ideas in these examples:

- description;
- giving reasons;
- giving definitions and examples.

In fact, there are many more methods for developing paragraphs. In the next task, other ways to expand paragraphs are explored. Students will discover that by developing their paragraphs using these methods, they are providing concrete evidence for the topic sentence. The concrete, supporting evidence occurs as a result of teasing out the idea from the first sentence using one of the methods presented.

## Task B: Methods of development of paragraphs, *continued*

SB P.80

### Answers

1 Study the examples, noting the methods outlined for you in bold type. Copy down the methods below:

A—cause and effect.

B—listing of details.

C—analogy.

D—comparison and contrast.

2 Locate the exact language that shows you that the method named is the method used.

A—the language used that demonstrates **cause and effect**: *This is because; Therefore, if a balance …; the inevitable result could be …; thus.*

B—the language used that demonstrates **listing of details:** details about *tofu—light on the stomach, full of protein, versatile to prepare, derived from soybeans, costs less.*

C—the language used that demonstrates **analogy:** *very much like, like.*

D—the language used that demonstrates **comparison and contrast:** *is like; as does; they both have to; the writer needs … and a songwriter needs …; they differ in that—but.*

3 Write four more paragraphs of your own, using the methods of development from the models A through D.

Again, student writing will differ. Peer marking of their answers using the models and the language used for each method of development will assist students.

# Creative writing

## Task A: Learning some conventions of poetry and writing your own poems

SB P.83

Literature would not exist without creative writing. The *purpose* of this section is for students to observe and note a little more obscure English than is usual and to write with freedom from convention using poetry to explore their own feelings. Theme is also revisited.

### Answers

1 a] Spring.

b] Love and ladies (women), men begging to be chosen (pluck'd).

c] Seven syllables in each line.

d] 1. seen; 2. blue; 3.view; 4.green; 5. blow; 6. pull; 7 snow; 8. full; 9. cry; 10. die.

e] 1 and 4 seen/green; 2 and 3 blue/view; 5 and 7 blow/snow; 6 and 8 pull/full; 9 and 10 cry/die.

f] Sometimes every other line rhymes and then two lines next to each other rhyme.

g] That $16^{th}$ century poetry often dealt with the outdoors, love and praise of women. It used rhyme in a structured pattern with seven syllables in this poem in each line.

h] Students should have fun using the poem as a guide.

**2** Students can use any words chosen from the circle in any order to compose anything they like, such as creative writing or poetry.

**3** Display work if possible. Have a poetry reading.

## Task B: Writing to develop the theme or main ideas

SB P.85

Students should be able to read *A holiday* … and link the method of development paragraph to paragraph before writing their own descriptive piece. The topic sentence in paragraph 1, *What a surprise! All our careful plans were not realised in this holiday adventure, but what occurred was far more exciting and fun,* establishes the remainder of the text. The writer **must** go on to explain what was *a surprise* and what *plans* were *not realised* and *what occurred*. They must also explain why it was *more exciting and fun* perhaps than the original planned holiday.

The purpose of the model is to teach students to think about their writing before they begin and to be certain that they actually place their main, most important idea (ie the theme) first!

Look at this example from a student's writing. When the student understands that the theme was not the word *Also*, (the student was reminded that the *theme or main idea is all the words up to the first verb*) but actually *the level of education*, the sentence becomes more coherent:

Original sentence:

*Also is very high the level of education and the people like to study.*

**Teacher:** Is *also* the main idea?

**Student:** No.

**Teacher:** But *also* is the only word up to your first verb which is *is*, so that makes *also* the main idea or theme of your sentence. So, what is the main idea?

**Student:** Mmm—the level of education | is very high and the people like to study.

New sentence:

*Also, the level of education is very high and the people like to study.*

# Grammar

✓ *Cause and effect: discourse markers or signals*
✓ *Ellipsis and substitution*

The *purpose* of this section is for students to:

- understand and identify discourse signals of cause and effect;
- understand and follow ellipsis and substitution.

## Cause and effect: discourse markers or signals

Students use the texts from the Reading *Writers talk about writing* to complete the first task on discourse markers.

Although there are not a great many of the discourse signals from the chart used in *Writers talk about writing*, the students should observe that the most common ones in speaking are: *so; but; because; as* ... These recur in almost every speaker's texts, yet the texts are varied. (The texts also include some writing as well as speaking.)

### Task A: Noticing discourse markers and how they function in texts

SB P.86

**Answers**

1 In comparison to real life, ... fiction frees us from ourselves and helps us revel in the muddle of life. (When writing)... Fictional time is wonderfully flexible. It can be stretched so that we can look about and take in every detail of the scene, then consider every option, as we never can in reality. (David Malouf)

2 The only piece of advice I can give (about writing) is that if you feel passionately about something, go with it and follow your heart and tell something that moves you as best you can. (Nicholas Evans)

3 When (my mother) left I sat down and I thought about my own life and thought this was a story worth telling. That's how I started writing this story. (Jung Chang)

4 So when people ask me why I write, the answer is not to become rich and famous—because … if you set out to do that, then you're never going to be either of those things. It's just that the bug bites you, it itches so badly and only one thing will stop it itching and that's to scratch it with a pen. (Wilbur Smith)

5 …because ever since I was a child if there was one thing I knew that if I could do, would do, it was write a book. But when I was in my teenage years, it was the last thing that I would ever have the luxury of being able to do and so the other things were really just ways of keeping my head above water. (Arundhati Roy)

6 The reason … (that my work is a little bit unpleasant or prickly)… is that my mind was warped when I was very young by being deprived of any knowledge of sex. (Roald Dahl)

7 Provided that a person had space, quiet, money and an understanding family (or no family at all), I believe anyone who really wished to become a writer, could become a writer. Admittedly, I make this claim only for those who love writing. I suppose this is depending upon whether you think that talent is everything or not. Dedication is equally important if not more so. (Nom de plume)

## Ellipsis and substitution

When English leaves things out and/or substitutes other words, it is done in order to avoid repetition. There are differing types of ellipsis: noun ellipsis, clause ellipsis and verb ellipsis. You may wish to go into this kind of detail with students, or you may only find it necessary to acquaint them with the fact that in English, words are left out and others are substituted.

The following examples are provided as a more detailed introduction that you could use **in addition** to the three examples provided in the Students' Book.

**Noun ellipsis:** I have read that many writers have stated that a routine is necessary for success. Some^ though, manage to just write when it suits them!

Noun left out after 'some' is *writers.*

**Clause ellipsis:** That woman is absolutely wonderful! Don't you agree^? ( )

Clause left out after 'agree' is *that woman is absolutely wonderful.*

**Verb ellipsis:** My friend plays violin with an orchestra. She prefers early concerts but she doesn't worry about performing late at night when often, she has to^.

Verb phrase left out is *perform late at night.*

### Task A: Understanding ellipsis and substitution in English

SB P.87

**Answer**

(d) is the correct answer.

## Task B: Locating ellipsed words and substitutions

SB P.88

SB▷ The howling simply would not stop! I lay in my bedroom listening to the wind, certain, however, that it^(1) came from a different source^(2).

I had heard it^(3) before, one dark night when both my parents went to a dinner party and left me home alone. I had insisted^(4) because at thirteen, I am certainly old enough^(5)!

What was it^(6)? And why was it^(7) so eerie? I decided to contact my best friend, Sam, and ask him^(8) to listen^(9) over the phone. I picked it^(10) up and waited for the dial tone. There was none^(11). Strange^(12), I thought. I decided to use my mobile phone^(13) instead.

Now things got even stranger. My mobile had a message on the screen that said 'Welcome to the Howling'! I absolutely freaked out and threw the phone across the room before realising that answering^(14) was the only way I might ever find out what was really going on. I raced across the room, picked it^(15) up, then realised that I didn't know how^(16)!

### Answers

1 the howling
2 than the wind
3 the howling
4 on being left home alone
5 to be left home alone
6 the howling
7 the howling
8 Sam
9 to the howling
10 the phone
11 dial tone
12 that there was no dial tone
13 to contact my best friend, Sam
14 the message
15 the mobile phone
16 to answer the message

# Reading

✓ *Writers talk about writing*
✓ *Text types*
✓ *Note taking from reading*

The *purpose* of this section is for students to:

- identify various literary text types and their features;
- practise identifying important ideas and practise note taking.

## Writers talk about writing

SB P.89

**Answers** for this section are from Task A, *Noticing discourse markers and how they function in texts* on page 75 of this book.

# Text types

What do we mean when we say 'text'? What is a text? A text may be defined as a semantic unit. It contains and indeed is meaning. It has a function to perform and it also has to be considered as 'product and process'.

> The text is a product in the sense that it is an output, something that can be recorded and studied ... It is a process in the sense of a continuous process of semantic choice, a movement through the network of meaning potential, with each set of choices constituting the environment for a further set. (Halliday & Hasan, 1985:10)

Students are to analyse the differing language features, social contexts and purposes of various text types. Will they recognise a Greek myth and differentiate it from a crime fiction detective story as a native speaker who reads it would be able to do? How do readers recognise a song that is 'old-fashioned' or rather traditional? What language makes readers 'know' that a story is being told which is fiction rather than a scientific text? It is not all vocabulary because 'panda bear' could be included in a children's fiction or a crime story set in China or a New York Zoo, or ... as it is used in the Students' Book, as a scientific text.

The following *language features* which are shaded in the Students' Book on pages 94–95 are not all inclusive, but they are meant to assist students to locate some of the elements that make a text the text it is. Hopefully, as students work together and with you, you may find other features to add (such as more detailed staging).

SB▷

In English, as in all languages, different texts are written for different purposes and in different ways. The next tasks should assist you to learn about some of the language features that make these texts recognisable. You will try to discover what language features make a crime fiction a crime fiction, and what different language features make an informative or scientific text an informative or scientific text.

Isn't it all English? Yes, it is all English. But you use different participants (people/no people); different processes (kinds of verbs); there are different circumstances (situations) and they have different social purposes.

## Task A: Recognising different text types

▶ SB P.90

Task A asks students to match the text types with their titles.

### Answers

A Crime fiction 2

B Fiction 4

C Scientific text 5

D Greek myth 1

E College (university) song 3

F Biography

G News story 7

H Abstract for journal article 6

I Recipe

## Task B: Recognising the language features of differing text types

SB P.93

Task B in the Students' Book has set out the language features in boxes in order that students may begin to recognise some of the features of that text type and ultimately apply them. (Please note that the actual transfer of information back and forth using numbers (1, 2, 3) or names of numbers (one, two, three) is intentional practice for students in exam technique).

### Answers

A Crime fiction ___one___

B Fiction ___four___

C Scientific text ___three___

D Greek myth ___two___

E College (university) song ___five___

F Biography ______

G News story ___seven___

H Abstract for journal article ___six___

I Recipe ______

## Task C: Recognising different purposes of text types

SB P.95

Task C matches the text types with their purposes or social functions.

### Answers

1 Scientific text: to provide information about natural and non-natural phenomena.

2 News story: to provide information about newsworthy events to readers.

3 Journal abstract: to persuade a reader that something is the case and to report on theory and/or research.

4 Fiction: to entertain a reader and to describe a particular person or persons in a particular place or places.

5 College song: to engage a group of people in one act of appreciation in a ceremony using song and to relate historical events.

6 Crime fiction: to entertain a reader and to describe persons and events around a crime.

7 Greek myth: to entertain and enlighten a reader using ancient stories which may have a moral or warning.

For Biography and Recipe, no text type purpose is given.

The exercises are represented below in table form. You could use this as an overhead at the end of this *Reading* section or ask students to produce the table and then present it as an overhead for verification.

| Title of text type | Language features | Purpose | Social context |
|---|---|---|---|
| Crime fiction<br>Detective novel | ▪ First person narrative—the 'voice' of the narrator is evident and clear in the reader's mind<br>▪ Staging – introduction with time, location, setting the scene<br>▪ Past and past continuous tense<br>▪ Processes (verbs) are material and mental<br>▪ Participants are human<br>▪ Location (place) important<br>▪ Time important<br>▪ Descriptive details prominent—of objects and events | To entertain, perhaps to inform (for example if forensics are included) | Leisure reading |
| Fiction | ▪ Narrator – omnipresent (knows all but is not present)<br>▪ Participants are human<br>▪ Processes (verbs) are mental—non-verbal action<br>▪ Description is important | To entertain/ for pleasure<br>May inform | Leisure reading |
| Scientific—flora and fauna only | ▪ Explanation is statement of fact—factual text<br>▪ Participants are non-human<br>▪ Processes (verbs) are relational (to be—is/has, etc.) | To inform and provide information about natural and non-natural phonomena | Teaching or learning in school or some other educational context |
| Abstract for journal | ▪ Authoritative address to reader<br>▪ Participants are outside the text<br>▪ Processes (verbs) are relational<br>▪ Clauses are long and tend to have many nominal groups (more nouns than verbs)<br>▪ Presents an argument for the reader to consider | To inform and sometimes to convince of an argument or position | To report on theory and/or research |
| News story | ▪ Headline which signals importance<br>▪ Newsworthy event<br>▪ Verbs of action to retell<br>▪ Processes (verbs) which quote<br>▪ Circumstances of time and place<br>▪ Specific participants | To provide information on newsworthy events | To inform readers on a daily basis |
| Greek myth | ▪ Third person narrative<br>▪ Past tense<br>▪ Participants are gods/goddesses of Roman/Greek origin<br>▪ Processes (verbs) are material and action<br>▪ Content of story imaginary<br>▪ Resolution of story clear (coda)<br>▪ Sometimes a moral or lesson to be learned | To entertain a reader using ancient stories | Reading in school or for pleasure |
| College/university song | ▪ Personal—includes reader as 'we'<br>▪ Participants—people, things and events<br>▪ Processes (verbs)—present, present continuous, future<br>▪ Rhetoric | To learn of the history of an organisation and continue tradition | To sing together in an act of appreciation |

# Note taking from whole books

Students must take notes when listening to lectures but they also need to learn how to make the best use of their study time when reading assigned material. Taking notes from reading will assist them to recall information, study for exams and prepare assignments. The tasks from the Students' Book are meant to assist them to:

- improve their speed by skimming and scanning for what is relevant; and
- to make organised notes when reading.

Rather than provide texts for students, this section expects the teacher to use each student's own future area of study or discipline (or own interest if the previous is not available nor realistic) to practise the skills needed to make improvements.

*Ask students to bring in texts, or use the library if you have access to one or use materials you have at your disposal for practising note taking skills from books.*

## Task A: Getting a global view of a text

SB P.96

Students tick the boxes.

## Task B: Getting around a book—the whole book

SB P.96

Students follow the instructions contained in Task B concerning the book they are examining and write the page numbers noting where they found items such as the index or references. They should write that the index begins on page x and finishes on page y.

## Task C: Note taking from books

SB P.97

Students should take their own notes using the texts from their own fields. The teacher acts as facilitator and checker by walking around the room and checking that students are using a workable method.

## Task D: Practise summarising information in topic sentences

SB P.98

Students are asked to use their own texts. As mentioned above, these would be realia and chosen by them or by the teacher.

- The *purpose* of this exercise is to ask students to shorten the material by summarising the first and last sentences of each paragraph.
- Sentences should not be copied exactly and should be shorter than the original texts, incorporating the main idea of each topic sentence.

***Text 1***

- Topic sentence: ______________________________
- Revised summary: ______________________________

*Text 2*

- Topic sentence: ______________________________
- Revised summary: ______________________________

*Text 3*

- Topic sentence: ______________________________
- Revised summary: ______________________________

# Listening

## Listening for pleasure and listening for non-lingustic clues

SB P.99

The *purpose* of this section is for students to listen for enjoyment, practise discussing around the topic of the listening and to understand that meaning can be conveyed through non-linguistic means.

We have devised this listening to be for pleasure. You may wish to teach some vocabulary before listening commences and explain that the accents are Irish (well, as Irish as it was possible to make them!) because, in the notorious Kelly Gang, Ned, his two brothers and some friends were of Irish descent.

**Variation:** You could read the information about Ned Kelly to students or use it as a jigsaw exercise where you photocopy the information and distribute it around the room by giving half to one student and half to another. Students with one half (A) explain it to the other students who have the other half of the reading (B), then vice versa.

**Ned Kelly**

A Ned Kelly was a kind of Robin Hood in the early colonial days of Australia when the mounted police ruled with an iron hand, terrorised whom they wished and kept order using harsh means. Ned obviously hated authority and, once on the wrong side of the law, was never able to return to civil society. He dreamed of a free state of North-East Victoria where the common person had power. He was a horse thief and a bank robber who gave money to the poor. He was shot dead wearing armour that he had devised to protect him.

B In the play, Ned lets Curnow leave the hotel. Curnow lies and says that his wife is ill (because she is expecting a baby). Curnow was the local school teacher and Ned trusted him. Curnow betrayed Ned and 'dobbed him in' (reported him to the police) and the trap was set for the demise of the Kelly gang.

**Vocabulary:** Teacher to introduce as desired:

- armour—metal protection that fits over the face and body (like medieval knights wore);
- invincible—cannot die;
- Euroa—a town in the State of Victoria, Australia, where there was a bank;
- wombat heads—the police (a wombat is a furry, fat, slow animal);
- big, ugly, fat-necked, wombat-headed, big-bellied, narrow-hipped, splay-footed sons of Irish baliffs of English landlords—hmmm, an angry invective concerning the police;

- fat necks—the police;
- she's in a delicate condition—she is pregnant;
- apparition—a ghost.

Student's listen and enjoy!

## Recording script

(7) **RECORDING NUMBER 7 (8 MINUTES, 30 SECONDS)**

**TITLE: Goin' down fighting**

Every country has stories about ordinary people who have done extraordinary things. Their story is told and retold and they become folk heroes, legends ... and over time no one knows the real truth. One such type of hero is the wronged person who fights against the system, robs the rich and gives to the poor. Australia's folk hero is Ned Kelly. He was much loved by the poor and hated by the rich. This is a part of his story.

*(Banging of hammer on metal)*

*Ellen:* Ned, Ned, what are you doing out there in the shed?

*Ned:* Oh, nothin, Maw.

*(Door opens)*

*Ellen:* What in the world are you doing?

*Ned:* I've just about finished. Hand me that rag, will ya, and I'll give it a polish.

*Ellen:* I don't understand.

*Ned:* It's armour, Maw.

*Ellen:* Armour?

*Ned:* See? This goes over my shoulders.
*(Clanking sounds)* And this here's the head part. I can see out ... and no bullet from the fat necks will get me.

*Ellen:* Really?

*Ned:* Really. No bullet can go through this. I'll be invincible.

*Ellen:* Ned, you can't take on the whole police force. There are too many of them. Please stay out of trouble.

*Ned:* I can't, Maw. After the way they hauled you off to jail with the baby just to get at me, and that Constable Fitzpatrick making eyes at Kate, I have to. They are our enemies and I'll strike them down.

*Ellen:* But Ned, they'll never let you live.

*Ned:* I have a plan, Maw. We will establish a new country, the Republic of North-East Victoria, a place for the bold, the fearless, and the free. No policemen, no banks, no railroads, and no landlords. You'll see. But first we need money, I'm off to Euroa. That will be an easy bank.

*Ellen:* Oh, Ned. Please be careful.

*Ned:* *(Laughing)* Don't worry, Maw. I'll be back. I'm the best horseman in Victoria, they won't catch me.

*Ellen:* And the best horse thief too.

*(Music transition)*
*(Creaking of saddles and horses walking)*

*Ned:* Well boys, Euroa was easy, just locked the town up in the hotel and robbed the bank. It sure was good takings.

*Daniel:* It sure was, Brother. Too bad we can't do another.

*Joseph:* What about Jirilderie? They've got a bank.

*Steven:* It's not too far. Only a few days ride.

*Daniel:* If we ride hard we could be there in a week and away before the wombat heads even get to Euroa.

*Ned:* *(Laughs and voice gets angry as he continues)* The big, ugly, fat-necked, wombat-headed, big-bellied, narrow-hipped, splay-footed sons of Irish bailiffs of English landlords. There's only one policeman at Jirilderie. We'll tie him up, cut the telegraph wire and round up the town.

*Joseph:* The Royal Mail Hotel would be big enough.

*Daniel & Steven:* Let's do it.

*Ned:* OK boys, we're on our way

*Steven:* We can use our hideout in the Wombat Ranges and pass out some of the money from there. There are plenty of poor folks about who could use it.

*Ned:* Let's ride.

*(Sound of galloping horses)*
*(Music transition)*

*Steven:* Ned ...

*Ned:* What is it Steven?

*Steven:* I heard some gossip while I was in town today.

*Ned:* Oh ... what were they saying?

*Steven:* Well, they say there's a plan to assemble a trainload of fat necks to come up and get us. They say dead or alive.

*Ned:* And, do you believe it?

*Steven:* I'm afraid so. It was all over town. What are we going to do, Ned?

*Ned:* Well, fight them, of course.

*Steven:* But there are only four of us!

*Ned:* Well, don't you see? They'd be never expecting us to stand and fight, they only think we'll run. But I will wreak a terrible revenge.

*Steven:* How?

*Ned:* First, we won't be where they expect us. Second, we'll tear up the train tracks. We'll take out a whole section of rails and wreck the train. And then we'll round up the town and lock 'em up ... Mrs Joneses' hotel will be big enough. Then we'll pick off the fat necks like a shooting gallery and hooray for the Republic of North-East Victoria!

*Stephen:* What if something goes wrong?

*Ned:* Then we'll go down fighting.

*(Music transition)*

*(Crowd noises)*

*Ned:* It's alright folks, nobody is going to get hurt. We just don't want you running around loose. You know Ned. It's a party. The drinks are on me. Come on, Mrs Jones, Fill em up. Drinks for everybody. Come on, fiddler, strike up a tune! (*Irish melody, some join in the song, sounds like dancing and merriment)* What is it, Mr. Schoolmaster?

*Curnow:* Ned, Mrs Curnow is ill. You know, she's in a very delicate condition. Please let me take her home. She's feeling very sick.

*Ned:* Aye, me Maw used to get that way.

*Curnow:* I'll just take her home and put her to bed. I'll come back if you like.

*Ned:* No need, no need. Just you take good care of her. *(Calls)* ... Daniel, let them out the back.

*Daniel:* Let them out?

*Ned:* You heard me. Curnow's all right. Let them out.

*(Door opens and closes, sounds of merriment fade)*

*Maggie:* *(Whispers)* Oh, Thomas, I'm not sick. What are you doing?

*Curnow:* Shhhh ... I'm going to try to stop the train and warn the police.

*Maggie:* Oh, Thomas.

*Curnow:* I'll be all right, you just run on home. Now, go on now.

*(Sound of revelry increases as if it has been a long night. The sound of gunshots ring out)*

*Ned:* To the windows boys ... Shoot the bastards but don't waste any ammunition.

*(Shooting continues)*

*Daniel:* *(Sounding frightened and more childlike)* Brother, they've got us. Steven's been hit ...

*Steven:* I'm all right.

*Joseph:* We've got them covered from this side.

*Ned:* It isn't light yet. I think I can get out the back way and into the bush. I'll come in from behind shooting both guns and we'll have them in a crossfire. Don't worry. We'll get 'em yet.

*Steven:* Maybe your armour will protect you.

*Ned:* Too right ... Good luck boys ... At least we'll go down fighting.

*(Temporary silence; a morning bird twitters)*

*Whispered voices:* What's that in the mist? Some kind of apparition? A spectre ... a ghost?

*(Three shots ring out)*

*Voice:* I'm hit.

*Voices:* Shoot ... shoot!

*(Hail of shots)*

*Voice 2:* It's down. Come on.

*(Sound of running feet).*

*Voice:* It's a man ..., We got him in the legs. Take that thing off.

*Voice:* My God, its Ned.

*(Music)*

**Epilogue**

Narrator: Ned Kelly was hanged for murder on November 11th 1880. His reported last words were ... *Ah, well, I suppose it has come to this. Such is life.* The other three of the Kelly gang were burned to death when the police set fire to Mrs Joneses' hotel. Many thought it a just retribution for their wickedness. The Irish poor thought him a hero, in their eyes he had always fought against injustice, robbed the rich and fed the poor.

Ironically, his place as a folk hero has been ensured by the art works of Sidney Nolan. He was the hero in a play by Douglas Stewart and the 2002 Booker Prize novel by Peter Carey, *True History of the Kelly Gang.* The people and the world of art and literature have enshrined Ned Kelly. The man who wanted a country for the free, the fearless and the bold and who went down fighting would be pleased.

## Task A: Listening for non-linguistic cues which carry action forward

SB P.99

The second time students listen to the recording, ask them to listen for 'sound effects'. Make a list of every sound you hear which is not a voice speaking.

Here they are in order:

1 Clanking on metal, a hammer hitting metal.

2 Horse neighing, creaking of saddles and horses walking.

3 Horses whinnying and galloping off.

4 A crowd in a hotel, glasses clinking.

5 Irish tune playing.

6 Door opening and closing.

7 Two shots ringing out.

8 Many shots ringing out.

9 Early morning bird call.

### Task B: Discovering—what is the point of these non-linguistic cues?

SB P.99

1 Present action taking place that you cannot see (Ned making his armour by hitting metal with a hammer).

2 Actions that have been mentioned are completed (such as robbing a bank)—you know this because the horses gallop off and the next speech is *'Well, Eurora was easy takings ...'*

3 Highlight location changes:

- in the hotel with crowd sounds and music
- outside the pub after the sound of the door opening and closing.

4 Show time passing (bird call in the morning mist = Ned leaving and returning through the woods (bush).

### Task C: Discussion using students as cultural informants

SB P.100

SB▷

1 Does your country have a villain who is a hero? Discuss.

2 What is the person's name?

3 When did they live if they are no longer living now?

4 Is the person male or female?

5 Are their deeds social, political or creative?

6 What makes a hero?

7 What makes a villain?

9 What cultural qualities does your nation have that makes this person famous and popular?

# Critical thinking

## Considering writing styles

The *purpose* of this section is for students to compare the writing styles they have studied in the Unit with those of their own countries.

**Variation:** Before doing Task A, students could answer questions like:

1 What similarities are there in the types of texts you examined to those you know about?

2 For example, myths—what language features can be matched from the 'language features 2' box on page 94? What is different about myths from your culture?

3 What other types of writing are prevalent in your country? (Religious writing may be significant and it is not included here as a Western genre.)

### Task A: Comparison of text types from your own language with English

SB P.100

Students' answers will vary and hopefully lead to discussion based upon their different cultures. Even if the class composition is one culture, it will be different from the English models provided earlier in this Unit.

# Speaking

## Tutorial participation skills 1

Some tutorials do not provide students with a great deal of opportunity to speak unprepared, but others do. Some students find themselves at a great disadvantage in this situation. The purpose of the task is to:

- assist students to learn how to take turns and to better understand the concept of turn-taking;
- anticipate when they might 'jump in' and begin to speak.

In Task B, the short (one minute) possibly humourous 'speech ideas' are for getting students used to speaking unsupported in front of others (in case some of them are not used to doing so) and to provide practice for other students in being concise and accurate. (It is also useful practice for the International English Examination Testing System or IELTS test.)

In order to teach some of the most common turn-taking discourse cues, the topic 'Western literature today', has been used for a short 'mock tutorial' in which five students agree, disagree and add to one another's position.

At the end of the task, it could be useful to ask students to work in groups to agree or disagree about any topic that is current in your classroom at the moment. They could also discuss literature in their own countries and what their favourite type of reading is, trying to get other students to feel the same way (that is, convincing them). Students should have enough differing opinions and knowledge to at least get one round of agreement or disagreement going. The point is to get them using the ***turn-taking language.*** The issues can vary. Try to give them five or six different contemporary topics. (Examples could include music taste; stem cell research; nuclear power as a good source of energy; living at home vs leaving home; young marriage vs waiting until older; the list is endless.)

## Task A: Using discourse cues to allow for turn-taking

SB P101

**Answers**

| Agree | Disagree |
|---|---|
| I agree | Yes, but … |
| Certainly | With respect … |
| Yes … | I don't agree … |
| | Hang on a minute … |
| | What makes you think that? … |
| | Well, you have a point there, but … |
| | Why not look at it like this? … |

## Task B: Practising speaking unsupported

SB P.102

The *purpose* of this task is to provide students with some practice in simply getting up in front of others and speaking without preparation.

Depending upon your group of students, you may wish to allow them to test each other using a timer to accomplish the speaking in groups, or they could tape record themselves speaking for one minute and play it back in groups; or, if the class is quite small, they could take turns speaking in front of the whole group.

# Learner independence & study skills

## Time management

Although a great deal of both research and writing has centred around the subject of time management, one wonders how many students have actually embraced either the concept or a system for implementing it. Have you ever asked a student how many weeks they have left in their course? Often, they do not know. And yet, what an important (and possibly expensive) time of their lives this is!

The *purpose* of this section is to:

- encourage each individual student to devise their own weekly time schedule for their lives;
- examine and consider what they do with their time.

## Task A: Examining your use of time

SB P.102

Students write next to the times one sentence explaining everything they did and will do today and fill in a timetable showing what they do throughout the week.

## Task B: Creating a personal timetable that includes 30 hours of study

SB P.104

Students revise their timetable to include 30 hours per week of study if it is not there now.

**Additional class work:** You could model how to note important events on a yearly calendar. A wall calendar devised for the class noting one important event for each of them, for example, examination dates or even their birthdays would provide a good visual display and acquaint them with the concept of monthly and yearly planning if they are not familiar with this already.

# English for the Internet Age and Critical thinking

## Evaluating academic credibility of information on the Internet

The purpose of this section is for students to consider factors pertinent to the academic credibility of information from web sites.

### Task A: Can Internet information be trusted?

SB P.104

If possible, put at least one computer-literate person in each group.

**Answers**

1 Publishing an Internet page is much easier than publishing a book. With a book, the author either has to convince a publisher to take it on, or is chosen by the publisher. Publishing an Internet page is just a matter of sending it electronically to an Internet service company—usually no human would even see it before it's available for anyone to access on the Internet. A publisher, having a financial interest in the book, will want there to be little danger of a loss of credibility affecting sales. However, an Internet company is just a 'host' for the site, gains fees from the author, not the readers, and loses nothing if the page loses credibility.

2 Usually information on the WWW should be considered very carefully before using it.

3 This depends both on who runs the websites and the publishers. Websites of well-respected organisations could possibly be treated similarly to books in terms of credibility, and self-published books as well as books published by potentially biased organisations should be treated with the same sort of scepticism as with websites. The important points are that students should think critically before believing published information, and that information on the Internet requires special care.

### Task B: Critical thinking—predicting bias and accuracy

SB P.104

Groups are useful for this activity as well.

**Answers**

1 (a), (b), (c) and possibly (d) all have clear reasons to present a biased view. Bias is also possible in the others!

2 Possibly (e) is the most likely to have had care taken to be accurate, but all except (d) would lose credibility or reputation if they contained inaccurate information, although it is quite possible that this may happen. However, it's unlikely but quite possible that (d)'s information is better than anyone else's.

3 The research in (e) may apply only to the countries investigated. Questions should be asked such as: which ones are they? Which other factors may apply to other countries? With (f), it would be interesting to know how the police collect their statistics—many gun owners may try to hide their guns from the police. Other questions are also possible.

## Task C: Evaluating website credibility

SB P.105

Having two students per computer means that issues and choices about which link to follow are discussed, enabling more critical thinking and speaking practice.

These websites have been chosen partly because they have been stable over a period of several years.

Accept all reasonable answers.

## Task D: Searching and evaluating

SB P.106

The students can choose their own issue(s). This can be done individually, in groups or as a class.

unit 5

# the news

The wolf preys upon the lamb in the dark of the night, but the blood stains remain to accuse him by day.

KAHLIL GIBRAN

## Skills focus: In this Unit, students will learn and use the following skills:


**Speaking:** oral presentation skills and oral discourse markers; oral presentation assignment 94

**Writing:** compiling bibliographies 97

**Grammar:** pronominal referencing and participant tracking; tense review—perfect tenses; register revisited 99

**Listening:** distinguishing between fact and opinion 105

**Reading:** newspaper editorial; purpose or intention of writer—identifying bias, connotations and attempts to influence 109

**Critical thinking:** language as power—becoming a critical reader 112

**English for the Internet Age:** refugees—Internet research project 113

**Learner independence & study skills:** assignment research skills; vocabulary for tertiary purposes—university word list 114

In this Unit, students will be asked to challenge authority, question texts, analyse messages for ideological content and critically consider whether news is informative or manipulative, or both.

They will also learn about oral presentations, tracking participants within texts, how to recognise and write bibliographies and carry out correct referencing, and where to locate university word lists.

The *purpose* of this section is to:

- assist students to critically examine media texts; and
- improve reading and writing skills by understanding what creates a cohesive text.

It is wise to emphasise both the structure and the social context of all texts so that students begin to think of texts in a context, not as isolated 'bits' or things. By understanding structure and social context the student/reader can be empowered to 'denaturalise' or expose the 'taken-for-grantedness' of ideological messages as they appear in the news and print media (Kaplan, 1993).

Texts are produced by *socially situated speakers and writers* (Kress, 1993). Students need to learn to analyse where texts originate, the possible purpose for their origin, and whether the writer wishes to persuade or convince them of something. Writers make language choices which readers can dissect in order to find the ideological position if it is not overt. Often, media texts present themselves as authorities on any subject they are discussing and the ideological content is reflected by the structure of the text. In other words, if I present something to you authoritatively then you should believe it and accept it, perhaps without question. Many students are used to accepting written texts as truth. Perhaps the *Listening, Reading, Critical Thinking* and *Internet* sections of this Unit may assist them to challenge that assumption.

Like the rest of this book, it is intended that individual teachers will utilise realia and newspaper editorials containing current issues from the news for students to analyse, deconstruct and discuss.

# Speaking

✓ *Oral presentation skills and oral discourse markers*
✓ *Oral presentation assignment*

## Oral presentation skills and oral discourse markers

SB P.108

As stated in the Students' Book, sometimes as much as 40% of a mark from subject may be based upon oral presentations, either alone or as a participant in a group.

We have tried to lighten the mood of this section with a little humour. Who has not seen a poor presentation where a student holds notes in front of their face, turns to the white board and speaks to it, or reads the whole presentation in a boring monotone? (The odd lecturer at university has been known to do the same, wouldn't you agree?)

## Task A: How to prepare and present an oral presentation (or maybe how *not* to)

SB P.108

### Answers

How to make a fool of yourself and get a low mark.

The numbers of the false advice are given below.

- Preparation and research: b and d.
- Presentation: a and e
- Delivery on the day: a, d and e
- Question time: a and b

## Task B: Using discourse cues to recognise stages of a presentation

SB P.109

Students should work in pairs—one to read the 'cues' aloud while the other places them under the correct heading in the table. They could then work on a simple oral presentation around a familiar and easy topic, utilising as many discourse cues as possible.

| Introduction | Body | Conclusion |
|---|---|---|
| ■ Today, I would like to ...; | ■ There are three main points | ■ In conclusion |
| ■ In order to define 'cactus' it is important to consider | ■ In 2002, Barker and Johnston | ■ To summarise |
| ■ This talk will cover two current theories around the topic of | ■ It would appear that one solution might be to | ■ Thus, it is obvious that the government should provide |
| ■ It is beyond the scope of this presentation to include everything around the topic of forestry, so | ■ Actually, there is not a great deal of research that has been carried out around this subject | |
| ■ Let me begin by | ■ A great deal of research has been carried out around this aspect of the subject since 1922 | |
| | ■ Next | |
| | ■ However | |
| | ■ It is worth considering | |

SB▷

### Discourse cues/markers

Today, I would like to ...; In conclusion; There are three main points ...; In 2002,Barker and Johnston ...; To summarise ...; In order to define'cactus' it is important to consider ...; This talk will cover two current theories around the topic of ...; Thus, it is obvious that the government should provide ...; It is beyond the scope of this presentation to include everything around the topic of forestry, so ...; It would appear that one solution might be to ...; Actually, there is not a great deal of research that has been carried out around this subject ...; Let me begin by ...; A great deal of research has been carried out around this aspect of the subject since 1922 ...; Next; However; It is worth considering ...

## Oral presentation assignment

The *purpose* of this assignment is for students to:

- gain experience preparing and giving an oral presentation;
- find for themselves resources that may be useful in their future field of study;
- carry out extensive library research;
- review aspects of writing considered earlier in this book;
- give an oral presentation demonstrating an ability to:
  - present a coherent argument with adequate support throughout
  - follow common academic conventions in the staging and organisation of the presentation
  - define key concepts and terms
  - critically analyse the issue
  - provide full and appropriate referencing and reference list.

Students will prepare and give an oral presentation to other members of the class. Oral presentations are introduced in this Unit; more work will be done in Unit 6; and the actual giving of the presentations is supported in Unit 7.

It's important that students gain experience in giving an oral presentation before they begin their tertiary course. This project should resemble as closely as possible the process of researching and preparing such an assignment, but with more support. It's best if other procedures, such as applying for extensions, are also kept realistic; for example with the use of a form. See Unit 1, *Academic Requests* 1, page 2.

The students should know as much as possible about the requirements for their presentation before commencing the project. Give them information to fill in the form in their books, and emphasise the importance of finding out as much as possible about assessment requirements as early as possible when doing any assignment, especially in tertiary education. To this end, they need to know:

- which of the assessment/observation worksheets in Appendix C will be used;
- that the presentation must give an opinion and be supported with evidence from their reading, and with logical argument;
- that they should show they have read from several sources to prepare;
- that they should show they have critically analysed the information they read.

**Some other points**

- A useful topic is the student's future field. This will allow each student to become familiar with some basic resources in their field, if they haven't already started their intended course.
- Twenty minutes is usually an appropriate length, though the length requirement you choose will depend on your student's aims and abilities. Different requirements for individual students are possible.
- If possible, take the class to a university library, or at least a large public library.
- At least three references, including one journal, should be a minimum requirement.
- Emphasise that in tertiary education, the minimum penalty for plagiarism is **fail**, and it could lead to expulsion from the university.
- Four weeks, if the students are studying full-time, is an appropriate time period for doing an assignment. In this book, the assignments are assessed in Unit 7, page 169 (Students' Book). See also Unit 10, *Reading, Peer review of extended essays* at page 234 (Students' Book).
- They must be informed that other students will watch their presentations.
- During the project, it is a good idea to organise some lessons to be workshops in which students bring in their work on their project. During the workshop, they would work on it individually or with the help of other students, while you go round each person, answering questions and giving advice. Not only will this allow you to check progress and give assistance, but it will also provide an incentive for the students not to leave everything to the last minute.
- Students will probably ask many questions when this project is set up, and the teacher should allow time for discussion, as well as time to help students with choosing their topic and getting started on their research.

**Variation:** Allowing all students to research the same topic increases opportunity for collaborative learning. However, if your students are doing/going on to do study in different fields, it reduces their opportunity to form a link between their English study and study in their field. Teachers would also have to ensure that students do actually undertake some research on their own!

# Writing

SB P.111

## Compiling bibliographies

### Task A: Understanding bibliographies

SB P.112

**Answers**

1 Which citings (references) have page numbers at the end of the reference?

The first, second and last—Bassey, Burns, Elliott.

2 Why are page numbers shown on some references and not others?

The page numbers mean that that is the exact place the information was taken from. No page numbers means the whole book or journal article was read and the ideas came from it in general.

3 What does (eds) mean in the first citing?

(Eds) refers to the editors of the volume. The name of the person who wrote the quoted words must come first, then the editors of the book where it was found, then the name of the book where it was found.

4 Why does Bassey appear first and Zancor appear last?

Because all bibliographies must be placed in alphabetical order.

5 Why are *italics* used at the end of some references and at the beginning of others?

It depends on whether the title needs to come first. If there is an article title or chapter title which needs to be written, that comes first and is in ' ' marks, whereas the title of the publication is italicised.

6 In the first reference, is *Action Research in Classrooms and Schools* a book or a journal? How can you tell?

It is the title of a book. Students can tell because there is no volume number.

7 In the final reference (Elliott) is *Educational Action Research* the title of a book or a journal? How can you tell?

It is the title of a journal. You can tell because it has a volume number and no publisher details.

8 Did you notice more than one reference from the same author? Name the author.

Burns, R.

9 In what order are the dates of publication of the author from question 8 presented?

In chronological order—from the most recent to the oldest publication date.

10 Some disciplines suggest from oldest to most recent publication dates for the same author (the opposite of above).

This may vary—students should remember to be consistent.

## Task B: Analysing references in body texts

SB P.112

### Answers

1 Students will circle Bassey (1986:18) and Burns (1994:32)

2 a] One.

b] 1986.

c] The author of the second reference.

d] Page 32.

e] 1994.

In Text 2, the correct answer is that there are *no references* in the article. Students must write the reference when they quote or use the article from the paper.

## Task C: Writing bibliographic references correctly

SB P.113

Zeng, Min (2001) 'APEC meeting to promote regional economy'. *China Daily* 21/01, Vol 21, No 6701.

SB▷ Examine the bibliography below and fill in the missing blanks by referring to the bibliography above.

**Answers**

The original bibliography on page 111 of the Students' Book provides the correct text.

Ask students to write a number of references such as this one, using local newspapers from your own state which might commonly be used.

### Task D: Referencing from the WWW (World Wide Web)

SB P.114

This is further developed in the Students' Book, Unit 7, page 161. Increasingly, students will use the World Wide Web for research. Most universities now provide their own guide as to how to correctly reference from the web. Students need to understand that it is sometimes difficult to name pages and dates. Pagination is not relevant on the web and, for dates, the date that is found on the material may be the date cited. When in doubt, students should provide as much information as they possibly can. For more information, as stated in the Students' Book, students may refer to *The Columbia Guide to Online Style*.

# Grammar

✓ *Pronominal referencing and participant tracking*

✓ *Tense review: perfect tenses*

✓ *Register revisited*

## Pronominal referencing and participant tracking

In this section, students learn to keep track of the main idea or participants while reading and writing. When writing in English, writers refer back to previously mentioned participants and substitute other words for those participants (referencing and substitution—for more on substitution, see Students' Book, page 87 and Teacher's Book, page 76).

Readers must carry forward in their memory the first mention of a participant and recognise when that main idea or thing (the participant) is again being referred to. A simple example would be 'The garden has lovely flowers. They are in blossom now.' (*They* refers to the flowers previously mentioned.)

The *purpose* of this section is for students to:

- recognise the main participants in a text;
- follow (track) them throughout a text;
- differentiate between pronominal referencing and substitution;

By doing the above, students will be able to:

- improve their reading comprehension;
- write with greater clarity.

## Task A: Identifying main participants and tracking them in a text

SB P.114

### Answers

The main participant is *the body of a Japanese man* who was a keen fisherman.

1 The body of a Japanese man who was a keen fisherman.

2 The man.

3 He/Mr/John Suzuki.

4 Mr Suzuki.

## Task B: Tracking multiple participants

SB P.115

### Answers

Numbers refer to line numbers.

| London firefighters | The scene of a factory fire | Five workers | Work |
|---|---|---|---|
| 1 London firefighters<br>2 The firefighters<br>3 The brave and tired men<br>6 Firefighters<br>11 The men in red | 1 the scene of a factory fire<br>2 West London<br>2 the chemical blaze<br>4 the premises<br>5 on the factory floor<br>6 the blazing building<br>8 the premises<br>9 there<br>12 the building | 1 lives<br>3 five workers<br>4 who<br>5 They<br>8 the workers<br>9 (they)had arranged with one another<br>12 the men | 4 working overtime<br>9 work<br>10 This work |

## Task C: Practice in locating and tracking a main participant

SB P.116

### Answers

1 a] The USA.

b] a … death penalty study of 4,578 cases in a 23-year period (1973–1995).

c] The courts.

d] Serious, reversible error.

2 Seven of every 10 capital sentence cases that were fully reviewed.

3 a] (1973–1995).

b] The period.

# Tense review: perfect tenses

SB P.117

The *purpose* of this section is for students to:

- learn to use past perfect tense correctly;
- revise narrative and recount;

- track participants throughout a long text; and
- enjoy reading a true story told about the only whaling ship ever sunk by a whale and wondering about the cannibalism that ensued.

## Task A: Processes or verbs—choosing the correct tense

SB P.119

### Answers

Questions 1, 2 and 3

**Text 1**

- The Essex sailed (past simple)
- A whale rose and spouted (past simple)
- I made …, came up and struck (past simple)
- Feeling the harpoon, he threw himself …, giving a severe blow with his tail struck … stove (past simple), (past simple), (past simple)
- I … took up … and cut … was moving off (past simple), (past simple), (past continuous)
- I succeeded in getting clear (past simple)
- I … stuffed (past simple)
- We succeeded ... and shortly gained (past simple), (past simple)
- The boat which had been stove (past simple)
- was immediately hoisted in (past simple passive)
- I was (past simple)
- I observed (past simple)
- I could judge (modal verb)
- He broke (past simple)
- He was lying quietly (past continuous)
- He made directly for us (past simple)
- I ordered (past simple)
- The words were scarcely (past simple)
- He came down upon us … struck (past simple), (past simple)
- He gave (past simple)
- Nearly threw us (past simple)
- We looked (past simple)
- Many minutes elapsed … we were able … the whale started off (past simple), (past simple), (past simple)
- I dispatched orders (past simple)
- I again discovered (past simple)
- He was enveloped … I could distinctly see (past simple) (modal verb)
- He remained … and then started off (past simple), (past simple)
- I was aroused (past simple)
- Here he is—he is making for us again (direct speech, present and present continuous)
- I turned around and saw him (past simple), (past simple)
- It appeared to me (past simple)
- The surf flew (past simple)
- His course towards us was marked (past passive)
- He made (past simple)
- His head was … (past simple)
- He came … (past simple)
- He struck … and completely stove … (past simple), (past simple)

- In the last paragraph, the author addresses the reader directly: Not a moment, however, was to be lost in endeavouring to provide for the extremity to which it was now certain we were reduced … We were more than a thousand miles from the nearest land with … and so forth.

**Text 2: Answers: see Task E, page 103**

Questions 4, 5 and 6

4 The simple past is used the most because it is a first person recount of past events. The writer moves the action forward by telling the story and using the simple past tense more than any other.

5 The past perfect is used in the second recount because the person telling the story is not the person who experienced it. It is a second hand recount about events. The writer was not there and is merely explaining something that happened to others in the past.

6 If you have time for your students to complete this writing, they may do it in class. Otherwise, it would make a good homework assignment.

## Task B: Comparison of a first person account with a third person narrative

SB P.120

SB▷

| **First person narrative** | | **Third person narrative** | |
|---|---|---|---|
| **Narrative of the Most …** | | **What happened to the crew …?** | |
| Author | Owen Chase | Author | Unknown |
| Target audience | Present day historians; anyone interested in whaling | Target audience | The same audience |
| Purpose for writing (author's possible intention) | To share a very difficult experience with others. To set the record straight concerning the sinking of a whaling ship | Purpose for writing (author's possible intention) | To explain a story of the past and to let people know what the crew told their rescuers |
| Source | A book by Owen Chase | Source | unknown |
| Time | The actual time of the event (although we know it was written after) | Time | Many months or even years after the event |
| Place | The Pacific Ocean, a thousand miles from the nearest land off the Galapagos islands and the whaling ship *Essex* | Place | The sinking ship; the boats where the crew lived; the country where the crew ended up after being rescued |

## Task C: Learning the features of a narrative

SB P.120

### Answers

- Time and date: 12 August , 1819; three months, day after day, week after week.
- Place: Nantucket, the Pacific, Galapagos Islands.

- Chronological order with temporal sequencers: the narrative begins with the *Essex* sailing from the Galapagos Islands. The first sequencer is: presently, the past tense carries the action forward and sentences that include 'immediately' as the action progresses are also moving the action onwards. The specific participant, who is the narrator, uses 'I' at the beginning of many sentences or 'he' or 'the whale' and then explains what they did. This keeps a chronological order in the sequence of events.
- Description of events, but not many feelings: events are described but, on the whole, the feelings of the humans are not explained. The whale is described as 'distracted with rage and fury' but the fear and wonder that the crew must have felt is not prominent in this recount.
- Specific participants: the *Essex*, the whale, the crew, three whale boats.
- Verbs of action: these verbs will be the same ones circled or underlined in the previous exercise. Begin with 'sailed, rose and spouted, made all speed, came up, struck, stove, cut, was moving off—etc. Almost all the verbs here are verbs of action.

## Task D: Tracking a participant

SB P.121

Track the participant—the whale in Text 1—*Narrative of the Most Extraordinary and Distressing Shipwreck of the whaleship* Essex.

### Answers

a whale, him, him, him, he, the whale, him, a very large spermaceti whale, He, he, he, him, he, He, The whale, the whale, He, him, He, he, he, him, him, he, he, He.

Point out to students the personification of the whale by naming him with the male pronominal referents—'he' and 'him' are used in most of the narrative.

## Task E: Tense choices in context

SB P.121

### Answers – Text 2

1 The crew were … their ship was sinking. (past continuous)
2 They had had … (past perfect)
3 There was… the crew sadly watched. (past)(past)
4 Before the Essex went down … members … had gone aboard. (past)(past perfect)
5 They had taken. (past perfect)
6 they had (past)
7 They had … were (past)(past)
8 Those who were rescued … were rescued. (past passive)(past passive)
9 They told … how … boats had become separated. (past)(past perfect)
10 The winds had blown. (past perfect)
11 They told how … had run low … they were living. (past)(past perfect)(past continous)
12 They told … their crew mates had died … there were ... (past)(past perfect)(past)
13 They had looked. (past perfect)
14 They told how … they had eaten … (past perfect)
15 They told how … great storms had threatened … and how they had had to keep bailing. (past)(past perfect) (past perfect)
16 Their trust … had saved them … which leads. (past perfect)(present simple)

## Register revisited

### Task A: Recognising the features/requirements of a news story

SB P.121

SB

**Prime Minister supports higher university fees**

The Prime Minister said he was going right ahead with charging higher money costs to students who want to go to college. He reckoned that people can afford it and anyway if they can't it really doesn't matter all that much because most people who want to get an education will do something to get it. They can always borrow money must be his philosophy.

Fees are too high now according to many students that I talked to. They figure they will have to quit going and get a job instead. It's terrible and rotten, I think. It's like education will only be for the very rich really soon. It's getting like that now.

| Questions | Answers |
|---|---|
| 1 Does the article read like a news story? | 1 No, it does not read like a news story. |
| 2 What is the usual format for reporting the news? Fill in the spaces below using the story and then comment upon what is missing or different in this news item. | 2 The usual format must include answers to questions such as *who, what, where, when and how!* |
| 3 Headline | 3 *Prime Minister supports higher university fees.* |
| 4 Name of reporter | 4 Missing, not stated. |
| 5 Summary of the event | 5 *The Prime Minister said he was going right ahead with charging higher money costs to students who want to go to college.* |
| 6 Time and place stated | 6 Missing, no time nor place is stated. |
| 7 Background to the event | 7 No background is given. |
| 8 Grammar—action verbs | 8 There are some verbs of action but the writer rambles on in the first person which would never happen in a news story unless they were being quoted. |
| 9 Processes (verbs) of thinking and feeling | 9 There are none except for the narrator's personal opinion which has no place in a news report or news item (unless it is an editorial where personal comment of the editor is allowed). |
| 10 Higher lexis (vocabulary) written language | 10 The lexis is too low. Vocabulary is spoken and the narrator does not belong in the text at all. |
| 11 If it is not a news story, what does it read like? | 11 It reads like an interview or a conversation between two people with one person's speech being recorded. |

# Listening

## Distinguishing between fact and opinion

### Task A: Listening for key phrases which signal opinions

SB P.122

The *purpose* here is for students to listen (Recording number 8) for the key phrases which signal opinions. People tend to say things such as 'I think' or 'I know' even if it is not fact. When a speaker has more authority, they may say 'In fact' or 'The fact of the matter is ...' This does not make it fact, but it is more likely that they will have something to substantiate what they are going to say.

## Recording script

8 **RECORDING NUMBER 8 (7 MINUTES, 4 SECONDS)**

**TITLE: Talk back radio program: Fast food around the world**

*Announcer (Jim):* All rightie, this is Jim Lord coming to you with *Your views matter—the best of talk back radio!* Now, this morning we're going to be talking about fast food restaurants, take-out and food to go franchises around the world. These days, everywhere ya go, you can get food to go or eat in restaurants run by companies you can trust. Now, we're taking calls from anyone who has a comment to make about these food chains and who wants to share their experiences with us.

Now, while we're waiting for those calls ... and before we start, I want to tell you that I have travelled to a whole bunch a' countries and it's fantastic the way I can always get a hamburger and french fries, tacos and chicken no matter which city I'm in. I never have to eat the local muck they call food in some of those places and I can always count on quality and never getting sick. And that's terrific! And it always shows some of these Third World back waters how to run a darn good business!

(*Pause*)

Our first caller is Barry, from Smallville.

*Caller 1, Barry:* [Male, older businessman, American accent, agrees with Announcer] Hello, Jim?

*Jim:* Yeah, you're on, Barry.

*Barry:* Yeah, well, I just wanted to say that I've travelled a lot too and I think it's a changing world, changing for the better alright, because, like ya say, we can buy good food no matter what country we're in. You know, I had to go to China just last year, and I ate at the biggest hamburger chain in the entire world right there in Beijing. It was amazing. Mind you, I thought that the hamburgers were pretty small and the bread tasted a little different, but, well, it was clean, ya know ... and cheap and, I uh, I uh ... really appreciated something familiar from home.

One thing, though, ya know how I said it was cheap? Well it was to me, of course, but for the Chinese, it's real expensive; it's like a treat to eat there. So that's kinda unusual because for us, we think of fast food as super cheap, ya know?

*Jim:* Yeah, thanks Barry, price is a big thing. I reckon it's still very good value to feed a family on a bucket of chicken with gravy, fries, coleslaw and buns. Now, ya couldn't cook it yourself for the price. I don't know about China, haven't been there myself, but I did go to Bali, Indonesia, before that bombing and my driver said he and his family couldn't afford to eat at any of the chains there either. Ain't that weird?

(*pause*)

OK—our next caller is Nerrida and she says she's worked in the industry.

*Caller 2,* [young girl with a U.S. accent]
*Nerrida:* Hi Jim? [Jim: Hi Nerrida] I just wanted to say something about—from the last caller and what you said, Jim. He was saying it's cheap and all ... well, I've been working since I was 15 and we get pretty low wages, ya know, and I think, maybe that that one of the reasons that the company can sell cheap food is that maybe ...

*Jim:* Are you just calling to whine and complain, Nerrida? You said you were working since you were 15. Well, you're lucky to have a job, aren't you?

*Nerrida:* Well, yeah. But I'm $17\frac{1}{2}$ now and I lost my job when I turned 17, and did ya know we can't join the union and mostly we get fired as soon as we're 17 and can get adult wages? We worked a lot of unpaid shifts, too and I know it keeps the prices for customers down, but we don't make a living wage.

*Jim:* Yeah, well, Nerrida, ya know, people like you are never happy. Ya get all that free training and experience and ya want top dollars too. Well, thanks for your call [*deprecatingly, sarcastically*].

Our next caller is Luke Simon, a scientist from Pronucky. Hi Luke!

*Caller 3,* [A serious sounding Scottish caller with factual information and quotes]
*Luke:* Good morning, Jim. Ay, well, before I start, I just wanted to mention the fact that around 70% of the work force in fast food chains are adolescents, like Nerrida.

*Jim:* Yeah right, whatever ... What's your point Luke?

*Luke:* You stated that you could count on not getting sick when you ate in fast food restaurants overseas and at home and I'd like to point out that that's not at all true. You can actually get very sick from eating fast food. In fact, fast food contamination is one of the big problems for modern societies, especially the wee children. Have you heard of *E. coli* 0157:H7?

*Jim:* Can't say that I have, Luke. What are you getting at?

*Luke:* Well, the fact of the matter is that *E. coli* is a bacteria and it is found in a fair bit of hamburger meat that leaves the big meatpackers. If you even eat a tiny portion of contaminated hamburger, you can get very sick with diarrhoea. In some cases, the toxins from *E. coli* can kill you. You get kidney failure, anaemia, internal bleeding and organ damage. Plenty of kids have actually died—I'm talking hundreds here with thousands requiring hospitalisations just as a result of this *E. coli* bacteria.

*Jim:* Hey, c'mon, that's a pretty strong statement to make, buddy. You're not suggesting that eating hamburgers can give you a disease and that you can even die from it, are ya? I can't see any facts backing that up. There's been nothing in the news to support what you're saying there, and I've eaten 'em all over the world and I've never been sick once. You sound like some sort of drama queen getting in some corporate bashing to me.

*Luke:* I'm not going to argue with you, Jim. But believe me, the facts are there. I refer you and your listeners to a book called *Fast Food Nation* by Eric Schlosser. He's done the research and it's true as the sun rising. There's indisputable evidence that the practices of fast food production are leading to more contaminated meat problems. There are, in fact, cases of real people and they have had settlements from food chains over the deaths of their wee children from eating contaminated meat. Not only that, *E. coli* spreads another way and that is from the hands of workers who don't wash them. It's a big issue, Jim, and not something to be swept under the carpet. If you ever watched a child die starting with abdominal cramping, blood in the stool, brain swell ... (*speaker is cut off and music is inserted for just a second*)

*Jim:* Cut that—that's plenty of that nonsense. Thank you very much, my God some people are just so negative, well, it's incomprehensible, don't you think? I mean, honestly, what a load of rubbish comes out of some people's mouths. Like I say, I've been eating good ole fast food for ever and I think it's just fine.

And now, to take us out, here's a word from our sponsors. (*Music comes up*) Chicken Pickin' home lickin'—We deliver!

## Answers

| (Task A) | Number of instances |
|---|---|
| a] I want to tell you | ✓ |
| b] I think | ✓✓ |
| c] I reckon | ✓ |
| d] I know | ✓ |
| e] In fact, | ✓ |
| f] The fact of the matter is | ✓ |
| g] You're not suggesting | ✓ |
| h] But believe me, the facts | ✓ |
| i] I refer you and your listeners to | ✓ |
| j] There's pretty indisputable evidence that | ✓ |
| k] I mean | ✓ |
| l] Like I say | ✓ |

## Task B: Facts, opinions and power relationships

SB P.122

- Students should consider the power paradigm and the way the radio announcer uses his unequal status in the situation to manipulate listeners to his own viewpoint. He does not really listen to, nor does he acknowledge, any other opinions.
- Additionally, **for critical analysis**, you might ask students to consider whether there is a relationship between the announcer's comments and the sponsor of the program (chicken ... etc) and whether sponsorship is appropriate considering the topic. (There are instances of 'neutral' talk back radio announcers using their influence to endorse products and being paid to do so without disclosing their financial link.) Are students familiar with this from their experience in their own countries?

### Answers

1 a]

2 He misuses it by being nasty and opinionated to Nerrida and kind to Barry. Barry shares his opinions and so he is reasonable to him. The announcer says, 'Yeah, Thanks for that, Barry' at the end of his call but at the end of Nerrida's call he accuses her of whining and then attacks her by saying 'Ya get all that free training and experience and ya want top dollars too. Thanks for your call.' It is here that intonation belies the words. Although the announcer says, 'Thanks for your call', his tone is not gracious.

3 Abrupt.

4 All of them (a, b, c, d and e).

5 Yes, the announcer is rude.

6 Students could choose a number of examples. One obvious one is, *You sound like a drama queen getting in some corporate bashing to me.*

7 Most students would answer *Yes.*

8 and 9 Student answers will vary.

10

| Most likely to be an opinion | Most likely to be a fact |
|---|---|
| 2—A | 1—B |
| 3—D | 4—A |
| 10—A | 5—A |
| 11—D | 6—B |
| 12—D | 7—C |
| 13—D | 8—B |
| | 9—A |
| | 14—C |

(Letters refer to answers to Task C.)

## Task C: Discovering if truth is necessarily fact

SB P.124

**Answers** as per table above.

## Task D: Factual evidence

SB P.124

### Answers

Nerrida and Luke.

# Reading

✓ *Newspaper editorial*

✓ *Purpose or intention of writer: identifying bias, connotations and attempts to influence*

## Newspaper editorial

Newspaper editorials are the section of a paper where opinion is allowed. The editor of a paper has the right to express her/his opinion concerning any current issues of interest to the public and which are present in the news. Opinions, even from editors, are not necessarily factual and students must learn to distinguish between a statement that is supported with evidence, and one that is not.

The *purpose* of this section is for students to:

- understand that issues have more than one side and opinions are taken, argued for and debated around issues;
- recognise when support for a statement is given;
- recognise when that support is factual, not just opinion;
- understand the main purpose or reason that a text is written.

### Task A: Defining an issue—global examination of text

SB P.124

#### Answers

1 *Issue*: a point in question or dispute, as between contending parties in an action at law. 6. A point or matter the decision of which is of special or public importance: the political issues *(Macquarie Dictionary)*.

2 What does the bold lettering beneath the name of the paper say and what does it mean or imply?

**News for those who care about the real issues**: The meaning is that the readers of this paper care about issues in society. It implies that other papers do not tell the truth as they do not discuss 'real issues', rather some other sort of information and their readers may not care enough.

3 After reading the title, what issue do you believe is going to be discussed in the article?

Discussion will be to do with refugees.

4 Examine the title and tell your partner what else you think the article is going to discuss.

It may discuss the refugees losing something as a result of being stranded somewhere.

5 From the title, can you guess which side of the issue the editorial will take?

It might take the side of the refugees.

6 What does the title *Stranded refugees lose again ...* imply?

'Stranded' implies being left somewhere with no help or assistance and so does the word 'lose'. 'Again' means it has happened before, so it seems the editor may be on the side of the refugees and feels sorry for them.

7 Identify the author of the editorial.

The author's name is not given. The author is the editor of the newspaper and the reader would have to find it in the paper somewhere else.

8 Examine the name of the newspaper. Are there any clues in the name of the paper that might give you an idea of what the editor may say in this article?

In English, the words 'social and left' would imply the left wing. Traditionally, the left wing is concerned with society and social causes of the less fortunate. They often stand for the worker, the protection of the environment and social welfare.

9 Who is the possible audience for this editorial?

The audience would be newspaper readers who wish to read about social issues.

### Task B: Vocabulary in context 1

SB P.125

**Answers**

| | |
|---|---|
| a] 4 | b] 8 |
| c] 6 | d] 10 |
| e] 12 | f] 1 |
| g] 2 | h] 11 |
| i] 5 | j] 9 |
| k] 3 | l] 7 |

### Task C: Vocabulary in context 2

SB P.126

**Answers**

| | |
|---|---|
| a] 8 | b] 5 |
| c] 1 | d] 2 |
| e] 6 | f] 3 |
| g] 4 | h] 7 |

## Purpose or intention of writer: identifying bias, connotations and attempts to influence

SB▷ Bias indicates looking at something in a way that is one-sided or prejudiced in its presentation. Bias is an opinion disguised as fact.

### Task A: Discovering a writer's purpose

SB P.128

**Answers**

1 What opinion does the topic sentence in the introductory paragraph express?

That the country has taken a position which is unfortunate and perhaps illegal.

2 Write the adjectives and noun groups used to express this opinion.

Unfortunate; illegal; a position outside international and UN determinations.

3 Write the adjective from sentence 2 that describes the editor's opinion of the people seeking refuge.

Desperate.

4 Write the adjective from sentence 3 that describes the editor's opinion of the country's reputation.

Tarnished.

5 What does the writer imply and intend you to think about the military in para 3 when he or she writes '*Leaking boats were rescued by the military (which currently has quite a different agenda) from the seas nearby our shores, …*'?

The writer implies that the military has changed its behaviour in a big way—('quite a different agenda') and that the writer disapproves of the current behaviour.

6 When you read '*humanitarian care was taken with these asylum seekers and processing of their claims for refugee status was carried out efficiently and quickly*' does the past simple passive 'was taken' and 'was carried out' imply that this is not happening now but it did happen in the past?

Yes.

7 In para 3, what is the implication of using ' ' (quote marks) around the word *guard*?

The punctuation implies that guarding is not necessary or that the act of guarding is in some way different from the correct definition of what to guard ought to mean.

8 In para 3, ' ' is used again around '*border protection policy*'. Why?

It is used to imply that border protection is not needed because of the punctuation around 'guard'. We do not need guarding and we do not need border protection by the military from leaking boats of weary people who are seeking protection.

9 Why does the author choose to write so-called 'border protection policy' rather than simply border *protection policy*?

'So-called' is a value judgment. It marks the words that will follow as untruthful as far as the writer is concerned. If we say that something is 'so-called', it means it is named that by someone else, but not us. We do not agree with the calling or naming of it.

10 In para 3, find the exclamation mark and explain what is implied by its use.

The exclamation mark follows the sentence 'Worse, still, if they do get onshore, the processing times for their claims for refugee status have taken years!' Like all uses of exclamations, it is used for emphasis. It is to make the reader realise the wrongness or rightness of something. In this case, the writer wants the reader to believe it is wrong. It is a dramatic way to point out the sentence and connote seriousness.

11 In para 3, what is the writer's view of the government?

The government is heartless, and perhaps even racist.

12 In the final paragraph, what statement does the writer make concerning the opposition party?

That the opposition is not offering any solutions.

13 How does the writer attempt to influence the reader?

Throughout the article, the writer makes many statements. These are presented as factual. The writer's position is clear from the beginning when he or she states that 'It is unfortunate, if not downright illegal …' and so forth. At the conclusion of the article, the writer makes it clear that he or she wants support for a particular party.

14 In the last paragraph, the intention of this writer is revealed. Look at the text after the summation or conclusion cue—*Thus*. Write what the author believes is our only option.

We, the readers, are to reject both parties.

15 Based on your reading of the entire editorial comment, what was the author's intention? In other words, why was this article written? You may choose from the following comments:

The answer is (e).

## Task B: How language creates meaning and how language choices help a writer to express an opinion

SB P.129

### Answers

1 What opinion does the topic sentence in the introductory paragraph express?

That despite a commotion by some people concerning immigrants, there is, in the writer's opinion, a better view.

2 Write the nouns and noun phrases used to express this opinion.

The current commotion/a small minority/the government's policies/a wiser, more financial view.

3 What purpose does the word 'Despite' serve as the first word in sentence 1?

Despite means 'in spite of' or 'notwithstanding'—it serves to discredit the 'commotion' and 'debate' that is raised by others.

4 What purpose does the word 'thankfully' serve in sentence 1?

It shifts the sentence's focus to what is coming next, it signals to the reader that the author is glad to tell you there is a better view coming and it links with the word 'despite' in the same sentence.

5 The writer uses an argument beginning in para 2. How does this argument begin?

'The cost burden of processing illegal immigrants ... is becoming an increasing encumbrance upon the taxpayers ...'.

6 What does 'sensible' refer to?

The government's border protection policies.

7 What is the writer's view of the government's border protection policies?

That they are sensible and preferable to anything else.

8 What is the financial effect of the government's border protection policies according to the writer?

That there has been a large increase in the defence budget, and a temporary budget deficit has been caused. Also, financial markets have improved.

9 Since the writer says that the policies will lift the defence budget (more money will be spent) and create a budget deficit (the country will be in debt), he or she still argues that they are a good thing. What one key word signals to the reader that this is going to be the argument?

Although.

10 Why are the border policies preferable?

Because, according to the writer, the country could not afford to have a lot of people enter the country.

11 Is the statement 'This country could ill afford an influx of the magnitude that other less prudent policies might give rise to' a fact or an opinion?

An opinion.

12 Is the above statement in Question 11 worded like a fact? How do you know that it is not necessarily factual?

Yes. There is no evidence to support the claim.

13 What evidence is there that refugees are actually 'queue jumpers' as the editor states?

There is no evidence to support the claim.

14 How does the writer attempt to convince the reader to agree with him/her in the last paragraph?

The writer states that the 'wider community', ie a majority of people, think the same way as the government does; thus, if the reader wants to be accepted and be in the mainstream of thought, they should go along with what everyone else thinks. The writer also says that financial markets will be better as a result of the confidence in the government's reforms, thus implying that in order to make money from the financial markets, you should support these ideas.

# Critical thinking

## Language as power: becoming a critical reader

### Task A: Discussion

SB P.129

Students are to think about and answer questions concerning refugees in their individual countries.

- You could use this as a group or class discussion and create an activity at the conclusion of the discussion around the students setting up their own virtual country and government and creating policies for dealing with the increasing issue of homeless peoples fleeing countries around the globe.
- They could create a 10 point plan for their virtual country with them at the head of it to identify and solve problems.
- Doing the research in the section titled *English for the Internet Age* of this Unit (Students' Book, page 131) prior to students carrying out the critical thinking and discussion would be useful, especially if your students have access to the Internet and have time within their course to do this.

**Answers** will vary.

### Task B: Considering language as power

SB P.130

**Answers**

1 a] Language is constructed, and the status quo is maintained by controlling language and making it serve the powers that wish to control society.

2 The writer wants readers to become critical and to question and not believe **everything** they read.

3 Rules are constructed by 'dominant meanings'. These meanings serve institutions like governments, the military and even universities. They have power.

4 How are language rules created? By social convention.

5 a] There are many examples: a student asking a question in class—the convention has a time limit on it, a student may not ask a question that takes half the class time; a job interview—the candidate must not speak too much, the employer will do the asking and the candidate must use the 'correct' amount of time in the answer, and so on.

b] A person may write an article for a newspaper, but this does not mean it will be published; books; in some of the students' countries, they may point out that they are not allowed to write critically of their governments.

6 A person can become a critical reader by questioning what they read. They can become critical by not automatically believing everything that is printed. They need to look for bias and persuasion. They need to look for supporting evidence to prove that a statement is factual, not just an opinion.

# English for the Internet Age

## Refugees: Internet research project

### Task A: Finding out about refugees

SB P.131

In this section, the entire project is self-explanatory within the directions in the Students' Book. Students look up the websites and then follow links to answer the questions. It is an autonomous learning experience but it can be done in groups with the teacher as facilitator.

# Learner independence & study skills

## Assignment research skills

### Task A: Using an assignment from this course

SB P.134

Students are given advice as to how to keep track of their references.

The advice concerning research for accurate bibliographic referencing arises from the bitter experience of the authors.

## Vocabulary for tertiary purposes: university word lists

### Task A: University word lists to expand lexis (vocabulary)

SB P.134

This site happens to be LaTrobe University's linked site to an ESL resource. It will acquaint students with one university word list. There are other sites that could be found by typing in the words University Word List. Students find this information quite useful as they are usually keen to learn more vocabulary.

# unit 6 a global connection: the environment

As between the soul and the body there is a bond, so are the body and its environment linked together.

**KAHLIL GIBRAN**

## Skills focus: In this Unit, students will learn and use the following skills:


**Speaking 1:** what do you know about environmental issues? **116**

**Writing:** research reports **116**

**Writing and Speaking:** mini-research project **118**

**Learner independence and study skills:** reading outside class **120**

**Listening and Speaking:** listening for main purpose—tutorial questions; tutorial participation skills 2—asking questions in tutorials **121**

**English for the Internet Age:** using university library catalogues on the net **126**

**Speaking 2:** using visual aids in presentations **127**

**Critical thinking:** distinguishing between fact and opinion **130**

**Grammar 1:** reporting verbs in citation and paraphrasing **131**

**Reading:** skimming and scanning **132**

**Grammar 2:** future predictions **133**

The linking theme in this section is the way in which the destiny of all parts of the world is related through the environment. This theme is used to introduce research reports, followed by a group project in which students carry out their own survey research and learn report writing. Students also continue their oral presentation project, focusing on using library catalogues on the Internet to aid their research, visual aids, and also on asking questions, either after a presentation or as part of a tutorial discussion. Further practice is also provided in skimming and scanning, and the grammar of citation and future predictions is covered.

# Speaking 1

## What do you know about environmental issues?

### Task A: Sharing knowledge about the environment

SB P.136

The *purpose* of this section is to:

- orient students to the field of the unit and consider causes and solutions;
- activate background knowledge related to the field;
- provide an opportunity for students to learn vocabulary from each other/activate some passive vocabulary;
- carry out group work.

**Variation/extension:** Students list as many other environmental problems as they can and put them in order of seriousness.

# Writing

## Research reports

The *purpose* of this section is to:

- introduce students to research reports, including their staging and language features;
- provide a model of a research report for present and future reference.

### Task A: Orientation to research

SB P.136

The questions are deliberately open-ended to allow students with a wide range of previous knowledge about research to be able to answer.

**Suggested answers**

1 Basically, research is the process of finding out something new. Many more sophisticated definitions are possible, a useful one being 'a systematic process of inquiry consisting of three elements or components: (1) a question, problem or hypothesis, (2) data, and (3) analysis and interpretation of data' (Nunan, 1992:3).

2 All disciplines use research.

3 Students with less background knowledge may mention market research, scientific research, etc. Others may talk about secondary research (eg in the library, from books) and primary research, which can be roughly divided into qualitative (focus groups, ethnographic observation etc) and quantitative (using questionnaires, experiments, statistics etc).

## Task B: Stages in a research report

SB P.137

### Answers and comments

1 Initially, accept any order for which students can show logical thinking. Students refine their answers in the next question.

2 Students check their answers to Question 1 by looking at the headings in the model research report.

- Background
- Aims
- Method
- Findings
- Conclusions

Point out that there is quite a lot of variation between possible headings in a research report, and that different disciplines favour different groupings and names of stages. For example, sometimes the *aims* stage is included in the *introduction*.

3
- Background = Context = Introduction
- Method = Procedure
- Findings = Results

4 This question helps students to relate previous knowledge about how research reports are written in their own language to what they are learning about research reports in English.

5 Students match the given sub-stages to the stages already introduced. No subheadings are given for the Aims and Findings sections.

- Introduction/Background/Context
  - Definitions
  - Literature review
- Method/Findings
  - Research design
  - Questionnaire design/Data collection
  - Data analysis techniques
- Conclusion
  - Commentary/Discussion/Analysis
  - Recommendations or implications

6 Students read the whole report and try to work out for themselves the purpose of the abstract. It should be clear that the abstract gives an overall summary of the whole report. If you have students who are going to study in the field of business, point out that in this discipline the abstract is called an executive summary.

## Task C: Identifying language features of reports

SB P.137

This is a good place to incorporate tense work if your students need it.

### Answers

1

| | |
|---|---|
| **Background** | In this case, present perfect is used to describe changes and trends from the past to now. However, present simple is often used to describe things that are generally true, give definitions etc, and past simple is used to describe things that are now finished. |
| **Aims** | Past simple tense is used here to describe the aims as chosen at the beginning of the research, ie in the past |
| **Method** | Because the research was done before the report was written, past simple is generally chosen here. |
| **Findings** | Again, these were obtained in the past, so past simple is commonly used. |
| **Conclusions** | Present simple is used to describe situations that are generally true, and the use of this tense here implies that the conclusions of this research are generalisable to the wider situation. However, if it is felt that the conclusions only apply to the specific situation of this research, the choice of tense would be past simple. In this example, past simple is used mainly to mention the results on which the conclusions are based. |
| **Recommendation** | Modal verbs such as 'should' or 'must' can be expected here. Present simple passive with verbs such as 'recommend' is also useful. |

2 Background, aims and findings have mostly discourse markers of addition, contrast and example, whereas the method section often has sequence markers (though not here) and the conclusion stage has markers to show cause and effect.

3 'Participants' and 'respondents' are the individual people who took part in the survey, and 'sample' is a singular word used for the whole group. Other research related words are: 'questionnaire', 'investigate', 'find out', 'a representative sample', 'trialled', 'sample size' and 'bias'.

In the next section, students carry out their own research and write it up as a report.

# Writing and Speaking

## Mini-research project

The *purpose* of this section is for students to:

- work as a group to conduct an informal mini-research project;
- write a research report from their own research.

Many tertiary courses require students to undertake group projects, and this section provides an opportunity for students to practise and prepare for this. The interaction that this requires also provides good speaking and listening practice.

Before beginning, let students know whether they will be performing their research on other students in the institution, or going outside to ask the general public. This project may be spread over several days, with other work mixed in between.

Many students may already be familiar with this kind of research. If so, they could be used as a resource to help other students—distributing them evenly between groups should help.

**Extension:** Such students could also be constructively used to introduce discussions about the methodology, such as bias in the sample.

## Task A: Research questions and hypotheses

SB P.140

SB

A research project often tries to either:

- answer particular questions (called *research questions*); or
- presents a statement (called a *hypothesis*) and tries to find out whether it's true or false.

### Answers

1 The research questions for the research in the previous section are:

- How much knowledge does a representative sample of people have about environmentally sustainable behaviour?
- How much has this knowledge led to a positive change in behaviour?
- Which factors are most effective at encouraging people to make their behaviour more sustainable?

2 Students could choose an environmental issue, a topic related to one of their oral presentations, or, if the group is going on to study in the same field, the project could relate to this field.

To provide another example, students can also look back at the families research covered in Unit 2, re-listen to Recording number 3 or read the recording script (Teacher's Book, page 49), in which the research questions were 'What is a "normal" family?', and 'Is there such a thing as a "normal" family?'.

## Task B: Devise the questionnaire

SB P.141

Students write a questionnaire with between five and eight questions to investigate their research questions or test their hypotheses. For example, for the research presented on environmentally sustainable behaviour starting on page 138 of the Students' Book, one of the questions on the questionnaire may have been 'How often do you recycle?'

## Task C: Pilot survey

SB P.141

Students trial their questionnaire (conduct a pilot survey) within the class. This is to identify any problems there may be with the questionnaire. For example, there might be more than one way of understanding the question, or they might find it's impossible to draw conclusions from some of the questions.

Students then negotiate together about how to adjust the questionnaire after looking at the results of the pilot survey.

## Task D: Main survey

SB P.141

Students carry out the survey!

If students go outside the college, this can be a valuable opportunity to speak with ordinary native speakers. However, students should be advised how to approach people politely (eg *Excuse me, could I ask you some questions. It'll only take a couple of minutes ... I'm doing some research as part of my English language studies ...*) and to expect some rejection.

## Task E: Write a report

SB P.141

This can be done individually, or different sections of the report can be allocated to different people in the group. In this case, the group can be told to organise a meeting to collate the final report in their own time, and to simulate what would happen in a real project.

**Note:** For those who want to read more about doing research:

- www.ukans.edu/cwis/units/ coms2/vra/door.html is a site that claims to give a tutorial on conducting social science research, focusing on qualitative techniques.
- http://gsociology.icaap.org/methods/ is another site intended to help with doing different kinds of social research.
- www.clearinghouse.net/div/subject/browse/soc00.00.00/ may provide further references.

# Learner independence & study skills

## Reading outside class

The *purpose* of this activity is for students to look at:

- the importance of reading practice outside class;
- ways of making their reading more focused and motivating.

## Task A: Focusing your reading outside class

SB P.141

**Answers**

1 Reasons, depending on the focus and level of the students, include that extensive reading, best focused on out of class, is important for language development because:

- it extends vocabulary knowledge;
- for people who enjoy reading, it can be a low stress, pleasurable way to immerse oneself in English;
- it provides exposure to culture; depending on what's being read, this could range from the culture of the country to the academic culture of the field of study;
- it can expose students to extra subject specialist language beyond that possible in general EAP classes.

Emphasise that even after the EAP course finishes, extensive reading is still necessary.

2 Aims could range from focusing on motivating themselves to read, to looking at academic texts in the field of their future studies. Suggest some aims and emphasise that each individual will be different.

3–5 These steps should help students to choose interesting reading ideas which fit their aims. You can also give suggestions, such as:

- Internet newsletters on a subject of interest, such as a 'what's on' or movie information site, eg www.yourmovies.com.au
- graded readers for lower-level students—these are widely available at 'upper Intermediate' and 'Advanced' levels
- novels may provide motivation for higher level students who don't like reading academic texts.
- Internet directories for subject-specific articles.

**Extension 2:** Discuss ways of overcoming a time shortage (see Students' Book, Unit 4, page 102), such as:

- reading on public transport
- allocating a certain time each day to read
- choosing something more interesting to read to provide motivation.

**Extension 2:** One problem that often comes up is dealing with unknown language. Discuss strategies to cope with this. For example:

- reading ahead to see whether the difficult section was unimportant or the meaning becomes apparent from the later context
- improving skills at finding meaning of words from context
- using graded readers to help improve language level.

# Listening and Speaking

✓ *Listening for main purpose: tutorial questions about business and the environment*

✓ *Tutorial participation skills 2: asking questions in tutorials*

## Listening for main purpose: tutorial questions about business and the environment

SB P.142

The *purpose* of this section is for students to:

- have the experience of listening to a tutorial discussion;
- practise listening and identifying the purpose or function of specific language;
- find out the range of purposes of questions that are acceptable in tutorials within English-medium tertiary education;
- practise intensive listening for the form of such questions;
- practise using these questions in discussions.

**Note to teacher:** Students will need to listen to this tutorial conversation three or four times to complete all tasks.

## Task A: Orientation to topic—alternative energy sources

SB P.142

9 It's important to give the context of the conversation (situation and topic)—this is given in the Students' Book. Play up to the end of the first student question (Recording number 9). Students listen for topic, which is alternative energy sources. Then in groups they tell each other what they know about this topic: for example, sustainable power production or alternative fuels for cars. This aims to provide practice at something students at this level need to get used to (orientating themselves very quickly to a conversation) while still facilitating the activation and sharing of background knowledge.

### Answers

1 Alternative energy sources.

2 Brainstorming—there will be a variety of responses.

3
- Four.
- Most people would consider so! They have read outside of class, bring their ideas to the tutorial and participate actively in it.

## Task B: Listening for purpose—why are questions asked in tutorials?

SB P.143

This is a tricky task, so if you have a lower-level class, expect to play the recording more than once. Students may have to read the script.

### Answers

Only 1 to 3 are dealt with at this step.

F = Female

M = Male

| | Speaking order | | | | | | |
|---|---|---|---|---|---|---|---|
| | 1st | 2nd | 3rd | 4th | 5th | 6th | 7th |
| **Main purpose** | Stu 1<br>F | Stu 2<br>M | Stu 3<br>M<br>Daniel | Stu 1<br>F | Stu 4<br>F<br>Japanese | Stu 2<br>M | Stu 3<br>M<br>Daniel |
| 1 Contradicting the tutor's idea (tutor's reply will help clarify understanding) | ✓ | | | | ✓ | | |
| 2 Giving an example supporting a previously mentioned idea | | | ✓ | ✓ | | | |
| 3 Asking for further explanation or information | ✓ | ✓ | | | | ✓ | ✓ |

In some academic traditions, it may be rare for students to contradict the lecturer. Students from these traditions may need reassurance that this is not only OK but often encouraged in Western education, as a way of gaining greater insight by probing the presented knowledge and testing it against other ideas.

Also, again depending on the background of your students, it may be important to reassure them that admitting to not fully understanding something is not only OK but encouraged, because it gives opportunities for further learning. Students who do this won't necessarily lose face.

## Recording script

(9) **RECORDING NUMBER 9 (5 MINUTES, 26 SECONDS)**

**TITLE: Tutorial discussion about business and the environment**

*Tutor:* Good morning, folks. You were all at yesterday's lecture, weren't you?

*All:* (Muffled) Yeah.

*Tutor:* Well, let's start by talking about the content. Does anyone have any questions?

*Student 1:* Yes, yes, I do. I'm not sure what you meant when you said that oil companies could gain advantages from investing in other energy sources. Surely other energy sources are their competitors!

*Tutor:* Well, it's just that, because the oil supply will fall below demand within the next few years, it's going to be very difficult for the oil companies to keep increasing their profits when the supply of the product they're selling is limited. In that case, the sensible thing to do seems to be to become expert in whatever products will replace it ...

*Two students:* Mmmm.

*Tutor:* ... the companies that can get ahead in this earlier will be the most successful ones later on. After all, as we've seen throughout this course, most companies now realise it's more effective to keep the same customers and change the product to suit, than to stick rigidly with a product that has an uncertain future. I know which companies I'd be buying shares in!

*Student 1:* OK, I see. Clear now.

*Tutor:* Any more questions?

*Student 2:* Yeah, yeah, well, I understand what you say about it being sensible for fossil fuel companies to look at alternative energy sources, but it seems to me that there isn't much of this happening! You know how the big oil companies keep pushing to get permission to explore national parks and wilderness areas such as the Alaskan National Wildlife Refuge. Yet you mentioned before that there were grounds for optimism with oil companies, energy companies and car companies looking at alternative energy sources. Now what did you mean by this?

*Tutor:* Well, it does seem that many companies are stuck in a short-sighted mindset that stops them from innovative thinking. However, there are some that are developing a bit more foresight. For example, Royal Dutch Shell is changing its policy and beginning to switch investment to alternative energy research. As for car companies, several of them are working on hybrid cars now, using battery electric power as well as a traditional internal combustion engine.

*A student:* Mmmmm.

*Tutor:* Honda, Toyota have been especially keen to develop these, and General Motors in the USA recently showed a concept car involving fuel cells, which we mentioned earlier. Can anyone expand further on this?

*Student 3: (Daniel)* Yeah, I read in a newspaper the other day that Honda is selling tens of thousands of hybrid cars, just in the USA, and they're just the same as normal cars to drive!

*Student 1:* Yeah, and I also heard that Ford, again in the US, um, is planning a four-wheel drive with a hybrid engine.

*Tutor:* Yes, I believe it is. It sounds like you've been keeping yourself informed about relevant news—and that's great! Now, does anyone have any more questions?

*Student 4:* But isn't it the case that alternative energy simply isn't economically viable, that is, it's just so much more expensive than energy from traditional sources that no one will choose to buy it?

*Tutor:* That's exactly what many companies and governments argue, yes, but the way to get it cheaper is to put more money into research, and also for people to start buying them now! It'll become economically viable when oil prices start going up, and by then the companies that are ahead in the research will have a massive commercial advantage!

*Student 4:* I see!

*Student 2:* I guess it all depends on when production actually does reach its peak and start falling. Could you tell me where I could find out more about the predictions that the peak will be earlier than people used to think? I want to write about it for my assignment.

*Tutor:* Mmmm, yes, Colin Campbell's book called *The Coming Oil Crisis*, that'll be a good place to start. I think it was published around '98, and I know there are a few copies in the university library. Come to my office if you can't find it, and I'll dig out the full bibliographic detail for you. It's probably a good idea to do a search for some of his more recent stuff as well.

Daniel: Yeah, I remember reading that, well, within a decade or two, the Persian Gulf countries will be producing half of the world's oil. Could this lead to the potential political issues you mentioned in the lecture?

*Tutor:* Mmm, good thinking and good background reading, Daniel. Now, I hope you have a reference to that source, because it'll be useful if you decide to include it in your assignment. But to go back to your question, yes, there are serious questions to be asked. Many industrialised countries depend on oil from this part of the world, so perhaps there'll be some re-balancing of the world's power away from the western and east Asian industrialised countries. Dr. Dorothea el Mallakh in Colorado has done lots of research on that question, and that may be an interesting one to read. There's some stuff by her in the library.

*Student 1:* Maybe they ...

**Note:** An interesting website about the predicted peak in oil production, and reasons for discrepancy in when this may take place, is www.hubbertpeak.com/. www.honda.com, www.toyota.com, www.ford.com and www.hybridcars.com have interesting information about hybrid cars.

# Tutorial participation skills 2: asking questions in tutorials

## Task A: Expressions for tutorial questions

SB P.143

**Answers**

1
- I'm not sure what you meant when you said that oil companies could gain advantages from investing in other energy sources. Surely other energy sources are their competitors!
- I understand what you say about it being sensible for fossil fuel companies to look at alternative energy sources, but it seems that there isn't much of this happening! ... What did you mean by this?
- But isn't it the case that alternative energy simply isn't economically viable, ...
- Could you tell me where I could find out more about the predictions that the ... +[reason].

2

| Expression | Number of purpose |
|---|---|
| When you said that ..., did you mean that ... | 4 |
| You mentioned before that ...but what about ... | 3 |
| Do you mean that ... | 4 |
| So you mean ... | 4 |
| If it's the case that ..., why can't/doesn't ... | 1, 3, 4 |
| Could you give me an example? | 3 |

## Task B: Speaking—asking tutorial questions

SB P.144

These topics, although different from tertiary level tutorial topics, allow discussions with minimal preparation by the student and give opportunities to use the questions from Task A. Their relevance should also keep the interest level high.

**Variation:** To make the discussion more realistic, instead of using the questions given, students could be asked to do some research before the discussion (this could be done after the next section of this Unit, *Using university library catalogues on the net*, or done after Task D on page 145 of the Students' Book, *Using visual aids in a mini-presentation*.

# English for the Internet Age

## Using university library catalogues on the net

### Task A: Searching library catalogues

SB P.144

The *purpose* of this section is to:

- build awareness about the information available on library Internet catalogues;
- allow students to practise skimming and scanning websites to locate appropriate links.

**Note:** If students have plenty of experience of using libraries, this section may be run through quickly, with an emphasis on the extension activity below.

If each student uses a different university's catalogue, they could afterwards compare the different information that's available from different universities.

**Answers and comments**

1 From the title of this section, students can guess that they can find the book using a university on-line catalogue. Most universities appear to have them, and they are usually accessible by the general public.

2 a] The CALL number (or Dewey number) is used to locate books on the shelves, though beware of oversize books being located on a separate set of shelves! Beware as well of catalogues that cover several library sites.

b] 'On loan' means currently borrowed, and 'for loan' means available in the library. What a difference a preposition makes!!

c] There are two ways to find books on the same subject. There is often a list of subjects under which the book is categorised—clicking on a subject will take you to a list of books on this subject. Alternatively, clicking on the CALL number usually produces a list of books with similar CALL numbers, ie also on a similar subject.

d] All books with the search criteria should be listed. If more than one edition is available, this will be visible. This is something for students to be aware of!

3 Many students are unaware of what academic journals are. Therefore, students should be required to find at least one journal as a means of increasing their awareness.

4 Further information necessary to cite the work is:

- Year of publication
- Publication company
- Publishing place (city)
- Possibly editor's name, article title and volume and issue number.

**Extension 1:** If you can obtain a password to access on-line databases, it would be very useful to show the students how these work.

**Extension 2:** Students could be asked to go to the library home page and find out such things as how long they can borrow books, special rules for the reserve collection, etc. Note that basic information about libraries was given in the listening in Unit 1 (Students' Book, page 26).

# Speaking 2

## Using visual aids in presentations

The *purpose* of this section is for students to:

- practise the oral presentation skills introduced in Unit 5;
- increase their awareness of visual aids and their usefulness;
- practise designing and using visual aids to supplement an oral presentation.

This section builds on Unit 5, *Oral presentation skills*, Students' Book, page 108, in which the concept of visual aids, specifically OHPs and computer presentations, was introduced.

Here, 'slide' refers to both a single OHT (overhead transparency) and a slide in a computer presentation. In the UK, OHTs are often known as 'acetates'.

### Task A: Sharing knowledge about visual aids

SB P.145

The *purpose* of this task is to:

- ensure that all students share some common knowledge about visual aids, in preparation for the next task;
- bring out the students' own ideas and previous knowledge about visual aids, again in preparation for the next task.

**Answers**

1 Visual aids include:

- OHTs
- computer presentations (for example, PowerPoint)
- the blackboard/whiteboard, preferably with colour chalk/markers
- posters
- handouts
- real objects mentioned in the presentation
- a flipchart.

2 Visual aids are useful to:

- provide prompts for the speaker, reducing the need to refer to notes and therefore allow a more fluent, smoother presentation;
- make the structure and main ideas of the presentation clear to the audience;
- convey concepts which are better illustrated using pictures than words;
- allow for the fact that the audience will probably have a variety of thinking/learning styles, and visual aids can provide for the more visual thinkers;
- take some of the pressure off the speaker.

3 In this question, learners' prior knowledge is acknowledged and used as a resource in a way that leads smoothly into the next task. There's no need to give answers that the students don't produce themselves at this point—plenty of advice will come out of the next section.

## Task B: Useful techniques for using OHTs and computer presentations

SB P.145

This task provides advice and helps students to see the reasons behind it. Manipulating the information, as the task requires, also helps them remember it.

**Variation:** This is a variation on a running dictation.

1 Give each pair a copy of the advice grid.

2 Attach the comments to the wall at enough distance that students can't read them—perhaps even outside the room!

3 During the game, one person from each pair runs to the comments on the wall, reads one idea and tries to remember it, and then runs back to their partner to explain it. The partner then writes it in the appropriate box on the advice grid.

4 This is repeated. Pairs should swap runners half way through the activity.

5 The first pair to write all comments in the correct boxes is the winner.

Meanings must be accurate, but don't have to be in exactly the same words as the comments from the book.

### Answers

Table 1: **Making your own slides**

| Advice | Comments |
|---|---|
| 1 Design your slide with plenty of 'white space'—that is, don't fill it completely with text. | This is common graphic designers' advice for good layout. |
| 2 If possible, use pictures, flowcharts, organisation charts, tree diagrams, tables or other visual representations, depending on the topic. | 'A picture is worth a thousand words', as long as it's clear and well captioned! |
| 3 Write only important ideas. Note form, with bullet points, is fine. Indenting is a useful way to show which ideas are the main ideas. | It's very difficult for an audience to read and listen at the same time, so too much writing on the OHT will take attention away from what you're saying. Therefore it's important for the OHT to be concise, clear and focused. It's not necessary to write in complete sentences. |
| 4 When you have finished making your OHTs, number them in sequence in a corner of the transparency. | A simple trick that will make things much easier when setting up for the presentation! |

Table 2: **Setting up and giving up your presentation**

| Advice | Comments |
|---|---|
| 5 Make sure your OHTs are in a pile, in order, next to the OHP, before you start your presentation. | It's very embarrassing to interrupt your talk to look for the right OHT! |
| 6 Before you start make sure your projector is positioned so that everyone in the audience can see the screen, and that it's focused. | Making sure that your audience can see comfortably is important. |

| Advice | Comments |
|---|---|
| 7 At the beginning of your talk, cover up everything except the title. During the talk, uncover one point, speak about it, then uncover the next point, explain that, and so on. | This helps the audience to focus on the point you're making, and creates a sense of anticipation about what's coming next. |

## Task C: Preparing an OHT/computer presentation slide; identifying main ideas

SB P.147

The *purpose* of this task is for students to:

- practise preparing an OHT slide;
- practise reading or listening for main ideas.

3 By doing step 2 in pairs, and then doing step 3, students get the chance to develop not only their skills at producing presentation slides, but also their skills of identifying main ideas and of critical analysis.

Students may have to be shown the recording script (Recording number 3), from Unit 2, pages 49–50 of this book.

**Suggested answer to step 2**

2 Henry (1989) — experiment

- students swapped families
- controlled for
  - age
  - gender
  - ethnicity
  - socio-economic group
- Results
  - all confused
  - other families 'not normal'
  - own family 'normal'
- Conclusion
  - no 'normal' family

Step 4 brings to consciousness any new insight into the usefulness of visual aids gained from this task.

## Task D: Using visual aids in a mini-presentation and review of oral presentation stages

SB P.147

This is best done in groups of three or so, with the OHT sitting on the table, slowly uncovered as the presenter works his or her way through. It's even possible to use paper instead of OHTs.

Stage 5 is useful to allow learning from peers. It's good preparation for English-medium tertiary education to encourage a classroom atmosphere which values peer feedback.

# Critical thinking

## Distinguishing between fact and opinion

The *purpose* of this section for students to:

- improve their ability to distinguish facts and opinions;
- develop awareness of how to make facts appear factual in their own writing.

It's important that students know that this essay (*Our world is one place*) is not a model for their own writing, neither in structure nor support.

### Task A: Orientation discussion

SB P.148

These questions allow students to share ideas, opinions and vocabulary as a lead-in to the next text.

### Task B: Distinguishing between fact and opinion

SB P.148

Refer to Students' Book for text titled *Our world is one place*.

#### Answers and comments

1 Both—there is some fact and some possible opinion. It might all be fact but the reader cannot know this because of the lack of academic referencing.

Facts must be verifiable.

2 There are several. The best would be the referenced sentence which states that 'radioisotopes were detected over Sweden within minutes … etc.' as this can be verified.

3 Again, there are many to choose from. Sentences with 'every' or 'all' might be closely examined as to their truth or otherwise. Basically, if a statement has no reference, one does not know if it is fact or not, because there is no way to test the truth of it.

4 Only one. Usually this is not sufficient. Academic writing of this length would require more references, and a bibliography which gives clues about the credibility of the references, eg published in a refereed journal or by a respected publisher.

5 In the final paragraph of the writing (the recommendation stage) there are clues—words like 'need' show passion and the personal appeal to the reader ('Is that what you want?') are inappropriate for this type of text. The register changes when the reader is 'spoken to' by the author.

6 Despite the answer above, most certainly, factual writing can be shocking or surprising. Consider, for example, the numbers of humans who were gassed in concentration camps during World War II.

7 No author is stated. Thus, there is even less possible verification of facts as the author's credentials cannot be checked. Academic texts must show an author. We also don't know who the author is working for or who commissioned the writing—fees for articles may be a major source of bias regardless of the merits of an argument.

8 Although there is high lexis and some factual material presented, it is not academic because it is not referenced; it appears opinion-based and the writer is unknown. The lack of a detached feel to the text also reduces the credibility.

9 Answers will vary.

10 By answering this question, students will summarise all the things mentioned above.

11 Answers will vary.

12 Research could begin with the one reference of sourced authors, Gordon and Suzuki (1990), and this source could probably be found using a library catalogue, even though no references list is given for the essay. A subject search could also be done using key words such as 'nuclear', 'uranium' or 'butterfly effect' at a university library.

# Grammar 1

## Reporting verbs in citation and paraphrasing

The *purpose* of this section is for students to:

- develop their understanding of how ideas are reported in academic writing;
- practise reporting ideas in the same way;
- understand and practise paraphrasing.

### Task A: Meaning and use of reporting verbs

SB P.151

#### Answers and comments

1 There are other ways to write the Gordon and Suzuki reference, such as:

'... an explosion, radioisotopes were 'detected over Sweden within minutes and over Canada's Arctic in hours (Gordon and Suzuki, 1990:57)'; or the word 'report' in line 8 of the essay can be replaced with other reporting verbs such as 'claim' or 'state'

2 If other journals aren't available, teaching journals which are available in the staff rooms of most colleges are highly useful. This section allows students to pull the appropriate language out of real world texts.

3 'Ask' is used to report questions.

'Assert' indicates a strongly stated view.

'Claim' conveys a hint of suspicion about the idea being reported.

'Deny' is used to report statements that are disagreed with.

'Maintain' has a feeling of persistence or going against accepted thinking.

'Report', 'state' and 'say' are the plain vanilla flavour reporting verbs and have approximately the same meaning as each other.

'Suggest' is used for proposals or suggestions.

4 Students may need help with identifying which name is the family name. As a general rule, if there is no comma in the name, the last name given is the family name, whereas a comma indicates that everything before it is the family name.

If students have difficulty with paraphrasing, suggest the following:

- read the idea;
- close the book;
- write it;
- open the book to check you haven't used the same words.

Answers will vary, but for an example (in case the students require it):

a] Harvey Weis, and Raymond Bradley (2001) assert/claim/maintain that 'the end of civilisations in the past has often been caused not by political or economic change as previously supposed, but by climatic change'.

b] Chakraverty (2000) asks 'whether logging should be stopped in Govindia's north west'.

Any answers are OK as long as they contain the same idea as the original quote, and contain a reporting verb. Work could be marked using the two-stage correction system (see Appendix A and Students' Book, Unit 2, page 56; Teacher's Book, page 53).

# Reading

## Skimming and scanning

The *purpose* of this section is to:

- provide further practice of skimming and scanning, introduced in Units 1 and 2;
- orientate students to the next text.

### Task A: Skimming race

SB P.152

Before starting, review prediction and skimming strategies. (See Unit 1, page 20.) (*prediction*: use titles, heading, pictures, tables, charts etc and their captions; *skimming*: read the end of the introduction, perhaps looking for key phrases, such as 'this report summarises/shows/demonstrates …' and also read the first (topic) and perhaps the last (summary) sentence of each paragraph.)

#### Answers

The paragraph numbers are in brackets.

1 How countries are improving waste disposal in cities (para 3).
2 Amount of waste generated in a particular country (para 1).
3 Population growth in a particular country (para 4).
4 Predictions for growth in waste from cities (para 1).
5 Effects of dangerous untreated chemicals (para 2).

### Task B: Scanning

SB P.152

Review scanning strategies from Students' Book, Unit 2, page 37; Teacher's Book, page 31.

#### Answers

1 How many contaminated sites are there in New Zealand?
7800 (para 1).

2 What problems are affecting the South Pacific?
'Serious waste management and pollution problems' (para 3).

3 Which Chinese cities are 'Environmental Star Cities'?
'Dalian, Zhuhai, … and Weihai' (para 6).

4 What percentage of Asia's solid waste is expected to be produced in East Asia in 2010?
60% (para 1).

5 What's the expected total population of Chinese cities in 2025?
832 million (para 4).

6 What's the average proportion of GDP spent on water and sanitation in Asia?
Around 1% (para 5).

# Grammar 2

## Future predictions

The *purpose* of this section is to:

- build awareness of verb forms used to express the future in academic writing;
- provide practice of incorporating predictions in writing;
- provide practice which is useful for Task 1 of the IELTS writing paper, academic module.

### Task A: Tenses for future predictions

SB P.154

**Answers**

1

| Tense | Number of times used |
|---|---|
| 'will' | 0 |
| present simple active | 0 |
| present simple passive | 4 (para 1, 4 and 5) |
| present continuous | 0 |
| 'be' verb + (**adverb**) + **infinitive** | 1 (para 5) |

2 Many students are surprised to find that 'will' isn't often used in academic writing for future predictions, and that present simple passive, such as 'is expected to', often is. The key to the explanation is the choice of verb—predictions, forecasts, expectations etc, which are current in the present, in fact refer to the future.

3 **infinitive** = infinitive with 'to', eg 'to eat', 'to go'.

**bare infinitive** = infinitive without 'to', eg 'eat', 'go'

Verbs used in the text are:

- is likely + **infinitive** (is likely to …)
- is expected + **infinitive**, … can be expected + **infinitive**
- is anticipated + **infinitive**

Other verbs that can be used like this are:

- is forecast (not) + **infinitive**
- is predicted (not) + **infinitive**
- is projected (not) + **infinitive**

Other expressions, such as:

- is unlikely + **infinitive**
- will probably + **bare infinitive**
- will possibly + **bare infinitive**
- probably won't + **bare infinitive**
- possibly won't + **bare infinitive**
- could + **bare infinitive**
- may + **bare infinitive**
- might + **bare infinitive**

can be used to indicate different degrees of certainty in the future (see Students' Book, Unit 7, page 172; Teacher's Book, page 154 for more information).

4
- 'is predicted not to …' means there is a prediction that something won't happen.
- 'is not predicted to …' could have the same meaning, though with a weaker emphasis, but could also mean that no prediction has actually been made.

## Task B: Reading to identify predictions

SB P.154

This task encourages students to look actively at language in authentic material, relate form to function and to use language in their own writing which they have found in their own reading. It may also increase their feeling of 'ownership' of new language if they find it in texts chosen by themselves rather than by the teacher.

One advantage of using the Internet is that searching may help students to find relevant articles faster. Useful key words are 'future trend', 'survey' and 'prediction'. Newspaper articles, including those on the web, often include surveys designed to look at future trends.

## Task C: Writing

SB P.154

Warn students that they must use their own words! Plagiarism is unacceptable! Students should paraphrase and reference statements and ideas, please.

# unit 7 on campus

The difficulty we meet with in reaching our goal is the shortest path to it.

KAHLIL GIBRAN

**Skills focus: In this Unit, students will learn and use the following skills:**


**Speaking 1:** campus vocabulary 136

**Listening and speaking 1:** academic requests and replies 2 137

**Speaking 2**: further oral presentation skills 142

**English for the Internet Age:** referencing from Internet sources 144

**Reading:** examining texts from different points of view; using texts to assist in making and supporting judgments 145

**Speaking and Listening:** giving constructive criticism; critical listening and peer marking of oral presentations 148

**Critical thinking:** what is the purpose of education? 150

**Listening and Speaking 2:** tutorial participation skills 3—various discussion techniques 151

**Grammar:** hypothesising and speculating; conditionals 154

**Learner independence and study skills:** speaking outside class 156

**Writing:** extended essay assignment 157

**Writing and Speaking:** issues in education 158

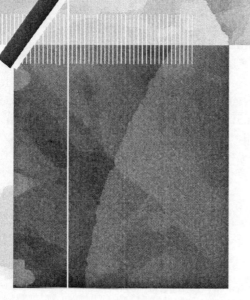

The topic of this Unit extends and builds on that of Unit 1 but the focus is narrowed to the tertiary sector, and some of the specific issues that students will encounter in their future studies are dealt with. The reading text explains concepts of equity that commonly apply to tertiary institutes, and students examine it from several different angles. They also develop tutorial skills after listening to a discussion about a controversial issue affecting tertiary education, and are encouraged to think critically about various issues, including the purpose of education.

Sensitivity in language choice is dealt with in two sections—*Academic requests* and *Critical listening*. Additional language choice, this time in order to speculate, is the focus of the grammar section. Extra practice opportunities to use this grammar are found in the section *Issues in education*.

Oral presentations are the culmination of a project students began in Unit 5. Students display the techniques they've been working so hard on and have the opportunity to refine them based on seeing each other present. The project is followed with an extended essay project, to be completed by the final Unit of the book. Both the oral presentation and the extended essay project are supported by a reminder about referencing, looking specifically at those elusive and tricky websites.

# Speaking 1

## Campus vocabulary

The *purpose* of this section is for students to:

- extend their vocabulary in the area of campus life;
- compare and contrast tertiary education systems in traditionally English-speaking countries with education in their own country.

### Task A: Extending campus vocabulary

SB P.156

- This builds on the vocabulary introduced in Unit 1.

#### Answers

1 Note the following abbreviations: BrE = British English, AuE = Australian English, AmE = North American English.

a] A **faculty** is a group of **departments**, eg the faculty of science may cover the department of physics, the department of chemistry, etc. A **school** is similar to a department. However, in the generic sense in AmE, '**school**' is also used to refer to any level of education. In AuE and BrE, it only refers to institutions for people aged about 5 to 16 or 18.

b] **Arts** covers languages, history, philosophy, music etc; **social science** includes economics, geography, politics, psychology etc; and **science** covers chemistry, physics, biology, computing etc. **Humanities** includes history and geography.

c] An **applied science**, such as electronics, engineering or computer science, has direct application to industry or government service. However, a **pure science**, such as physics or botany, is studied in order to get a better understanding of the universe in which we live.

d] **Recognition of prior learning** is a system by which students who can prove they have already covered the content of a subject or part of a course, either through work or a previous course, can receive a **subject exemption** for it.

e] Most degrees require students to take **core** or **compulsory** subjects, which everyone on the course must take, together with a few **elective** or **option** subjects. Some subjects require students to have already taken another subject, which is then called a **prerequisite** for the later subject.

f] In order of level: Bachelor/Honours/Master/Doctorate = PhD (Doctor of Philosophy). Note the use of capital letters and apostrophes: a **Master's** in Business Administration, … a **Bachelor's** degree, … an **honours** degree (= a higher level Bachelor's degree)

g] These are both divisions of an educational year. There are two **semesters** in a year, but in BrE, three **terms** comprise a year.

h] In Australia, the levels of grades, from lowest, are: **pass**, **credit**, **distinction** and **high distinction**. Other terminology, more common in the UK, is: **third**, **lower second**, **higher second** and **first**. As a final grade, we can say, for example, that someone has a 'first class honours degree'.

**2** Discussion should focus on, and use, the vocabulary from Question 1.

# Listening and Speaking 1

## Academic requests and replies 2

The *purpose* of this section is:

- for students to practise listening for purpose, and intensive listening;
- for students to examine and practise the stages of a typical request;
- to ensure students are aware of some of the things they can request and services normally available in Western tertiary education.

10

### Task A: Listening for purpose

SB P.156

Before each recording, make sure students are aware of who is involved in the conversation, because these requests may be dealt with by a different person in the students' own countries.

Stop the recording after each conversation to give students time to fill in the answers.

**Variation:** Higher level students could listen to identify the function without first looking at the list of functions in their book.

**Answers**

| | |
|---|---|
| a] Special time off from your course (leave of absence). | *Conversation 1* |
| b] Help with the English in your assignment. | |
| c] Special treatment in an exam due to injury or disability (special dispensation). | *Conversation 2* |
| d] Help with understanding an assignment. | |
| e] A particular form. | *Conversation 4* |
| f] An exam/assignment to be marked again. | *Conversation 3* |
| g] Explanation of marking system. | |

h] Information about using the institution's counselling service.

i] Information about which subjects need to be taken to finish a course. *Conversation 5*

j] Information about special resources available for your subject in the library.

## Recording scripts

(10) **RECORDING NUMBER 10, (4 MINUTES, 17 SECONDS)**

**TITLE: Academic requests**

**CONVERSATION 1: Requesting leave of absence**

*Student:* Errr, excuse me. Er, am I interrupting you?

*Lecturer:* Oh, no, not at all. How can I help you?

*Student:* Yeah, oh, well, it's quite complicated, I'm afraid.

*Lecturer:* Would you like to have a seat?

*Student:* Ah, yes, thanks very much. Well, it's like this, you see, my mother has been ill for some time and er ...

*Lecturer:* I see ...

*Student:* ... Well it was my mother who was supporting me. But that's the problem—she just isn't able to run the family business by herself now that she's in hospital ... so I need to go back to look after her for a while.

*Lecturer:* Oh, I see now. I'm sorry to hear it.

*Student:* So what should I do about my course? I don't want to drop out and then have to apply again, and organise the visa, all this stuff, and I certainly don't want to have to restart the course again, and then repeat the first few units!

*Lecturer:* Oh, don't worry, there's no need for all of that. All you need to do is to complete a Leave of Absence form, and put all your reasons on that, and get it to me to sign, and, er, then we'll send it off to the admin section. I hope your mother gets better soon!

*Student:* Thank you very much.

**CONVERSATION 2: Requesting special dispensation in exam due to disability or injury**

*Student:* Well, the problem is that I broke my arm in a soccer game and I can't write properly ... so I just don't know how I'm going to write the essays in the exam!

*Lecturer:* Mmmm, OK, I'm sure there's a way around that! I think we should be able to get someone to do the writing for you—they'll just write exactly what you say, and of course that'll be done in a special room. I'll contact the course coordinator for you and I'm sure we'll be able to sort something out.

## CONVERSATION 3: Requesting re-mark, and asking for explanation of a procedure

*Student:* Professor, umm, I wonder if you can help me.

*Lecturer:* Mmmm?

*Student:* Well, I've been getting good marks on my assignments so far, and my tutor seems quite happy with my progress, but you know the exam we did recently?

*Lecturer:* Yes.

*Student:* Well, I've just got the result back, and I'm really disappointed with it. I was sure I'd done much better than that. Could I ask another lecturer to mark it again?

*Lecturer:* Well, sometimes it works—there's no harm trying, I guess. Just go to the admin office and ask for a Reassessment Request Form, fill it in and then take it back to the office.

*Student:* And what happens after that?

*Lecturer:* Well, what'll happen is that two more lecturers will look at it and, umm, they won't see the original mark, but if their marks are very different from what you got first, then you'll get the average of the two new marks.

*Student:* Ohh, I see. Thanks very much.

*Lecturer:* Good luck!

## CONVERSATION 4: Asking for a form, and asking and confirming directions

*Student:* Excuse me

*Admin assistant:* Yes?

*Student:* Could I have a Reassessment Form, please?

*Admin assistant:* I'm afraid you'll have to go to the faculty office for that. This is just the department office.

*Student:* So how can I find it?

*Admin assistant:* Just go straight down Johnston Street until you come to a pub. I think it's called Shane O'Reilly's, anyway, it's an Irish pub. Then hang a left, go straight for a few blocks and it's across from Woolworths, in the big Chomsky building. Can't miss it!

*Student:* The one with the orange stripes?

*Admin assistant:* Yeah, that's the one!

*Student:* Oh, cheers, thanks ...

## CONVERSATION 5: Finding out what subjects can be studied next year

*Student:* I'm trying to plan my studies for next year, but I'm rather confused about which subjects to put down.

*Lecturer:* OK. Well, let's have a look. You're doing a Masters in Anthropology, OK, and you've already done Social Anthropology I, Research

Methods, Clan and Kinship, and Social Organisation and Control, so you've completed four of the core subjects. So now you have to do Religion, Ritual and Systems of Belief, and for the other subjects, you can choose from this list. Oh, and of course you also have to do a research project.

*Student:* Can I have a look at that list ...

## Task B: Understanding replies

SB P.157

It's one thing to know how to ask a question, but quite another to understand the reply! The questions here are designed to bring out all the main points of the responses, without giving too many clues about the answer. However, a better **variation** for higher level students is to listen without the questions, taking notes (as detailed as possible) about each conversation. Playing the recording more than once is fine here because in a real situation, students would be able to ask for clarification.

### Answers

1 *Conversation 1:* What are the three steps the student must follow?

a] Fill in 'leave of absence' form.

b] Lecturer signs it.

c] Send it to admin section.

2 *Conversation 2*

a] What kind of help will the student get? Someone will write what he says.

b] Where will it happen? In a special room.

c] Who will the lecturer contact? Course coordinator.

3 *Conversation 3*

a] Where should the student go? Admin office.

b] What should she pick up? Reassessment Request Form.

c] How many lecturers will look at it again? Two.

d] In what circumstances will the mark not change? If new marks similar to original.

4 *Conversation 4*

a] Which office should she go to? Faculty office.

b] Which office is she at? Department office.

c] Which way should she turn when she sees the pub? Turn left.

d] Write two features of the building with the correct office. Two from: Chomsky building (name, accept any spelling!), opposite Woolworths (accept any spelling), has orange stripes.

5 *Conversation 5*

a] How many compulsory subjects has she done already? Four.

b] How many more compulsory subjects does she still have to do? Two.

## Task C: Language of requests

SB P.158

If students are unsure about the difference between orientation and problem, go through Conversation 1 with the class as an example.

### Answers and comments

1

| | |
|---|---|
| **orientation + problem + question** | 1, 3 |
| **orientation + problem** | 5 |
| **problem + question** | |
| **problem** | 2 |
| **question** | 4 |

2 These questions lead students to the following conclusions. If a hint is needed, ask students to think about what information is necessary in the situation.

a] There's enough knowledge by both speakers that the orientation wasn't necessary (in both cases, both the student and the lecturer know which exam is being referred to).

b] As with many routine, administrative requests, there was no need to explain any problem or background. No advice or permission was being sought.

c] The speaker's purpose is often clear to the listener before the speaker reaches that stage.

3 You may have to stop the recording after each expression, to focus students on the expression and to give them time to write.

**Variation:** With a lower level class, put these answers with gaps on the board before playing the recording, and ask students to write only the words that go in the gaps.

a] **orientation**

- Well, it's quite complicated, I'm afraid …
- Well, it's like this, you see, …
- I'm trying to … but…

b] **problem**

- But that's the problem …
- Well, the problem is that …

c] **question**

- So what should I do … (request for advice)
- Could I ask …
- And what happens after that? (request for information)
- Could I have …
- So how can I find it?
- The one with the orange stripes? (request for confirmation)

4 i] Relatively gentle intonation.

ii] More hesitation or tentativeness, with umms and ahhhs, and expressions such as 'well, it's like this, you see, …'.

## Task D: Role play—making academic requests

SB P.159

Monitor carefully and provide students with useful language when they get stuck. If they get into areas not covered by the boxed information in the appendices, encourage them to imagine the situation and guess what they think is realistic.

# Speaking 2

## Further oral presentation skills

The *purpose* of this section is to:

- extend what students learned about paralinguistic features of oral presentations in Unit 5 (Students' Book, page 108; Teacher's Book, page 94);
- provide students with strategies to involve their audience and make their presentations enjoyable to watch;
- relate what they have learned about oral presentations in western cultures to what they know about presentations in their own culture.

This section should be done at least a couple of days before students give their main presentation, see page 169 of the Students' Book.

## Task A: Further features of presentations

SB P.159

### Answers

The best choices from each pair of instructions are:

1 b] Hold your notes in one hand, to leave one hand free for gestures (a useful trick that helps students remember to use gestures!).

2 a] Use small notes, the size of your palm. On these, write only main points and any details that are difficult to remember, such as statistics and references. These are called palm cards.

3 b] Speak a little slower than your normal speed, but not too slowly.

4 a] Use gestures and move around. (Although some students overdo this, try to demonstrate a good balance as you go through these answers with your students.)

5 a] Ask questions during your talk to involve the audience, and respond to their answers. (Asking questions is a relatively easy way for students to make their presentations more interactive and lively.)

6 a] Make eye contact with everyone in the room, without lingering for too long on each person.

7 a] Make a special effort to make eye contact with people on the edge of the room as well as those in the middle, because people on the edge can easily get missed out.

**Variation:** A fun alternative is for the teacher to demonstrate a very bad presentation, and ask students to identify the bad features.

## Task B: Dealing with questions

SB P.160

Focusing on how to deal with difficult questions improves students' confidence with answering them, and also improves the quality of their answers.

### Answers

1 Clearly, guessing the answer is a big no-no! Students from some cultures may need reassurance that they won't lose face if they don't know the answer, nor will they cause the presenter to lose face if they ask a question that the presenter doesn't know the answer to. Doing (b) and, if possible, (c) or (d) together (admitting to not knowing and explaining why or suggesting where to look) would be the best policy for most people.

2

| | |
|---|---|
| i] I'm afraid that's beyond the scope of this presentation. | e] explain that the talk doesn't address the issue |
| ii] That's a very interesting question—but I'm afraid I don't know, though I think the answer might be in Richards and Rogers. | b] be honest<br>d] suggest where to look |
| iii] That would be an interesting research topic! I'm not sure anyone has done that yet. | c] explain why the answer isn't known |
| iv] I'm not sure, but I'll try to find out for you. | b] be honest |
| v] I think it might be around 80, but I'm not sure. I'll check for you. | b] be honest |

3 A homework activity. The answers will vary.

## Task C: Speaking—differences and similarities between presentations here and in your culture

SB P.160

This activity raises awareness of features that could be transferred to English, and also of features that aren't conventionally used in English language presentations, so that the students are aware not to use them here. This may require careful teacher monitoring to give feedback on any aspects of presentation technique the students aren't sure about.

## Task D: Practice!

SB P.160

This activity can be done in small groups working simultaneously. Give five minutes preparation time.

If this task is done in the students' home country the third topic in the Students' Book is possible, but other topics could include:

- An interesting educational experience;
- What do you consider the best (and/or worst) features of the education system in your country?

# English for the Internet Age

## Referencing from Internet sources

The *purpose* of this section is to

- review Internet referencing, first mentioned in Unit 5 of the Students' Book, page 111.
- give students a guided experience of finding the details about websites necessary for referencing

Emphasise to the students that the exact form of all citations, including those from electronic sources, needs to follow the form prescribed by the department or lecturer on the particular course and this varies considerably. All we are doing here is developing awareness of the importance of accuracy and consistency in referencing.

### Task A: Referencing from Internet sources

SB P.161

#### Answers

1 By adding the details from the reference to the table, students review and develop their awareness of what the different parts of the reference mean.

2 This will require a little detective work on the part of the students. A good place to look for the year of writing is at the bottom of the page. This may be prefixed 'last update' or with a © symbol. To find the title of the site, it may be necessary to go back to a previous page. There is often a link to the homepage of the site at the bottom of each page.

Note that for Questions 1 and 2 some details may vary as the sites get updated.

| Author | Year of writing/last update | Title of web page/ document | Title of website/ complete work | Web address | Date of access |
|---|---|---|---|---|---|
| Columbia University Press | 2002 | Basic CGOS Style | The Columbia guide to online style | www.columbia.edu… etc. | 8 Dec 2002 |
| Department of Education and Skills | 2002 | Higher Education | Department of education and skills | www.dfes.gov… | 8 Dec 2002 |
| Department of Education, Training and Youth Affairs | 2002 | Scholarships | Study in Australia | www.studyinaustra… | 8 Dec 2002 |

3 Department of Education and Skills (2002) Higher Education. *Department of Education and Skills*. www.dfes.gov.uk/highereducation/ (8 Dec 2002).

Department of Education, Training and Youth Affairs (2002) Scholarships. *Study in Australia*. www.studyinaustralia.gov.au/Sia/en/StudyCosts/Scholarships.htm (8 Dec 2002).

4 This provides students with more practice as well as being relevant to the oral presentations.

# Reading

✓ *Examining texts from different points of view*
✓ *Using texts to assist in making and supporting judgments*

## Examining texts from different points of view

The *purpose* of this section is for students to:

- use a text to make and support judgments;
- examine a text from different points of view;
- appreciate that people reading for different purposes may get very different meanings and ideas from the same text;
- practise skimming and scanning;
- practise note taking and reading for research;
- be exposed to attitudes to discrimination and harassment common in Western tertiary education;
- critically evaluate these attitudes in terms of their cultural context.

Although the text in this section, *Preventing discrimination and harrassment*, is quite long for lower level students (over 1100 words), the headings break it down well and the long lists also make it easier to read.

### Task A: Orientation discussion—what is discrimination and harassment?

SB P.162

#### Answers

Answers will vary, but here are some notes:

1 In addition to the most obvious: discrimination against the disabled, people from certain socio-economic groups or who live in a particular area, ageism, discrimination in favour of those who have certain family connections, etc.

2 Accept any reasonable examples.

3 *Oxford Advanced Learner's Dictionary* (6th ed): 'to annoy or worry [somebody] by putting pressure on them or saying or doing unpleasant things to them'. Common opinion in traditionally English-speaking countries is identified from the text in the next section.

4 Students' own opinions. However, it should be noted that (c) provides an example of harrassment that may not be apparent—to either side—firstly, the woman is not expressing dislike of the situation in a way that the man recognises, and secondly, she might not even recognise it as harassment.

**Additional question:** It may be interesting for students to compare notions of discrimination and harassment in their own cultures. Are perceptions of discrimination universal or dependent on culture (or other factors)?

### Task B: Reading—skills practice

SB P.163

See Students' Book, Unit 1, page 20, *Skimming*.
See Students' Book, Unit 2, page 37, *Scanning and skimming*.

### Answers

1 No written answer.

2 The first three are in section 1. The definition of harassment is in section 3.2.

3 'Permanent expulsion', 'dismissal' or 'formal warnings', given in section 4. Skimmers will find 'disciplinary action' right at the beginning of this paragraph, and scanning from here will reveal the answers.

4 Go to the Equity and Diversity Unit for advice and/or the Student Services Unit for counselling. This is section 4.1.

5 This question reinforces to students who skimmed and scanned that this is a valid strategy (some students are suspicious of doing this) and for those who forgot, a reminder here will help.
Question 1: skimming.
Question 2: scanning.
Question 3: skimming and scanning.
Question 4: skimming and scanning.

# Using texts to assist in making and supporting judgments

## Task A: Using the text when making and supporting judgments

SB P.166

### Answers

| Situation | Mark if yes | | | Support for your answer | |
|---|---|---|---|---|---|
| | Discrimination? | Harassment? | Neither? | Section no. | First and last words of section of text supporting your answer |
| a] A well qualified and experienced woman trying to get a job but a man is always chosen | X | | | 1.2, 1.4 | UTS is committed to ensuring the elimination of any discrimination … on the grounds of … potential pregnancy' |
| b] A man with a scruffy hair style and rough manner having difficulty finding a job | | | X? | None | No mention in the text of dress, style etc |
| c] A male students who often touches female students | | X | | 3.2 | 'discrimination … uninvited physical contact' |
| d] Someone who has a different political opinion from her boss is repeatedly passed over for promotion | X | | | 1.4 | 'discrimination … political conviction' |
| e] A male in an office who makes sexual jokes in front of female colleagues | | X | | 3.2 | 'discrimination … offensive communications' |
| f] A student in a wheelchair who can't do a particular course | X | | | 1.4 | 'discrimination … disability' |
| g] A student applying for a scholarship who is omantically involved with the lecturer | | | X | 2 | 'A relationship … mutual attraction, friendship and respect … not … discrimination', 'However, consensual relationships may lead to conflict of interest' |
| h] Charging a high fee that only the rich can afford | | | X? | None | No evidence in text |

Another pertinent quotation for (c) is 'Unlawful harassment can occur even if the behaviour is not intended to offend … differing social and cultural standards may mean that behaviour that is acceptable to some may be perceived as offensive to others.'

## Task B: Critical thinking—analysing the cultural content of a text

SB P.167

Texts are created in a particular social context and reflect that context. This activity asks students to compare the text titled *Preventing discrimination and harassment* within the context of their own culture and, in so doing, develop an ability to critique a text in relation to its cultural context, eg to say 'the ideas in this text apply to this cultural context, and while I might be sensible to follow them while I'm here, I don't have to take such attitudes back to my own country if they're not appropriate', or 'this says ... because it was written in ...'.

## Task C: Reading to research an assignment: note taking practice

SB P.167

This reviews the note taking techniques from the Students' Book, Unit 2, page 50 and Unit 4, page 97. In doing this, students will look at the text from a different point of view from the previous tasks.

If some students are struggling, suggest one or two of the ideas below.

### Suggested answers and comments

1 and 2

- *def$^n$ of indirect dscrmntn;*
- *can appear non discriminatory;*
- *some egs;*
- *list the areas of dscrmntn covered in the policy;*
- *can be detected by looking at impact of rules, procedures, their intention;*
- *may take big effort to detect—the university has to 'examine all its policies and practices'. How do organisations implement this?*
- *not illegal if 'reasonable'—what is 'reasonable'?*
- *the Equity and Diversity Unit useful in helping people affected by indirect dscrmntn. Find out more about this unit?*

3 A quick awareness-building point. The questions raised may suggest the direction of future reading. Phoning the Equity and Diversity Unit may be the best strategy!

4 Encourage students to think critically and constructively about their own and their partner's note taking. Students with particularly clear or effective techniques could show examples of their work around the class.

### Task D: Reading from a different point of view

SB P.168

**1** Again, being able to go rapidly to relevant sections of the text will help students to do this quickly.

**2** A quick task. It won't be a radically new revelation for most students, but does serve to build awareness.

# Speaking and Listening

✓ *Giving constructive criticism*

✓ *Critical listening and peer marking of oral presentations*

The *purpose* of this section is for students to:

- practise giving oral presentations;
- critically appraise their peers' presentations in a sensitive manner;
- practise language useful for giving polite feedback.

## Giving constructive criticism

### Task A: Constructive criticism

SB P.168

#### Answers

1 Most people would prefer not to hear—

- You should have made clearer OHTs.
- I didn't understand your OHTs.

2 **Positive feedback**

- I liked the way you (explained the …)
- It was great how you (made it clear with your OHTs)
- (Your OHTs) really helped me to understand your presentation because …
- It was an interesting presentation because …
- … I'll do the same in my presentation

**Suggesting alternatives**

It might be useful next time to make the OHTs clearer.

- (I think) it might help to …
- One thing you could do is work on …
- How about …
- What do you think about …
- It might be useful to …
- I would suggest …
- It'd be better to …

**Replacing negative words with positives**

Your OHTs weren't so clear.

- It was difficult to understand that section → It wasn't so easy to understand …
- There were very few references → There weren't so many references.

**Mitigating the not-so-good by also mentioning the better**

Your talk was generally good … but making the OHTs clearer would help.

- Your first point was easy to follow because you used plenty of discourse markers, but the next section, I think, needed a few more of them.

**De-personalising**

- Your OHTs could have been better … → The OHTs could have been better …

3 The point of this activity is to remind students about sentence stress. Most of the nouns, verbs, adverbs and adjectives above could be stressed, depending on the emphasis the speaker chooses.

4 Answers will vary. Monitor closely, focusing on intonation and sentence stress.

# Critical listening and peer marking of presentations

## Task A: Observing oral presentations

SB P.169

Refer to the oral presentation sheets in Appendix C.

### Variation

- Ideally, students should have the chance to practise their presentation with a partner, as pair work, before commencing Task A in the Students' Book. Then they can revise it in the light of feedback from their partner. Later, they would give the real presentation to the class.
- The observation sheets have been designed to give the audience a focus to their listening.
- If the group is large, spread the presentations out over time, and make sure students know the benefits of actively listening to others. Ideally, in this situation the class would be split with presentations taking place in parallel.

### Suggested assessment guide

If assessment is required, some suggestions are presented below.

*Alternative 1: Competency based assessment*

To assess by outcomes/competencies, use the *Oral Presentation Observation Sheet: Outcomes* in Appendix C.

*Alternative 2: Giving a percentage*

A percentage can be calculated by simply adding together the marks in the following categories. Weightings may be adjusted.

| Content | |
|---|---|
| Staging of introduction | /10 |
| Staging of body | /10 |
| Staging of conclusion | /5 |
| Answers to questions | /5 |
| Coherence and logic of argument | /10 |
| Evidence and quality of research | /10 |
| **Total content mark** | **/50** |
| **Technique** | |
| Signposting | /10 |
| Use of visual aids | /10 |
| Gestures, eye contact etc | /10 |
| Involvement of audience | /5 |
| Voice and clarity of expression | /10 |
| Timing | /5 |
| **Total technique mark** | **/50** |
| **Total mark (content + technique)** | **%** |

### Task B: Reflecting on oral presentations

SB P.170

Through these questions, as well as the boxed points in the Students' Book, we are trying to instil the attitude that improvement in oral presentations, as all other areas of learning, is an on-going process that continues after students have moved on to tertiary education.

# Critical thinking

## What is the purpose of education?

The *purpose* of this section is:

- to expose students to ideas about education that they may not have considered previously;
- for students to critically evaluate these and other ideas and to challenge their views.

### Task A: Evaluating purposes

SB P.170

Small groups, preferably of mixed nationality, are appropriate for this discussion in order to bring out as many ideas as possible. This task aims to respect values from the students' own cultures rather than imposing the values of just one country.

This activity can smoothly flow into Task A of the next section.

# Listening and Speaking 2

## Tutorial participation skills 3: various discussion techniques

The *purpose* of this section is for students to:

- gain further experience of listening to a tutorial discussion;
- practise listening for gist, listening to identify opinion and argument, and intensive listening;
- look at the functions of the speech acts in a tutorial discussion;
- learn and practise using expressions and techniques from the tutorial discussion they heard.

### Task A: Orientation discussion and predicting

SB P.171

Questions 1 and 2 should lead students into the topic, to help them predict arguments (Question 3).

11

### Task B: Listening for main ideas

SB P.171

**Answers**

1 *Eleanor:* governments should provide funding for a wide variety of subjects.

*Hamid:* public funding should be focused on vocational subjects.

2 Providing funding for a wide range of subjects:

- increases quality of entertainment
- expands whole of society's knowledge/experience of arts
- enables learning of skills which are transferable to the workplace
- provides benefits to society from the diversity of its members
- makes people more interesting.

(Eleanor's arguments)

3 Restricting government funding for the study of arts/pure science:

- reduces burden on taxpayer
- increases future earnings and therefore tax revenue
- provides economic benefits to the country.

Study of arts or pure science:

- is a luxury
- there should be a few funded places, but with careful selection of candidates.

(Hamid's arguments)

## Recording script

(11) RECORDING SCRIPT 11 (3 MINUTES, 11 SECONDS)

### TITLE: Tutorial discussion: Funding for education

*Dr Lee:* So, then, do you think it's OK that many governments are reducing funding to university arts and pure science departments?

*Hamid:* Well, yes, of course, it sounds like common sense to me! The money to fund them has to come from somewhere—and ultimately, it must come from the taxpayer, doesn't it? [*asking a question that expects agreement in reply*]

*Dr Lee:* Yes, ... [*indicating understanding, but not agreement*]

*Hamid:* Well, you know, how many taxpayers do you think would be happy to pay for people to study literature or sociology, just for their own pleasure? [*asking a question that expects agreement in reply*]

*Eleanor:* Mmmm [doubtful intonation] [*signalling doubt, but will let the other person continue talking until the point is made. Also avoids answering the question.*]

*Hamid:* If you are studying something that society values enough that it leads to a job with a good salary, I think you have a much stronger right to government support. When you are earning a good salary you'll automatically pay back what the government gave you because you'll be paying the higher tax. And of course you'll always provide some economic benefit for the country [*steps in a logical argument*]. But those arty people doing it just for fun—that's a luxury—and why should governments give money for people to buy luxuries? [*another question that expects agreement*]

*Eleanor:* [aggrieved] But what about the arts and pure sciences? Where would our society be without them? [*responding with the same technique—asking questions that expect agreement*] We'd be in a cultural black hole! There'd be nothing in the way of art except for the mass-market stuff like Hollywood movies that simply follow the same old boring formula [*illustrating point with a hypothetical situation*]. Not to mention ...

*Hamid:* [interrupting] No, no, no, no, no, I don't mean those subjects shouldn't be studied at all [*correcting other person's understanding of a point he made earlier*]—just that students on those degrees should be selected very carefully, and the numbers should be kept low, unless students can pay their own way. Now, that way, the resources could be moved to more productive departments [*more logical reasoning*].

*Eleanor:* But don't you think that expanding society's knowledge and experience of arts has its benefits? [*responding to Hamid with a question that asks for agreement*] I mean for everyone in society, not just the elite? [*focusing/clarifying the previous statement*] But I'd also like to make a point about transferable skills [*making a new point*]—things you learn on an arts or pure science course which can be later used in any situation, even business. Things like analytical skills, and the ability to argue a point of view with the support of solid evidence [*supporting the point with examples*]. All these are important for just about anything you do!

*Dr Lee:* Excellent point!

*Hamid:* Yes, yes, yes, I take your point there [*accepting the other's point*]—these skills are all things that universities should develop and encourage [*showing that he understands by restating the point in his own words*]—but I see no reason why that can't be done with subjects that have benefit to business [*modifying the point to his own purposes*]. That, surely, would make it easier for the students to transfer their skills later on and they'd be killing two birds with one stone! Learning the subject and the skills at the same time [*supporting the point with logical argument*].

*Eleanor:* Ah, I have to disagree with that—for the reasons I gave before—society as a whole benefits from diversity [*referring back to the argument that she didn't get chance to address, bringing up a previous point}*] and people who've had a variety of experience, and who haven't just studied and worked in the same thing, are not just more rounded but also more interesting to be with ...

## Task C: Listening to identify tutorial discussion techniques

SB P.171

11

In this task, students identify some tutorial techniques not already covered earlier in the book, as *well as their linguistic realisation*.

Questions 1 to 5 ask the students to gradually build up the expressions used in the listening. A big factor in making this activity work is the fact that the teacher can check and give confirmation—an essential function. If it is taking too many listenings, you can give more help to the students.

### Answers

1–5 Answers are on the recording script above, indicated in italics.

6 There may be some confusion amongst overseas students about the tutor's role. This varies from tutor to tutor and department to department, but generally they facilitate, guide and encourage discussion and ensure that the ideas discussed are critically analysed. There will be times, like here, when the tutor's input is minimal.

## Task D: Speaking and critical thinking

SB P.172

If students find this difficult, referring them back to the ideas in Task A should provide them with inspiration.

## Task E: Tutorial discussion practice

SB P.172

This provides practice at using the techniques and language found in Task C.

**Variation:** Students work in groups of four or more and discuss the issue. One member of each group is an observer and doesn't take part in the discussion. Instead, he or she keeps track of which functions are used, and lets the group know if some have been missed out. The role of observer should be rotated regularly so that everyone gets a turn.

### Task F: Further discussion practice

SB P.172

This task can be done to review the functions in a different lesson. It can also be done with any topic chosen by the teachers or students—a good opportunity to use a topic suggested or chosen by the students.

# Grammar

✓ *Hypothesising and speculating*

✓ *Conditionals*

The *purpose* of this section is for students to:

- review the verb forms used for hypothesising and speculating, including those used in conditionals;
- practise using these in speaking.

## Hypothesising and speculating

This is not intended to be a comprehensive overview. Instead the point is to emphasise the tenses used to describe and explain hypothetical situations; something that is common in academic English, especially speaking, and which students frequently have trouble with.

### Task A: Verb forms for hypothesising and speculating

SB P.172

Questions 1 and 2 are best done in open class discussion. For most students, this will be review.

#### Answers

1 Students may be able to pick up, either from instinct developed through experience, or previous knowledge, that the second example is the more hypothetical.

2 The first describes a 'timeless' situation—the condition applies whatever the time (within reason!). However, the second condition applies only in the future.

3 Table A

| | real/likely | hypothetical/ speculative |
|---|---|---|
| **past time reference** | various (past simple, present perfect, past perfect and continuous versions of these tenses, plus used to, and would for past habits). | would have + **past participle** |
| **'timeless' time reference** | **present simple** | would + **bare infinitive** |
| **present or future time reference** | **various** (Any tense using 'will', and going to, present simple, present continuous etc.) | would + **bare infinitive** |

4 'Would' is often contracted to /d/ and written as 'd', and 'would have' is often contracted to /dəv/ or /wʊdəv/, but normally the only written shortened form is, 'd have'. 'Wouldn't' is often pronounced /wʊdnt/ and 'wouldn't have' is pronounced /wʊdntəv/, and again, the written forms given here are the only ones in normal use.

# Conditionals

## Task A: Verb forms in conditionals

SB P.173

The previous task is now extended to embrace conditionals. Again, this task reviews knowledge that most students at this level already have, but which many have trouble with using in speaking and writing. By approaching conditionals from a different angle from most texts, it is intended that students may obtain a deeper insight into how conditionals work, and see that the tense used in the main clause of conditionals is the same as would be used if there were no 'if' clause. Even though the focus is on hypothetical meanings, real and likely meanings are also included as a contrast.

### Answers

Table B

| | real/likely | | hypothetical/speculative | |
|---|---|---|---|---|
| | 'if' clause | main clause | 'if' clause | main clause |
| **past time reference** | N/A | **various past tenses** | **past perfect** | would have + **past participle** |
| **'timeless' time reference** | **present simple** | **present simple** | **past simple** | would + **bare infinitive** |
| **present or future time reference** | **present simple** | **various future tenses** | **past simple** | would + **bare infinitive** |

'Will' and 'would' can be replaced by other modal verbs, and other tenses are possible, eg *If it's raining later, I might not go out.*

**Extra note:** How the traditional way of looking at conditionals, as zero, first, second and third conditionals, fits in to this can be seen by comparing the table below with the one above.

| | real/likely | | hypothetical/speculative | |
|---|---|---|---|---|
| | 'if' clause | main clause | 'if' clause | main clause |
| **past time reference** | N/A | | third conditional | |
| **'timeless' time reference** | zero conditional | | second conditional | |
| **present or future time reference** | first conditional | | | |

## Task B: Practice

SB P.174

Questions 1 involves students constructing controlled examples that they can refer to later. Questions 2 and 3 allow more natural use of the language in which students use it to express their own opinions.

In Question 2, emphasise to students that they should give extended answers, not single sentences. You may choose to monitor the responses especially for pronunciation of weak forms. In Question 3, if students find it difficult to choose issues, they can refer to earlier Units in this book.

**Answers**

1 A: Imagine if by some chance our language were more popular in the world than English, and if people from many countries came to our country to study our language. That'd be interesting, wouldn't it!

B: Yeah! It'd be great! We wouldn't have come here, would we! I guess we'd already be at university, without spending all that time it takes to learn English

A: But the great thing is that … it'd be easy to travel for fun if everyone in tourist resorts spoke our language … no problems! Or, for a career, we could teach our language to international students coming to our country to study … so we'd still be able to meet/we could still meet people from other countries.

B: Good idea! That'd be an interesting job … though we'd need to study another course!

2 and 3 Answers will vary.

# Learner independence & study skills

## Speaking outside class

### Task A: Sharing and evaluating ideas

SB P.175

The *purpose* of this task is to:

- help students to critically analyse, in terms of the quality of speaking practice, their opportunities to speak outside the class;
- help them to find new out-of-class opportunities for practice of spoken English.

If you aren't in a native English speaking country, this section could be used as preparation for living in the native speaking country if your students are going to do that, or could be adapted to take into account local English speakers, for example if you are near a tourist resort.

**1** The more ideas generated here, the better. Some suggestions:

- Join a club for a hobby or sport you enjoy;
- Work (with people who don't speak your language!);
- Live with native English speakers.

**2, 3** and **4** After these steps, whole-class feedback should enable each student to get more ideas from the other students.

# Writing

## Extended essay assignment

### Task A: Starting the assignment

SB P.175

The *purpose* of this assignment is for students to:

- experience writing an extended essay;
- find for themselves resources that may be useful in their future field of study;
- carry out extensive library research;
- review aspects of writing considered earlier in this book;
- write an essay demonstrating an ability to;
  - — present a coherent argument with adequate support throughout;
  - — follow common academic conventions in the staging and organisation of the essay;
  - — define key concepts and terms;
  - — critically analyse the issue;
  - — provide full and appropriate in-text referencing and reference list;
  - — follow the conventions of academic writing in terms of vocabulary and sentence structure choice.

It's important that students gain experience of writing an extended essay before they begin their tertiary course. This project should resemble as closely as possible the process of researching and writing such an assignment, but with more support. To help provide realism, Appendix C includes a cover sheet (page 224 of this book; Students' Book, page 257) similar to those required on the front of every assignment at many universities. It's best if other procedures, such as applying for extensions, are also kept realistic, for example with the use of a form. See also Unit 1, page 2, *Academic requests*.

#### The extended essay—teacher's role

- The topic could be the same as the student's oral presentation, introduced in Unit 5, although you could choose to require more detail, or a focus on one aspect included in the oral presentation. See also Students' Book, Unit 5, page 110.
- Genre must be argument, discussion or exposition—students will often try to write explanations, but this does not provide a realistic experience of what will be required of them at university.
- From 1000 to 2000 words is usually an appropriate length, though the length requirement you choose will depend on your students' aims and abilities. Different requirements for individual students in the class are possible.
- If possible, take the class to a university library, or at least a large public library. Unit 4, pages 96 to 98 (especially Task C) of the Students' Book has work relevant to this.

- At least three references, including one journal, should be a minimum requirement.
- Emphasise that in tertiary education, the minimum penalty for plagiarism is fail, and that it could lead to expulsion from the university.
- Four weeks, if the students are studying full time, is usually an appropriate time period for this assessment task. In this book, the assignments are assessed in Unit 10.
- Unit 10 includes a peer review task. If peer review is to be done, students must be informed that this will happen before they begin writing.
- During the project, it is a good idea to organise some lessons to be workshops in which students bring in their work on their project. During the workshop, they would work on their essays individually or with the help of other students while you go around to each person, answering questions and giving advice. Not only will this allow you to check progress and give assistance, but will also provide an incentive for the students not to leave everything to the last minute.

# Writing and Speaking

## Issues in education

SB P.176

The *purpose* of this section is to provide issues for further discussion, critical thinking and writing practice. This is an extra resource that can be used in any way the teacher feels appropriate.

unit 8

# a global connection: economics

Representative governments were, in the past, the fruits of revolutions; today they are economic consequences.

KAHIL GIBRAN

**Skills focus: In this Unit, students will learn and use the following skills:**


**Reading and Writing:** compare and contrast essays; cause and effect 160

**Writing:** exposition schema—discussion and argument 166

**Grammar:** nominalisation—moving towards more academic writing 169

**Speaking and Listening:** orientation discussion about global trade; listening to predict main focus, understand key points and take notes 174

**Reading and Critical thinking:** vocabulary and scanning; skimming for main ideas 176

**English for the Internet Age:** Internet research project 183

**Learner independence and study skills:** faculty requirements within different disciplines 184

In this Unit students expand their vocabulary around the theme of global economics and become aware of current social issues around economic policies. Grammatically, they (and you) will tackle a difficult and important aspect of academic and all other high order reading and writing—nominalisation.

They will learn to write comparison and contrast essays while thinking about the language features of texts as a whole. They will understand and be able to use language that creates cause and effect. From the readings, they must think critically and analyse statements, consider the sources and form opinions for themselves. Internet research and learner independence projects are included.

# Reading and Writing

✓ *Compare and contrast essays*
✓ *Cause and effect*

## Compare and contrast essays

SB▷

When a writer has two or more ideas about a topic, the writer must be able to contrast their ideas in such a way that readers can understand what is being compared and why. The reader must also be made to understand where and how the contrast begins and ends.

Should those ideas express different points of view, all viewpoints must be examined. A writer could begin by comparing a sunny day to a rainy day.

### Suggested answers

1 A sunny day is dry and it could be warm and bright with blue sky and light.

2 A rainy day is wet and the sun is often hidden. The sky is grey and dark.

3 *Whereas* a sunny day is warm, a rainy day may be cooler. A sunny day has blue sky and is bright *but* a rainy day is grey and dark.

### Questions

- You need contrast words in between the description—words like whereas, on the other hand, however, in contrast, why is it, but, although, in contrast to.
- You have to juxtapose ideas, descriptions and sentences against each other.

### Task A: Converting description into comparison

▶ SB P.178

### Answers

Answers will vary according to the student. In general, the comparison is apt to read something like the following:

1 Rich countries have (are characterised by) an industrial base as well as agriculture. They have the power to sell exports and buy products. The people have jobs and are fairly comfortable and they do not go hungry.

2 Poor countries often have an agricultural base without much developed industry. They have little currency for buying products. The people may live on farms and are fairly poor. In some countries, people go hungry.

As you can see from above, comparitives are not used, just statements. So, in their comparisons, students will need to juxtapose their thoughts and use connectives. Thus, their answer to Question 3 should read more like the following:

3 **Whereas** rich countries have (are characterised by) an industrial base as well as agriculture, and they have the power to sell exports and buy products, poor countries often have an agricultural base without much developed industry. **In contrast** to rich countries which have a lot of power to sell exports and buy imports and products, poor countries have little currency for buying products. In **poorer** countries, people may live on farms and are fairly poor and they may even go hungry, **but** in the rich countries, hunger and starvation are far less known.

## Task B: Orientation discussion and reading around world economics and global trade

SB P.178

The IMF is the International Monetary Fund, an international organisation set up by the United Nations and the International Bank for Reconstruction and Development, to stabilise relations between currencies of the subscribing countries.

The World Bank is an international bank set up by the United Nations in 1944 to economically assist developing countries, especially by loans. Its official name is International Bank for Reconstruction and Development. (*Macquarie Dictionary,* 1991)

**Vocabulary notes:** Photocopy the following and cut into cards so that students may walk around the room trying to match the words to the card carried by another student.

| | |
|---|---|
| **1** squander | **2** disposable income |
| **3** inequality | **4** debt servicing |
| **5** economic analysts | **6** national autonomy |
| **7** deforestation | |

**squander**—to waste

Governments are sometimes accused of waste because they

____________________________

taxpayer's money on luxuries for themselves.

**disposable income**—money to spare and to spend on whatever one wishes after necessities are paid for

People in the more industrialised countries appear to have a great deal of

____________________________

____________________________

to spend on fashion clothes, perfume, hair styles and other not so necessary things.

**inequality**—unequal distribution of wealth or other attributes between differing groups

When one person can afford an excellent education while another cannot attend school at all, it really shows the

______________________________

between them.

**debt servicing**—a country or individual must pay back a debt (something borrowed)

Many agriculturally based countries are locked into

______________________________

______________________________

due to the huge amount of capital they borrowed to get their economies up and running in an international market place.

**economic analysts**—people who analyse economies (money earned and spent)

Can we trust the analysis of our economies by the

______________________________

______________________________

who work for organisations like the IMF or the World Banks or are they driven by too much self-interest?

**national autonomy**—the independence of governments to act in ways that suit their own nations

It's certain that not many countries enjoy

______________________________

______________________________

due to influences and pressures linked to world trade. They are not free to make decisions based solely on the needs of their own people.

**deforestation**—the process of trees, forests being destroyed and disappearing, leaving bare land in their place

I think one of the more shocking and ugly sights I have witnessed was a vast track of forest which had suffered complete

______________________________

where, after logging, bulldozers with chains had knocked all the trees out and then the ground had been burnt.

## TITLE: Economics and governments: Who calls the shots?

1 Why do you think it is that a small, privileged group of people who live in developed countries squander food, drive enormous cars that consume huge quantities of petrol (gasoline), take 45-minute hot showers and buy consumer goods daily, while the majority of people in the world go to bed hungry, don't own a car, have little or no access to hot water and no disposable income? Why, too, do the people of many countries walk miles to collect drinking water that other countries would not even consider fit to wash their dogs in? Why in many countries do children as young as five or six years old have to work like adults do instead of going to school and playing games in their spare time?

2 If one acknowledges the inequality that exists in the world, the next logical step is to question the reasons behind it. There needs to be an exploration of cause and effect and a questioning of the powers that control the circumstances of people in all countries. Usually, governments are expected to find solutions to economic problems which may give rise to poverty, child labour, poor working conditions and low pay. Governments are meant to consider and address problems concerning environment and progress.

3 But do governments actually control their countries? Do governments have real power on the global stage? What forces lie behind governments? According to some historians, researchers and economic theorists, it is not individual governments that hold power, it is actually the world banks and/or international monetary funds. Debt servicing in terms of interest payments on money lent to entire countries is the largest single controlling factor on the planet.

4 According to some economic analysts, servicing debt to the so-called First World countries has meant the demise of those countries in the form of eroding social, economic and environmental conditions. These claims are supported by the following argument: the banks charge interest rates which cannot ever be paid. Some countries have been paying back loans for 30 years and have paid the initial debt back many times over. It is the interest that can never be met. Further, many countries are actually re-borrowing money from the same banks in order to pay that bank their interest payments. In other words, the World Bank and the IMF lend money to pay their own selves back. In these instances, so the arguments go, the lenders make decisions which affect the government policies of the countries in debt. Thus, it may be argued that national autonomy is seriously affected by debt servicing.

A few examples follow:

5 Tanzania, 1983: Farmers required imported sprays for their oxen against deadly ticks and tsetse flies and pumps to administer the sprays. 'To conserve funds needed to pay its foreign debt, the government has had to impose restrictions on these and other desperately needed imports' (George, 1990:101).

6 Brazil, 1984/2002: 'The country has been shedding jobs by the hundreds of thousands' (due to the government having to pay back debt). A parallel

economy of crime is the result and it may oblige shops and business premises to maintain armed guards ... (Ibid:128).

7 Indonesia, Zaire, Peru and Colombia: Deforestation is increasing due to loans from the World Bank and other sources. 'Environmental issues become totally marginal' when governments face huge debts (Christine Bagdanowicz-Bindert, an economist who used to work with the IMF, Ibid:167).

8 In Bolivia in the 1980s 'the government froze salaries for school teachers under pressure from the IMF' (statement from a Bolivian teacher to Susan George, Ibid:151).

9 On the other hand, there are those who argue that the IMF and World Bank lending policies have brought enormous benefits to countries that were barely developed. Their economies were lagging far behind the First World nations and their populations had little opportunity for any sort of industrial development. Without the aid, assistance and funds from these lenders, many countries could never have enjoyed the economic profitability that industrialisation and investment can bring.

10 There is evidence to support both positions. Solutions for difficult conundrums like those described are neither simple nor easy to discover. However, programs that concentrate on a shift to self-reliance, community action and production of local goods, less debt to governments by allowing longer times to pay back or by cancelling interest payments altogether could be, and presently are, a starting point.

## Task C: Global examination of texts for six main purposes

SB P.180

Questions 2, 3, and 4 have a variety of possible answers. Their *purpose* is to get students to:

- think about texts they read, and the possible sources of those texts;
- critically analyse the author's position.

### Answers

1 *Why* is the theme. It is the word up to the first verb, which is 'do'.

2 It could be an opinion piece from a newspaper. It might be an extract from a book about inequality in the world. It might be a text book essay.

3 An historian, a left-wing economist, a worker who is familiar with aid to countries.

4 The target audience would depend upon where the text originated. It cannot really be discovered, only speculated upon. It is meant to convince whoever is reading it that there is a great deal of difference in people's lives in the world.

5 The author seems to believe that developed countries are privileged and greedy at the expense of other countries and their populations.

6 'Why' personalises the text, the writer addresses the reader personally and engages the reader by demanding that they frame an answer in their minds.

### Task D: Contrast and comparison words—juxtaposition of ideas

SB P.180

**Answers**

1 **Why** do you think it is that a small, privileged group of people who live in developed countries squander food, drive enormous cars that consume huge quantities of petrol (gasoline), take 45-minute hot showers and buy consumer goods daily, **while** the majority of people in the world go to bed hungry, don't own a car, have little or no access to hot water and no disposable income? **Why**, too, do the people of many countries walk miles to collect drinking water **that** other countries would not even consider fit to wash their dogs in? **Why** in many countries do children as young as five or six years old have to work **like** adults do **instead of** going to school and playing games in their spare time?

2 People:

a] squander food/go to bed hungry

b] drive cars/don't own a car

c] take 45-minute showers/have little or no access to hot water

d] buy consumer goods daily/no disposable income

e] others would not wash their dog in it/walk miles to collect drinking water

f] go to school and play games/children work like adults

## Cause and effect

### Task A: Cause and effect; result and reason

SB P.181

Cause and effect are based upon result and the reason for that result.

*I'm cold (result) because (reason)—the window is open.*

*OR*

*The window is open and that's why (reason) I'm cold (result).*

**Answers**

1 Effect—(result) is that the farmers could not obtain the sprays they needed.

Cause—(reason) is that the government had to impose restrictions on imports.

2 Effect—(result) The country has been shedding hundreds of thousands of jobs and an economy of crime is occurring.

Cause—(reason) The government has to pay back debt (and cannot afford money for infrastructure which could avoid the problem).

3 Effect—(result) Deforestation is increasing.

Cause—(reason) The government has huge debts and cannot afford to worry about the environment.

4 Effect—(result) School teachers' salaries were frozen.

Cause—(reason) The IMF put pressure on the government (to pay back debts).

### Task B: Establishing reason or result

SB P.182

**Answers**

1 *in order* to is implied—(in order) 'To conserve funds needed to pay …'.

2 Effect = (result) = is the result.

Cause (reason) = due to

3 Effect = (result) = due to.

Cause (reason) = when

4 Effect = (result) = froze salaries.

Cause (reason) = under pressure from (these words are not cohesive signals, but they are the ones that tell the reader why the previous event occured). 'Under' means, as a result of, in this instance/example.

### Task C: Metaphor and simile

SB P.182

SB▷

Another way to compare or contrast is through **metaphor** and **simile**:

- a metaphor calls one thing, another thing;
- a simile compares two things using *like* or *as*.

**Answers**

1 Metaphor

2 Metaphor

3 Simile

4 Simile

5 Simile

6 Simile and personification

7 Metaphor

8 Metaphor

9 Metaphor

10 Metaphor

11 Metaphor

12 Simile

13 Simile

14 Metaphor (and personification)

### Task D: Writing contrasting texts

SB P.183

Students answers will vary. The criteria is that they include contrast words to set up their comparisons and use five differences.

# Writing

## Exposition schema: discussion and argument

SB▷

When undertaking tertiary study in an English-medium, you will be expected to compose essays using researched information which argues a case for something. When you argue, you must persuade. This happens in both speaking and writing. You must persuade your listener or reader that your point of view is correct. You must have a point of view and you must convince the listener or the reader of it. In argument, people are said to 'take sides'.

### Task A: Identifying an issue

SB P.183

An issue is anything where more than one belief is possible.

## Task B: Defining an issue

SB P.184

**Answers**

1 a]

2 Students will think of three current issues both/either in their own country and in the host country where they are now. Student answers will vary.

## Task C: Exposition: an argument that will express your belief, claim, contention, side or case!

SB P.184

**Exposition** is one of the most common essay forms that you will be required to produce. An exposition is a factual text which carries forward an argument or puts forward a point of view. You will write essays and give oral presentations based upon reading and the research of others.

An essay must be logical and the staging within its structure follows the pattern:

| | |
|---|---|
| **Introduction** | Introduction general statement<br>Position (thesis)<br>Scope or preview |
| **Arguments** | Individual points<br>Elaborate with support |
| **Conclusion** | Restate the initial position |

Notice that this includes arguments and discussion.

- Expositions often use simple present tense and logical sequencers rather than temporal (time).
- A model/an example of an exposition about the reasons for a successful international business follows Task D.

## Task D: Staging in exposition and predicting text content from a title

SB P.185

Read the model below and match the stages of the writing to the exposition schema provided above.

**Answers**

1 See page 168.

2 The title will be about the reasons for an international surf clothing company's success. These reasons can be tracked within the text.

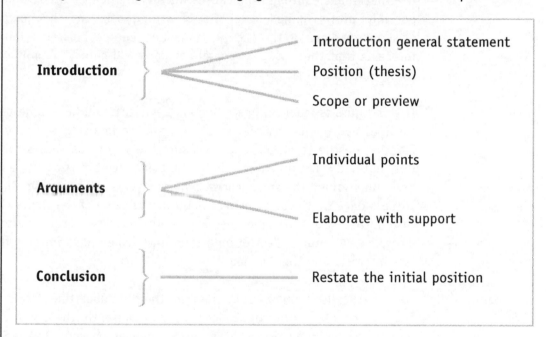

## TITLE: Causes of Aqua Blue Surfgear International's success in 2003

Introductory general statement →
Thesis statement or position →
Preview or scope of what will be argued →

1 Whenever a business is enormously successful, other companies and the general public want to know why. Aqua Blue Surfgear is an international success story for the first decade of the 21st century. For a business to be successful, it is necessary to have strong consumer sales, leading to big profits which in turn inspires investor confidence. Many success stories are also based around international expansion. These elements of strong sales and profits, plus investor confidence are really key components. A business example of these principles in action is Aqua Blue Surfgear International (ABSI).

Arguments: individual points elaborated with support →

2 Initially, ABSI was a Spanish company driven by local sales. They expanded offshore, and it was this expansion that really launched the group. Companies require continuing investor confidence and with ABSI, this confidence had waned. Now there is certainly renewed confidence in Aqua Blue Surfgear International's earnings. The causes for this confidence are strong sales, and a possible profit upgrade. Reports of strong sales in the company's major offshore markets of the US, Australia and Europe bolstered faith in market forecasts that the surfwear apparel company will earn $110 million in the year to 30 June, 2003.

Individual points elaborated with support →

3 If this figure is reached, or is even close to it, it will be a large profit upgrade for ABSI due to the fact that investors believed in a target of only $85 million. Floating on the stock exchange is a sure-fire way to be successful in business. But, naturally, it takes a certain amount of success to float in the first place. Aqua Blue joined the stock market only two years after forming. The measure of success once on the stock market is the rising value of the shares. Investors are thrilled because Aqua Blue company shares have risen this quarter more than 9% to $8.90 surging clear of long-term lows. When Aqua initially floated, there was interest, and then it died down.

Individual points elaborated with support →

4 So, what caused renewed interest in their product lines? One reason Paul Minnow, company director, believes is that presently there is a resurgence of interest in his company because surfing movies have hit the U.S. again, and young people are buying up big in a wave of enthusiasm and rekindled interest in the surf scene. Consumers have to enjoy the brand and repeat buy for a company to be successful and with ABSI, their consumers are girls, and girlswear is the primary driver in their remarkable recovery. The rally is predicted to continue for two to three years.

Conclusion—restates the initial position →

5 The company offices will expand to Los Angeles in July of this year providing evidence that success in retail business, and ABSI in particular is primarily based around consumer and investor confidence plus international expansion.

# Grammar

## Nominalisation: moving towards more academic writing

SB P.186

SB

In English, there is a specialised grammar of writing. This is 'a grammar that has evolved over hundreds of years, with science at its cutting edge, to construct the world in different ways than talking does.' (Martin, 1991:55).

In this writer's opinion, the use of nominal groups and nominalisation is one of the most important aspects of academic writing that you can help students to master. In academic writing, the use of nominal forms is highly regarded. The following points are important:

- Nominalisation creates a higher level of abstraction in writing and nominal groups allow more information to be 'packed' into the themes.
- English nominalises rampantly and no academic essay is possible without the use of many nominal groups and nominalisations.
- Students at this level can move from non-academic to academic with your help and by following a few steps.
- This is an ongoing process to be repeated in every text they write.
- This can be achieved using *multiple drafts* incorporating one step at a time.

In a moment, you will read an example from a student essay. It is a fairly good English sentence, but it is non academic. There are three main steps in changing it from non-academic writing to academic writing:

### The three steps (for teachers to understand)

1 Verb groups are changed to noun forms (or sometimes to passive voice).

2 Human participants which serve as the subject (or actor) of the sentence are changed to a non-human participant which then serves as the subject (actor). (I call this step removing the personals and often agency is shifted from a person to an abstract concept.)

3 The register (largely spoken) is changed to written by using higher lexis (words or vocabulary).

Remember to ask students to carry out **three steps** in their writing and to use multiple drafts.

### The three steps (for students to understand)

1 **Bold** all the personals (the human agents and pronouns).

2 <u>Underline</u> the verb groups (in order to change to passive and noun groups).

3 *Italicise* vocabulary which is too simple (*get, got, good, bad, big, we have to, I think,* etc).

Then, when students begin to rewrite their texts, they know to:

1 Remove the bolded personals;

2 Examine the verb groups for what it is they really wish to say—changing many to nouns and noun groups (this often requires use of the passive voice);

3 Change the vocabulary from simple and spoken, to more complex and written register.

Now read the student's sentence: 'The environment is an important issue in today's world because the scientists and researchers spend a lot of time about the environment, the problems and how to protect it.'

This example is taken from a student essay written on the topic: 'One of the single most important issues in the world today is the environment'. It is not bad English, but it is not academic, is it? Why not? How can you help students to change it?

Examine the model below:

'The environment is an important issue in today's world.'

| | |
|---|---|
| because | spoken register—tell student to use higher lexis, eg *as a result of* or *due to the fact that* (causal relationship changes) |
| the scientists and researchers | human actors—change to non-human *scientific research* (shifting the agency from human to more abstract causes) |
| spend a lot of time | verb form *to spend time*—tell student to change to passive voice: *time is spent*: use higher lexis—change *a lot* to *a great deal* = a great deal of time is spent (passive is sometimes used in academic writing) |
| about | spoken register—tell student to use higher lexis, eg *concerned with* (reach for the highest vocabulary) |
| the environment, the problems | nominalise—it becomes *environmental problems or environmental concerns* |
| and how to protect it | verb form—nominalise, change to *protection* |

After explaining this model or giving it to the students, students carry out the exercises in the Students' Book. They should try to remove the personals and attempt to re-write the text in a more academic style.

The sentence above will require reworking and a new organisation to create something along the lines of—'*Environmental problems are a huge issue in today's society. As a result, a great deal of scientific research is concerned with the environment and its protection.*'

It may be that the student really wanted to say that she felt that the evidence for the environment being important lay in the fact that many scientists are working on it as a problem. To create this agency, another text may be written, such as; '*Environmental issues are of huge concern to today's society. This is proven by the great deal of scientific research which is concerned with its protection.*' Or, '*The amount of scientific research concerned with the protection of the environment is proof of societies' growing concern around the issue.*'

### Multiple drafts

Speaking individually with each student to discover what it is they really wish to say is often the only way to improve drafts. If the student can work on a word processor and create multiple drafts, this is the ideal way to teach how to re-work essays. The first draft would see them using:

- Step 1—bolding the personals.

  The second draft would see them using

- Step 2—examining the verb groups, often shifting to passive.

  The third draft would see them using

- Step 3—reaching for higher vocabulary.

Students ought to embrace the idea of multiple drafts and keep each one to see their progress. This is made easy on the computer.

## Task A: Nominalising verbs—changing verb forms to nouns

SB P.186

### Answers

1 Eg. Education
2 Information
3 Distribution
4 Citation
5 Solution
6 Prediction
7 Communication
8 Introduction
9 Transportation
10 Production
11 Pollution
12 Conservation
13 Government
14 Development
15 Detainment

## Task B: Removing personals from writing—creating a more academic text

SB P.186

### Answers

1 In **my** country, there are very rich **people** and very poor **people. People** in the government are corrupt because **they** take bribes. **We** cannot live a good life and feel free all the time. **I** love **my** country because it is mine and many **people** feel the same way. **We** just wish **our** government would make more jobs and **peopl**e could be more equal in **their** lives.

2 In (name of some country), there are the very rich and the very poor. The government, because (or as a result ) of bribery, suffers from corruption. Freedom is restricted and life is poorer. Many love (name of the country), but wish the government could create more equality through job creation programs which would lead to higher levels of employment.

3 Answers will vary, but here are some examples.

| Active | Passive | Nominalisation |
|---|---|---|
| Next people strip the bark from the trunks | The bark is stripped from the trunks | Bark stripping is the next step |
| Saw the trunks into logs | The trunks are sawn into logs | Sawing the trunks into logs occurs next |
| Convey the logs to the paper mill | The logs are conveyed to the paper mill | Conveying the logs to the paper mill is next |
| Cut into small strips | Small strips are cut | Cut strips are produced |
| Mix the strips with water and acid | The strips are mixed with water and acid | Mixing with water and acid is the next step |

| Active | Passive | Nominalisation |
|---|---|---|
| Clean wood pulp | The wood pulp is cleaned | Then wood pulp cleaning is carried out |
| Bleach the pulp with chemicals to whiten it and flatten with rollers | Pulp is bleached with chemicals, to whiten it and flatten with rollers | Bleaching and whitening with chemicals before flattening with rollers |
| Produce sheets of wet paper | Sheets of wet paper are produced | Resulting in the production of wet sheets of paper |
| Press and dry sheets | Sheets are pressed and dried | Pressing and drying the wet sheets is the final stage of paper making. |

4 Paper making begins with the felling of trees. Next is the removal of branches and leaves from the logs and the transportation of logs to the sawmill. Bark stripping the trunks is the next stage, and the sawing and conveyance of the logs to the mill follows. At the paper mill, small strips are cut before mixing with water and acid, and wood pulp cleaning. Then, there is bleaching and whitening with chemicals before flattening the pulp with rollers, resulting in the production of wet sheets of paper. The pressing and drying of wet sheets is the final stage of paper making.

## Task C: Using multiple drafts—unpacking the meaning of noun groups and nominalisations

SB P.188

SB▷

The next text is a paragraph from the essay titled *Economics and governments: Who calls the shots?* from page 179, but it is the first draft before nominal groups and nominalisation were introduced.

Examine the table and continue to 'unpack' the meaning in the nominalised sentences. You are working from the academic back to the non academic to discover the writer's original thinking. This is the opposite of moving from the active to the passive to the nominalised forms as you did in the paper making exercise.

- Here you will put the personals back into the text, *eg people.*
- You will change nouns back to their verb forms, *eg solution = to solve.*
- You will change the higher language back down to lower language, more spoken, *eg – acknowledges = admits to knowing.*

The next text assists students to 'unpack' meaning. The text that they are to write by filling in the column 'Non-academic with personals' is the draft or the real ideas that were there, in the writer's mind, before nominal groups and nominalisation were introduced.

Students are to put the personals back into the text. This is harder than it sounds because students have to take the nominal forms and work backwards to discover the intent and meaning in the language.

The first six are done for the students as examples or models.

| Academic and nominalised | Non-academic with personals |
|---|---|
| If one acknowledges the inequality that exists in the world | If a person admits to know that in the world, people are not equal |
| the next logical step is to question the reasons behind it. | people need to ask why other people are not equal. What are the reasons? |
| There needs to be an exploration | People need to explore |
| of cause and effect | what causes things to happen |
| and a questioning of the powers | and people need to question the powers (powers are people who make decisions and who have power) |
| that control the circumstances of people in all countries. | people have circumstances, circumstances are their living conditions, their employment etc. These circumstances are controlled by someone in every country |
| Usually, governments are expected to find solutions | People expect governments to solve |
| to economic problems which | problems that are part of the countries' economies |
| may give rise to poverty, child labour, poor working conditions and low pay. | people are poor, children work, people who work have poor conditions at their work, people get paid a low amount of money. |
| Governments are meant to consider and address problems | Governments are supposed to think about and solve problems |
| concerning environment and progress. | about everything concerning nature and everything that is around people ... and about how we can move forward in our country. |

## Task D: 'Unpacking' meaning

SB P.189

These economic terms are nominalisations and require a tremendous amount of 'unpacking' to understand them. Unpacking is related to defining. However, with nominalisations, a student cannot look up the individual word/s or noun groups in the dictionary and gain a satisfactory explanation.

### Answers

1 *Debt servicing*—this means that someone or some country borrows money and is obligated to pay it back. To service a debt means that you must do whatever it takes to 'make the debt good'. In other words, whoever borrowed money must pay the money back.

2 *National autonomy*—to be autonomous means to be able to stand alone or to make decisions without being influenced by someone or something. National means a whole nation, which may be an entire country and which is made up of states or provinces, villages and people. All these people should be able to make up their own minds, they should be able to make decisions, or their governments can make decisions without being affected by outside interests.

3 *A country's self-determination*—countries could have the ability to think about and decide upon their own future. They would be able to make decisions for themselves. They can determine their own fate.

4 *Economic sanctions*—money, trade, import and export all make up economies. To sanction something in the economy is to prohibit or prevent it happening. It means that money is withheld, or goods and imports are not allowed to be imported, often as a punishment from one country to another.

5 *Dissuasive taxes*—to dissuade someone is to try to convince them not to do something. When a government imposes a tax that is too high, it means they want only a very few, very rich people to be allowed to have, buy, trade, import or whatever. Taxing like this means that the item or action has been taxed so highly that it causes people not to buy or carry out an action, ie people are convinced not to do something because of a tax.

# Speaking and Listening

✓ *Orientation discussion about global trade*

✓ *Listening to predict main focus, understand key points, take notes*

## Orientation discussion about global trade

### Task A: Discussion

SB P.189

Students are to continue thinking around the topic of global economics by activating any previous knowledge they may have, combined with the reading done so far in this Unit. The discussion is primarily to open up ideas before they listen to a relatively complicated and lengthy lecture.

Subjects they could explore are in the Students' Book as follows:

SB▷

- The public protests throughout the world that have taken place since 1998 concerning the European Union and the World Trade Organisation.
- What you can purchase in your own country.
- What you can purchase in the country where you are now.
- Whether it is possible to produce and buy goods made in your own country only, or whether we all need imports.
- If you try a web search titled 'global economics', use information from that search to add to your discussion.

## Listening to predict main focus, understand key points and take notes

**Teacher note:** This lecture is quite difficult. If you wish to introduce vocabulary from it, go to the *Reading and Critical thinking* section which follows this one. *Vocabulary and scanning* consists of learning tasks around the vocabulary. You could introduce the vocabulary and the text with exercises to students (prior to actually listening with the purpose of taking notes).

## Task A: Note taking

SB P.190

Refer to Students' Book, Unit 2, page 52 and Unit 4, page 98 for abbreviations for note taking.

## Task B: Predicting the focus of a lecture from the title

SB P.191

**Answers**

1 a] Students should be able to predict that topics around world trade will be discussed.

b] That there is an issue because someone says there is a 'fuss' or a problem around trade.

c] Some effects of trade in relation to global economics will have to be discussed.

2 Answers will vary.

12

## Task C: Listening for discourse markers to understand key points and main ideas in a lecture

SB P.191

- This is a reminder to students to think about the discourse markers they should listen for while they listen to the lecture.
- In this lecture, the speaker often signals an important point by using *'Now'*.

12

## Task D: Note taking from a lecture

SB P.192

Students listen to the lecture (Recording number 12) and take notes. The lecture is around fifteen minutes. This is lengthy by class standards and for a recorded lecture. But if you consider that at university or at a conference in business or academia, a person would listen for an hour or more, then fifteen minutes is still just a sample.

Here is a possible model for what a good note taker might have included within part of their notes:

**Title: Trade and more trade, what's all the fuss about?**

| Economies | Links between developed nations' and emerging nations | Benefits of Globalisation |
|---|---|---|
| Def: eco – pertaining to production, distrb. Use of $ | Free flow of trade, invest x borders & resulting integration of t internat. eco. | |

The script for Recording number 12 is in the Students' Book, starting on page 193, in the next section, *Reading and Critical thinking*. It is also on page 178 of this book.

# Reading and Critical thinking

✓ *Vocabulary and scanning*
✓ *Issues around globalisation*
✓ *Skimming for main ideas*

## Vocabulary and scanning

The following exercises are meant to add to students' vocabulary and assist them to scan for relevant information and skim in order to understand the purpose/s of a whole text. The text from Recording number 12 is used for all tasks.

### Task A: Three-part task

SB P.192

In this three-part task, students approach the text in a global way. They begin by gaining a thorough understanding of the nominalisations within the text, then place them in the text in their correct sentences. Subsequent tasks enable students to examine how the grammar makes meaning and constructs the message within this text.

SB▷

**1** There are three parts to this task. First, you are to scan the written version of the recording for the following nouns, noun phrases/groups and nominalisations contained in the text. They are underlined. Once you locate the words, write the number of the paragraph where you located the words next to the word in the list.

**2** With a partner, match the underlined word groups to their definitions on page 198.

**3** Last, place the underlined word groups into the correct sentences which contain blanks.

- Text of the lecture is in the Students' Book, starting on page 193 (and is also on page 178 of this book).
- Underlined words in the text of the lecture are the gap fill answers.
- Definitions are from 1–20.

**Answers**

**Part 1: Words and word groups list**

1 22 degradation of developing countries' environments.

2 13 a commodity.

3 1 globalisation.

4 1 consumerism.

5 3 global economic integration.

6 8 very good track record.

7 9 conspicuous consumption practices.

8 10 a cursory glance.

9 13 the maxim.

10 19 excessive higher dependence on foreign capital inflows.

11 20 the trade deficit.

12 3 liberalised trade.

13 4 advocates.

14 2 integration of the international economy.

15 23 the continuing advocacy.

16 23 the assumption.

17 13 prudent master.

18 1 emerging nations' economies.

19 3 deregulated global trade.

20 22 consumption poverty.

## Part 2: Definitions for words and word groups list

1 To degrade or lower the environment of a country which is emerging.

2 Any thing of value which may be bought or sold.

3 Describes the ongoing global trend towards the freer flow of trade and investment across borders and the resulting integration of the international economy.

4 To buy—the power to obtain goods and to do so.

5 Where economies join or become integrated into the world's economic policies.

6 A positive result of actions.

7 To consume a great deal, to purchase new things constantly and to have the buying power to do so.

8 A quick look at something.

9 The saying or belief

10 For a country to rely too heavily on other countries in terms of cash/money coming into the country.

11 Money owed to other countries as a result of trade.

12 Free trade or trade which is unrestricted, trade without controls.

13 People who believe in something and ask that it be accepted—to put up an argument in favour of something.

14 For economies around the world to become integrated, to work together.

15 For people to continue to advise and argue a case.

16 A belief.

17 Wise person.

18 The economy or money base of nations which are developing along an industrial line.

19 Trade around the world that is not regulated by governments.

20 When people do not have buying power and are poorer than others who consume a lot.

## Part 3: Gap fill

The answers are the underlined words in the recording script (starting on page 193 in the Students' Book and page 178 in the Teacher's Book).

# Recording script

(12) RECORDING NUMBER 12 (17 MINUTES, 5 SECONDS)

## TITLE: Trade and more trade, what's all the fuss about?

**Lecturer:**

1 *Good Afternoon* to students, visitors and guests...
In my talk today, I hope to clarify some of the issues that surround the topic of globalisation. A great deal of the world's focus over the past decades, has been concerned with developed and emerging nations' economies and the links between *them* and the more developed, *established* economies or countries which are capable of huge consumerism. So, what's meant by 'economy' and what do we mean when we mention 'globalisation'?

2 Well, let's start—according to the *Macquarie Dictionary*, a discussion of economics will be a discussion, and I quote, 'pertaining to the production, distribution and use of income and wealth'. Globalisation has not made its way into the dictionary as yet as it appears to be a term (a nominal or noun term—a nominalisation) based upon the noun, 'global' which pertains to the whole world. Now, according to an article at the Center for Trade Policy Study's website entitled, 'The Benefits of Globalisation', 'Globalisation describes the ongoing global trend toward the freer flow of trade and investment across borders and the resulting integration of the international economy'. So, let me repeat that definition for you....'Globalisation describes the ongoing global trend toward the freer flow of trade and investment across borders and the resulting integration of the international economy'.

3 Now, global economic integration is a goal of the policy makers who advocate liberalised or free trade around the world. Another common term for free trade or liberalised trade is deregulated global trade.

4 Advocates of free trade try to explain that the reason globalisation is so good for countries is that it expands their economic freedom and spurs competition thereby raising both the productivity and the living standards of the people in countries who participate.

5 Hmmm, and that's where the debate really begins. Because, if that's true, then the countries involved in globalisation over the past 10 or 20 years will surely be able to demonstrate those promises—that is that their productivity and living standards are raised or improved. And that there are fewer poor people and those who are poor have a better standard of life. Now, before we examine that aspect of the claims for a particular economic policy, I'd like to outline briefly what I intend to cover in the talk.

6 Now, there are three main points—

**1** First, I'd like to offer a brief overview of some positions concerning free trade.

**2** Secondly, I'd like to point out some examples of countries who are seen to benefit by advocates of globalisation policies.

**3** And, thirdly, I would like to point out some of the examples of countries who are seen not to benefit by reformers and critics of globalisation policies

**4** And then to wrap up, I would like to test the truthfulness or otherwise of the statement that globalisation raises both productivity and the living standards of the people in the countries who participate.

7 Now it's beyond the scope of this lecture to discuss in depth some of the economic policies which comprise globalisation, well, for example, open or closed capital accounts, capital controls, inflation targeting, reserves and supplementary reserves and so forth. So, I'll limit my talk to issues around trade and whether or not this most important aspect of globalisation is, in fact, delivering its promise.

8 Now, by whatever term you call free trade and the push to increase it, it either has a very good track record or a very poor track record, and that depends entirely upon which side of the fence you sit upon, be that politically, financially or academically.

9 So, let me explain this a bit further. The main drivers for free trade are the richer, industrialised countries led by the IMF, you know, the International Monetary Fund and the World Bank. Now these advisors meet at the World Economic Forum where changes have recently taken place. Interestingly, all of these organisations state that they are committed to reducing world poverty and to increasing the wealth and well being of the poorer, less industrialised or, let's call them, developing nations (as countries without the conspicuous consumption practices of the other nations are referred to).

10 Now, even a cursory glance at the World Bank's home page on the World Wide Web reveals that its position statement or motto, if you like, is 'Our dream is a world free of poverty'. Well, regardless of the side if I may call it that, that you are on, this is the stated aim of both the opposing sides. Now, the method for the achievement of that aim is the thing that seems to be in dispute.

11 Now, deregulated, liberalised free trade in order to integrate economies is the goal of both the World Bank and the IMF. For example, the World Bank in September 2001, argued that, and again, I quote 'globalisation reduces poverty because integrated economies tend to grow faster and this growth is usually widely diffused'. (World Bank: 2001a,1)

12 Now, the IMF's First Deputy Managing Director, Mr. Stanley Fischer, states that he believes that 'Asia needs the Fund if it is to continue to benefit as it has so spectacularly over the years from its integration into the global economy'. Well, his position is clear enough. The IMF has benefited Asia in a spectacular way. Korea, for example was one country that may have agreed, but only for a short while. They appeared to be benefiting until the Asian crisis in the late 1990's.

13 Another point of view, James Glassman, a columnist for the Washington Post and a fellow at the, what is it, the ... American Enterprise Institute in Washington stated that free trade creates wealth, which he says ... get this ... is 'more

important than jobs'. So, here he is entering a debate with fellow Americans in the United States who oppose free trade because many of their own industries and there are many (such as textiles)—are being destroyed. Now, in this theory, imports are why people trade and they are in fact the important factor. He uses Adam Smith's argument of 200 years ago that, and I quote Smith, 'It is the maxim of every prudent master of a family never to make at home what it will cost him more to make than to buy ... If a foreign country can supply us with a commodity cheaper than we ourselves can make it, better buy it off them.' So, in his view, exports are only traded in order to gain the benefit of imports.

14 So, just returning for a minute to claims that global economic integration has great potential to combat poverty and economic inequality ... and as I stated earlier in this lecture if this claim were true, then that could be demonstrated. But, it isn't. Listen a moment to these statistics which are provided in a research paper by Weller, Scott and Hersh in 2002. It goes like this ...' In 1980 median income in the richest 10% of countries was 77 times greater, 77 times greater, than in the poorest 10%; and by 1999, that gap had grown to 122 times. The number of poor people actually rose from 1987 to 1999. The world's poorest 10%, and that's 400 million people, lived on 72 cents a day or less. In 1998, that figure had increased ... to 79 cents and in 1999 had dropped again to 78 cents'. This represents no improvement for a decade of trade.

15 Now, while many other 'social, political and economic factors contribute to poverty, the evidence shows that unregulated capital and trade flows actually contribute to rising inequality and in fact impede progress in reducing poverty.' How? I hear you asking. Well, it goes like this ... when trade is liberalised there is more import competition—which in turn leads to lower wages for locals. Deregulated international capital flows can lead to rising short-term capital inflows certainly and increased financial speculation. But this causes instability which causes more frequent economic crises. We only have to think of the so-called Asian crisis back in the late 90's. Governments cannot cope with crises as they do not have the reserves. Now, as we all should know, any economic problems within any country harm the poor to a greater extent than others. Poor people are not being helped by free trade, even though that could be the desire and is, indeed, the stated claim of the IMF and the World Bank.

16 Hang on a minute, I hear you say .... What about somewhere like India and the IT industry there? Surely, this unrestricted globalisation there has proved to be a boon in India. Many business opportunities for India would be the result. And they now have lots of technology. Yes, but firstly, it does not belong to them and secondly, there is no infrastructure to provide it to people outside of a very small area of the country, and thirdly, only a very few workers benefit from it and even they work for far lower wages than they should.

17 In a detailed analysis of the IT revolution and the opening up of India to globalisation in South Asian Voice, it appears that FDI (that's Foreign Direct Investment) benefits the multinationals far in excess of the benefits to India and its own people. For example, the MNCs receive huge tax breaks that are not available to competing local companies. So not happy with tax breaks, the MNCs also evade tax.

The Minister of State for Finance in India named a number of very large and very well known companies as having been charged for serious income tax violations so obviously, this means that the government has lost money to these huge companies.

18 And, privitisation has meant that in areas such as power supply—companies like Enron charge double to the State Electricity Board than a local supplier. And also, Enron uses imported fuels, making India even more dependent on the international market. Now, it also means again that the Indian government has lost capital. This results in a lack of funding to important infrastructures within the country, the obvious ones like education and healthcare. So once again, the poor get poorer and the rich get even richer.

19 Now, in the same article from the *South Asian Voice*, we have Dr. DM Nanjundappa in the *Deccan Herald* in 1998, now he's a noted economist and also happens to be the Deputy Chairman of the State Planning Board in India, and he stated the following, and I quote from Dr Nanjundappa: *'Excessive higher dependence on foreign capital inflows and a rise in exports is likely to be dangerous. Unless there is a sustained growth in exports arising from improvement in the competitive strength of the Indian industry, our hope to recover will be the will o' the wisp'.*

20 And to support that, the trade deficit in India widened to a record four billion dollars in the last quarter of 2002. It grew by a staggering 27% and this was in spite of an increase in exports. And at the same time the rupee shrank in value as well. Africa has many similar tales to tell to the Asian situation.

21 Now, the point of all of these criticisms is that economists themselves are actually questioning the value to their countries of unrestricted and deregulated trade. Certain geographical areas may benefit and certain individuals will most certainly benefit from those policies. But in terms of the overall nations who are supposed to be assisted by having markets for trading—that is a place for their exports and the development of technology within their own countries, there's not really much concrete evidence to support that that is in fact happening. So, the benefits go to the rich countries and it is on the rich country's terms that the whole concept of globalisation is constructed.

22 Now, to the second point, as for combatting poverty, the World Bank has this to say in its own report published in 2001. And this is straight from the report, 'In the aggregate, and for some large regions, all...measures suggest that the 1990's did not see much progress against consumption poverty in the developing world' (Chen and Ravallion, 2001:18) and also the IMF, in its 2000 report, ... Part IV reports that progress in raising real incomes and alleviating poverty has been so disappointingly slow in many developing countries." It also states that "the relative gap between the richest and the poorest countries has continued to widen" (IMF 2000, Part IV, p.1). What is not mentioned in all of that is that not only has poverty increased, but the degradation of developing countries' environments has also increased dramatically. To put that another way, there is greater poverty of lifestyle conditions as well. Note the air, water and land pollution as a result of demand for exports produced cheaply and with great cost to the local environment.

23 So, and I'll close here, despite the continuing advocacy of rich nations that poor countries must trade and trade on the terms of the more powerful nations and that in turn this trade will and must lead to greater wealth, prosperity and more equality, it appears that the number of poor people has actually risen. So, the promises of poverty reduction and more equal income distribution have actually failed to occur. Now I'd like you to consider whether or not the economic policies need to be a little newer than 200 years old and could, in fact incorporate the economies they deal with, rather than making the assumption that there is but one way to create wealth and reduce poverty. It is not working. The evidence is there. Now, the theory may work, but the practice doesn't. It seems that the ideas for globalisation must take into account the infrastructures which currently exist in developing countries and work respectfully with them to create meaningful solutions to and for the ever increasing poor around the globe rather than exploiting them in an opportunistic way to create ever more poor. Thank you.

## Skimming for main ideas

Students may find slightly differing 'main ideas', but the most important aspect of the task is for them to relate scanning and skimming around the key language signals to locate sentences that contain main concepts.

### Task A: Skimming and scanning for key language signals

SB P.199

Students take 10 minutes to locate keywords in the recording script for the listening for this unit, on pages 193 to 197 of the Students' Book (pages 178 to this page of this book) using words such as those below:

1 Issues.

2 Sequencing words such as *first, second.*

3 Arguments and their counter-arguments—cued by words such as *however, but, now, let me explain.*

4 Conclusions and recommendations.

### Task B: Writing concepts

SB P.200

Students note down what words and phrases they find that match the keywords and concepts, beginning with 'issues'.

**Answers**

Answers will vary, but a guide is provided below.

1 Issues

- Globalisation.
- Free trade, liberalised trade
- Whether poorer, emerging nations benefit by policies created by richer nations in relation to trade.

- IMF and World Bank's influence on economies.
- Poor people and poverty throughout the world.

2 Sequencing words such as *first, second*:

- The lecturer uses these to set out what his talk will cover.
- An overview of various positions; give some examples of countries who are supposed to be benefiting from free trade policies; test if poverty reduction is actually happening; find out the truth of statements made.

3 Arguments and their counter-arguments—cued by words such as *however, but, now, let me explain:*

- (para 9)—'the main drivers for free trade are the richer ...'
- (para 12)—Korea was 'one country that may have agreed, but ...'
- (para 14)—'that global economic integration has great potential to combat poverty and economic inequality ... and as I stated earlier in this lecture if this claim were true, then that could be demonstrated. But, it isn't.'
- (para 16)—whole paragraph.
- (para 21)—third sentence 'But in terms of the overall nations who are supposed to be assisted by ...'

4 Conclusions and recommendations:

- (para 29)—'So, and I'll close here, despite the continuing advocacy of rich nations that poor countries must trade and trade on terms ... the promises of poverty reduction and more equal income distribution have actually failed to occur.'
- Recommendations—'It seems that the ideas for globalisation *must take into account* the infrastructures which currently exist in developing countries and work respectfully with them to create meaningful solutions to and for the ever-increasing poor around the globe rather than exploiting them in an opportunistic way to create even more poor.'

# English for the Internet Age

## Internet research project

### Task A: Issues and views, Earth Summit 2002

SB P.200

Students conduct an Internet research project based upon the *Earth Summit* held in Johannesburg in 2002.

**Answers**

1 What were the key issues set down for the summit and stated by UN Secretary-General Kofi Annan?

Water; sustainable development; energy; climate change and biodiversity.

2 Which two countries did not sign the protocol for the EU's (European Union's) renewable energy target?

The United States of America and Australia.

3 What was the reaction and action of Greenpeace activists to the *Earth Summit*?

They protested by wrapping Rio de Janeiro's Christ the Redeemer statue in rope with 'Greenpeace' displayed on it and scaled down the statue (rappelling) in order to protest the summit's outcome. They said that the environment was the big loser and it did not get mentioned.

The only thing covered was trade and trade at the present was contributing to ruining the environment of developing countries.

Answers to other questions will depend on the opinions of the students.

# Learner independence & study skills

## Faculty requirements within different disciplines

### Task A: Using a university/faculty handbook

SB P.200

If you, as the teacher are able to obtain (from local universities) some booklets from different faculties as to their requirements, you could provide them to students to examine for this section. However, it is quite legitimate for the students to be asked to locate this information for themselves. If Internet access is available, then they should type in the name of a specific university, find its home page and then go to the faculty of their choice in order to discover what faculty requirements there are in terms of:

- assessments;
- course materials;
- examinations and their dates for the current session;
- essay writing requirements;
- tutorial presentations;
- referencing style;
- bibliography requirements.

# unit 9 language

Every language is a temple, in which the soul of those who speak it is enshrined.

**OLIVER WENDELL HOLMES**

**Skills focus: In this Unit, students will learn and use the following skills:**


**Speaking 1:** languages quiz and introductory discussion 186

**Listening, Speaking and Critical thinking:** language of persuasion; critical thinking—reflecting on cultural aspects of persuasion; speaking—persuasion 187

**Grammar:** articles 2 192

**English for the Internet Age:** Internet directories 193

**Writing 1:** dissecting essay questions for meaning; expositions revisited and expanded 194

**Reading:** finding implied meaning 199

**Listening:** listening skills—interview with a student 200

**Learner independence and study skills:** listening outside class; poster session about language learning experiences 202

**Speaking 2:** explaining grammar features of languages other than English 203

**Writing 2:** short answer questions 205

**Writing and Speaking:** discussion and essay questions 205

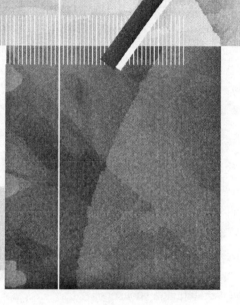

# Speaking 1

## Languages quiz and introductory discussion

### Task A: Languages quiz

SB P.202

The *purpose* of this section is to introduce some of the concepts and vocabulary covered in this Unit in an interesting way.

Students may not know answers to most questions: the point is that they speculate and give reasons.

#### Answers

1 c] Most authorities put the figure somewhere between 5000 and 7000.

2 c] Papua New Guinea has 832 languages. Other figures are:
- 731 in Indonesia
- 515 in Nigeria
- 400 in India
- 234 in Brazil
- just less than 300 each in Mexico, Cameroon and Australia

3 d] The eight countries listed in Question 2.

4 d] Various sets of statistics have been published, but the most recent we have found are:
- 1st: Mandarin Chinese: 885 million first language speakers
- 2nd: Spanish: 332 million first language speakers
- 3rd: English: 322 million first language speakers
- 4th: Arabic: 220 million first language speakers
- 5th: Bengali: 189 million first language speakers
- 6th: Hindi: 182 million first language speakers
- 7th: Portuguese: 170 million first language speakers
- 8th: Russian: 170 million first language speakers
- 9th: Japanese: 125 million first language speakers
- 10th: German: 98 million first language speakers

5 a] Amazingly, around 100!

6 b] Around 1100, or around one-sixth to one-fifth of all the languages in the world.

7 c] Once every two weeks.

8 All of them. Hebrew existed only as a written language 100 years ago, but is now spoken by 5 million people in Israel. Welsh has become common through strong support by the Welsh and British governments: now, in many parts of Wales most government documents and road signs are bilingual (Welsh and English), the medium of instruction in schools is often Welsh, and children often learn Welsh before English. There are many children who can speak both languages but whose parents can speak only English. The number of Hawaiian speakers has increased from below 1000 to nearly 10,000 in the last ten years. Irish Gaelic has also been supported by a strong nationalist movement in Ireland.

9 d] 66%—indicating that bilingualism and multilingualism are more natural than monolingualism. It will be interesting to know how many students in your class were raised in this way, and also what the circumstances were.

10 a] 350 is probably the most realistic here—perhaps more! According to Crystal (2000: 35), 'there are over 350 living languages listed in the etymological files of the *Oxford English Dictionary*'.

**Sources for answers:** Questions 2–6, 8 and 9: Superville (2001), who bases her data relating to Question 4 on SIL International (2001); Questions 1, 7, 8 & 10: Crystal (2000); Question 5: SIL International (2001)—this website gives some of the most detailed statistics about language available; Question 8: Phillipson (1992).

# Listening, Speaking and Critical thinking

✓ *Language of persuasion*

✓ *Critical thinking: reflecting on cultural aspects of persuasion*

## Language of persuasion

The *purpose* of this section is for students to:

- practise listening for main ideas;
- listen to and identify techniques for persuasion;
- think critically about these techniques;
- be empowered by improving their ability to recognise attempts to persuade them;
- practise using one or more of these techniques.

### Task A: Discussion—orientation to the topic

SB P.204

This task orientates student to the topic and activates any previous knowledge, thoughts or opinions they have about it.

**Answers**

Answers will vary.

13

### Task B: Listening for main ideas

SB P.204

**Variation:** If you need to make this task easier for your students, you may want to put a limited number of ideas from Task A on the board or OHT, for the students to choose from. Limiting students' choices will make the task easier for them.

**Answers**

Ideas a, d, e and g are used in the discussion.

## Recording script

13 **RECORDING NUMBER 13 (6 MINUTES, 6 SECONDS)**

**TITLE: Saving languages**

*Roger:* So, why bother to save languages? It sounds to me that when a language dies, life will be easier anyway—there'll be one less language to cause confusion.

*Kate* (surprised): Oh!!! Do you think so?

*Roger:* Well, the fewer languages that're spoken, the more that people will speak just one language—probably English—and the easier people will find it to communicate.

*Kate:* Mmm, I don't ..., I'm not sure about that. Mmm, look, I know it sounds easier that way—but don't forget it's just, it's more normal around the world to grow up speaking two languages or more, not just one like we do. You know, knowing one language is just, like, something you find in a developed country ...

*Roger* (doubtful): Uh Aahaa.

*Kate:* Humans are naturally good at picking up new languages, especially if they do it early enough. And you know, like the majority of children around the world, they grow up thinking, well, it's normal and natural to speak more than one language, because everyone around them does, every day, so mmm, that's exactly what, like, most kids will do — without even thinking.

*Roger:* Aahaa.

*Kate:* So it's not really a problem for people—new generations, I mean, not people who're already adult, to know at least two languages. You know, most people know their local language, and also another language for communicating with people outside the local area, or in other countries.

*Roger:* OK, yeah, that's all very interesting, but, still, I don't see any good reason to go to all the trouble and expense of saving endangered languages!

*Kate:* Oh, typical Roger! Bringing money into everything! [laughs]. Look, one point is that languages like, they kind of like, I don't know, they kind of, like, cultural richness, they add cultural richness to human life—just like, you know, a painting, or music. Different languages have, like, different ways of expressing ideas, and different history, different folk tales, you know, anything to do with culture really.

*Roger:* So?

*Kate:* Well, look, Roger, if you lose a language, it's a bit like losing the Mona Lisa, or a Van Gogh painting—only with languages, it's, it's a bit different, because not so many people really know what they represent, because they take so much more time and effort to learn and appreciate, and so they just go away quietly without anyone paying much attention.

*Roger:* What do you mean, 'what the language represents'? Surely folk tales and things like that can be written down? Then we can keep them forever!

*Kate:* Well, you've got a good point, that's true, but don't you think there's something missing if it's just a s s s, a story in a book? I don't know, for me, it's just like looking at a dead animal in a museum, rather than seeing the real thing, live, in it's natural environment, which is bizarre.

*Roger:* Yeah, I suppose so. I guess it's just not the same, is it?

*Kate:* But well, for me, mmm, I think the most interesting thing really is how people express ideas. Don't you think so? Because every language has different ways of saying the same thing ... Have you ever studied another language, Rog?

*Roger:* Mmm, French at high school.

*Kate:* Probably not a good example—look, look, French is reasonably close to English but just a few things are a bit different. Like, do you remember, adjectives after nouns instead of before, all that kind of thing ... ?

*Roger:* Mmm, yeah, not so different.

*Kate:* But if you'd learned, say, an Asian language, you'd be thinking about a whole load of things in a different way. You know how English has all these different tenses, whereas, you know, with most Asian languages, mmm they use other ways to show time, like time words, or without so many changes in the verb as in English, or often just purely from the context.

*Roger:* Really?

*Kate:* Yeah but, if you're talking about your family, it's other languages' turn to give more information. You know how English has one word for any kind of cousin, whether they're male, female, on your mother's side of the family or your father's?

*Roger:* Yeah.

*Kate:* Well, Asian languages, they've got different words for different kinds of cousins. Isn't that amazing? And that's just a start. There are often different words for other relationships, such as, well, sometimes two or more depending on whether it's someone in your family or someone else's family, or whether you're older or they're younger than you, whatever. Like I say, it's like a totally different way of thinking.

*Roger:* Aaaah, I guess it is. I remember how people learning Japanese and Indonesian at school said everything was so different.

*Kate:* And that's just one set of languages. Just think of the richness and all those diverse ways of thinking that're being lost when languages die!

*Roger:* Mmm, I'm beginning to see what you mean.

*Kate:* Yeah, exactly. Look, I believe languages dying makes the world a less diverse place and therefore more boring. But there's an even more important reason than that—identity, or at least the part of that that's connected with people's origins. Just imagine how you'd feel if you picked up a letter from your grandfather had written, say, and you couldn't even read it at all, because it was in a different language.

*Roger:* Aaah, ... that must be weird. You'd feel kind of cut off, as if something was lost, I reckon.

*Kate:* Exactly, well, that's how people must feel when the language of their culture dies. They, they sort of lose connection with their past—you know, like their personal past as well as their cultural past. People feel lost. Just look in most countries, at mmm, who is at the bottom of society, and you'll find in most cases it's people from minority cultures —the people you see on the streets, such as alcoholics, etc—and you know blacks and native Americans in the US, say Aborigines in Australia. They're often the people ...

*Roger:* (interrupting) But not everyone ends up like that!

*Kate:* No, of course not, I was just generalising ... but they're proportionately far more than in the majority culture. But for many of them, one of the major factors is loss of their cultural identity, the feeling of just not really fitting in—not fitting into the dominant culture, and not having connections with their own culture. I guess it's difficult to understand unless you experience it, I suppose ...

*Roger:* Yeah, I suppose so ...

*Kate:* ... but just try and imagine for a moment—no connections with anything, nothing about your origins that you can have pride in or have any feeling of confidence in. Imagine what that would do to your self-esteem and your sense of security!

## Task C: Identifying techniques for persuasion

SB P.205

The *purpose* of this task is for students to:

- recognise persuasive techniques in spoken English
- prepare students to use these techniques if they so wish

After completing this task, your students may benefit from hearing the conversation again.

### Answers

| Persuasion technique | Linguistic realisation |
|---|---|
| a] Acknowledge another's point of view, but then refute it. | i] ... I know it sounds ______ er... , but ... |
| b] Ask questions which expect a positive answer. | iii] ... but don't you think there's something missing if it's just ... a story in a book? *[Tag questions and sentences ending in 'yeah' with an upward intonation; they have a similar effect to negative questions.]* |
| c] Use dramatic language, to give the argument more force. | iv] ... it's just like looking at a dead animal in a museum |
| d] Make strong statements of opinion. | No clear examples given |
| e] Add emphasis, for example, by repeating words or using a signposting expression. | x] ... not really fitting in—not fitting in to the dominant culture.<br>vii] ... But there's an even more important reason than that ...<br>v] ... the most interesting thing ... is how people express ideas |
| f] Relate the argument to the other person's experience, or to a similar idea that's more familiar to them. | ii] ... it's a bit like losing the Mona Lisa, or a Van Gogh painting ...<br>iv] ... it's just like looking at a dead animal in a museum ...<br>vi] Have you ever studied another language? → *answer* → *development of argument* |
| g] Appeal to the listener to imagine a situation. | viii] ... just imagine how you'd feel if ...<br>ix] ... just look in most countries at ... who ... |

**Variation:** There are other techniques on the recording, such as use of a modal of deduction to present something as a common sense conclusion—'That's how people must feel ...'. You could go through these if you want.

It's worth pointing out to students that, during a presentation or a talk, a good technique is to use rhetorical questions. These are questions that the audience answer in their minds, not out loud.

13

### Task D: Listening for intonation in persuasion

SB P.206

Stop the recording after each instance of the language from Task C, and discuss the intonation used.

## Critical thinking: reflecting on cultural aspects of persuasion

### Task A: Critical thinking—reflecting on persuasion; cross-cultural comparison; identifying attempts to persuade

SB P.206

Small groups work well for this task.

**Answers and comments**

If students run out of ideas for Question 1, give hints such as: politicians, advertisements, shop assistants trying to sell something, a doctor recommending expensive treatment, a multinational company and a government, etc.

Questions 2 and 3 ask students to reflect particularly on the language from earlier tasks in this section, with number 3 adding a cross-cultural comparison element. Suggestions for answers to Question 2 are: tutorial discussion, argument of any kind, and possibly even requesting an extension.

Question 4 is important not only because it allows students to relate their classroom learning to the real world, but also because it gives them chance to identify ways in which people attempt to persuade in real life outside the classroom.

## Speaking: persuasion

### Task A: Practice in persuasion

SB P.206

Before commencing this task, it may be useful (depending on your students) to do some sentence level grammar work on useful structures, such as those listed below against the letters of the persuasion techniques in Task C in the section above.

- **a]** Vocabulary and verb patterns: realise/know/admit/agree + **subject** + **verb**.
- **b]** Negative questions and tag questions to elicit positive responses.
- **e]** Qualifiers for comparatives (eg 'even bigger'), superlative review.
- **f]** Qualifiers for 'like' (a bit like/just like/exactly like).
- **g]** Unreal future conditionals, hypothesising (See Students' Book, Unit 7, pages 172–175; Teacher 's Book, pages 154–156).

Students should not be asked to use techniques they feel too uncomfortable about using.

Several of these questions have been chosen because they are related to the topics of previous Units in the book, and so provide opportunities to recycle vocabulary and ideas.

**Variation:** This activity could be made easier by focusing on just one or two of these techniques. For example, they could choose an opinion, select arguments for and against it, and then practise discussing, using signposting to indicate important arguments.

**Extension:** This spoken text is a useful one in which to draw attention to, or examine features of spoken English such as fillers ('you know', 'like', 'mmm', etc) and false starts.

# Grammar

## Articles 2

The *purpose* of this section is for students to become more familiar with when to choose 'a' or 'an', and the meaning constructed by the use of this article.

This section builds on the *Grammar* section of Unit 2 (page 54) in which the focus was on the use of '*the*'.

### Task A: When are 'a' and 'an' used?

SB P.207

Go through this explanation with the class.

### Task B: Practice

SB P.207

It's important to emphasise to the students that the feedback from this activity is likely to give them additional insight into the use of articles, but that it's usually better for them if they try to work out the answers first. Encourage pair work.

Encourage students to think about the difference in meaning when different articles are chosen. Providing contrast in this way can also provide good insight, and this is also true in feedback. The table below should help with this.

**Answers**

| Q | Answer | Change of meaning with a different article |
|---|---|---|
| 1 | **the**<br>'course' is previously mentioned (first noun group of the text) | 'a course' would imply a different course than the one mentioned before—the meaning of the sentence would be lost |
| 2 | **a**<br>the pattern mentioned in Task A: 'It is … a/an' | 'the' could only be used if the concept of a ten-week course had already been introduced earlier in the text |
| 3 | **the**<br>if the accreditation requirements are standard, there can only be one set of them | 'a' is impossible because 'requirements' is plural. It is also possible to omit the article, in which case the feeling would be that the requirements are more general |
| 4 | **a**<br>the focus isn't on which full time course. 'A full-time course' describes the nature of the course rather than specifying which course | 'the full time course' would imply the only full time course that exists, clearly rather strange in this context |

| Q | Answer | Change of meaning with a different article |
|---|---|---|
| 5 | **a**<br>very similar to 4 | very similar to 4 |
| 6 | **the**<br>as 1 | as 1 |
| 7 | **the**<br>the same college as in the first sentence | 'a college' would imply a different college than the one mentioned before—in fact, any college. The meaning of the sentence would be lost |
| 8 | **the**<br>as 7 | as 7 |
| 9 | **a**<br>introducing a new idea | 'the preference for Business English' would appear to mean that this preference was mentioned before |
| 10 | **the**:<br>as 7 | as 7 |

Some articles haven't been gapped, because knowing with certainty which article to choose can only be done by someone who knows about the particular college. For example, in the last sentence, 'the Upper Intermediate English for Business class' would imply there is one of these classes in the college, whereas replacing 'the' with 'an' in the same sentence would imply more than one such class exists.

**Additional note:** Students find it helpful to think of the following as common collocations (see Students' Book, page 41; Teacher's Book, page 35): the + superlative (-est/most + **adjective**), the same ... as, the UK, the USA, the first, the future, the present, the past ... There are deeper reasons for these, but thinking like this can provide an accessible and reasonably accurate guideline which may be refined as the students gain greater experience with English.

### Task C: Speaking practice with articles

SB P.208

If students are confident enough, they can repeat step 2 after completing step 4.

**Variation:** If you don't have access to enough cassette recorders for the whole class, pairs could be taken out of class to do this activity while students do other work such as writing.

This activity can be used with most grammar points which occur reasonably frequently in spoken English, and provides an intense learning experience that students often find highly worthwhile.

# English for the Internet Age

## Internet directories

The *purpose* of this task is for students to:

- find out about web directories/virtual libraries;
- evaluate which ones are useful for their field;

- practise skimming and scanning web pages;
- think critically about their choice of which links to follow.

### Task A: Demonstration of an Internet directory

SB P.208

Chinese culture was chosen because the information on this subject in this directory is quite comprehensive.

### Task B: Evaluating and selecting directories for your field

SB P.208

Question 1 encourages students to think critically about what information is useful in determining whether a site is worth looking at.

In Question 2, it may be useful to go through the first column as a class, perhaps using the Chinese culture page found in Task A, in order to ensure that all students understand the questions.

**Note:** The directories given here also give links to other, more field-specific, directories such as www.humbul.ac.uk, which specialises in the humanities. Early finishers could be asked to look for a similar directory for their field.

Question 3 is the main point and culmination of the task.

**Extension:** Students could use directories to research essay questions in the next section.

# Writing 1

✓ *Dissecting essay questions for meaning*

✓ *Expositions revisited and expanded*

## Dissecting essay questions for meaning

The *purpose* of this section is:

- to familiarise students with multi-part essay questions;
- for students to learn common conventions of meanings of words used in essay questions;
- for students to practise interpreting essay questions.

### Task A: Model of a multi-part essay question

SB P.209

This task gives students an example of a multi-part essay question, to set the context for later tasks.

### Task B: Key question words and genres

SB P.210

Encourage students to actually write the words in the gaps to make it easier for them to refer to the table later (students will often try to short-cut this by giving numbers to the words and writing only the numbers in the gaps).

The information report genre has not specifically been covered in this book because it is rarely required by itself at tertiary level. It is included in this table because sometimes a part of a question asks for it. An information report follows the schema: general statement (to state and classify the topic), followed by different aspects of the topic being described, in a logical order.

**Answers**

| Key question words | Meaning | Genre |
|---|---|---|
| describe | give information without analysis or judgment (answers most 'what' questions) | information report |
| explain | give factual information about how something works, how something is done, or why something happens (answers most 'how' or 'why' questions) | explanation |
| account for | give reasons for something | explanation |
| compare<br>contrast | show similarities (and sometimes differences)<br>show differences | compare and contrast |
| justify<br>assess<br>evaluate<br>yes/no question<br>to what extent do you … | make an overall judgment (perhaps by looking at strengths and weaknesses and deciding which are stronger) | argument or discussion (exposition) |
| comment on<br>criticise<br>(critically) analyse<br>critique<br>discuss | find strengths and weaknesses, advantages and disadvantages, etc | discussion |

## Task C: Analysing essay questions

SB P.211

**Suggested answers**

Show strengths and weaknesses of the model

**Critique** Porter's Five Forces model of competitive advantage. **To what extent** can it still be applied in today's rapidly changing business environment of globalisation, deregulation and increasing use of technology?

Give an opinion about how much Porter's ideas can be applied, referring to each of the three factors listed, eg aspects that can be considered are …

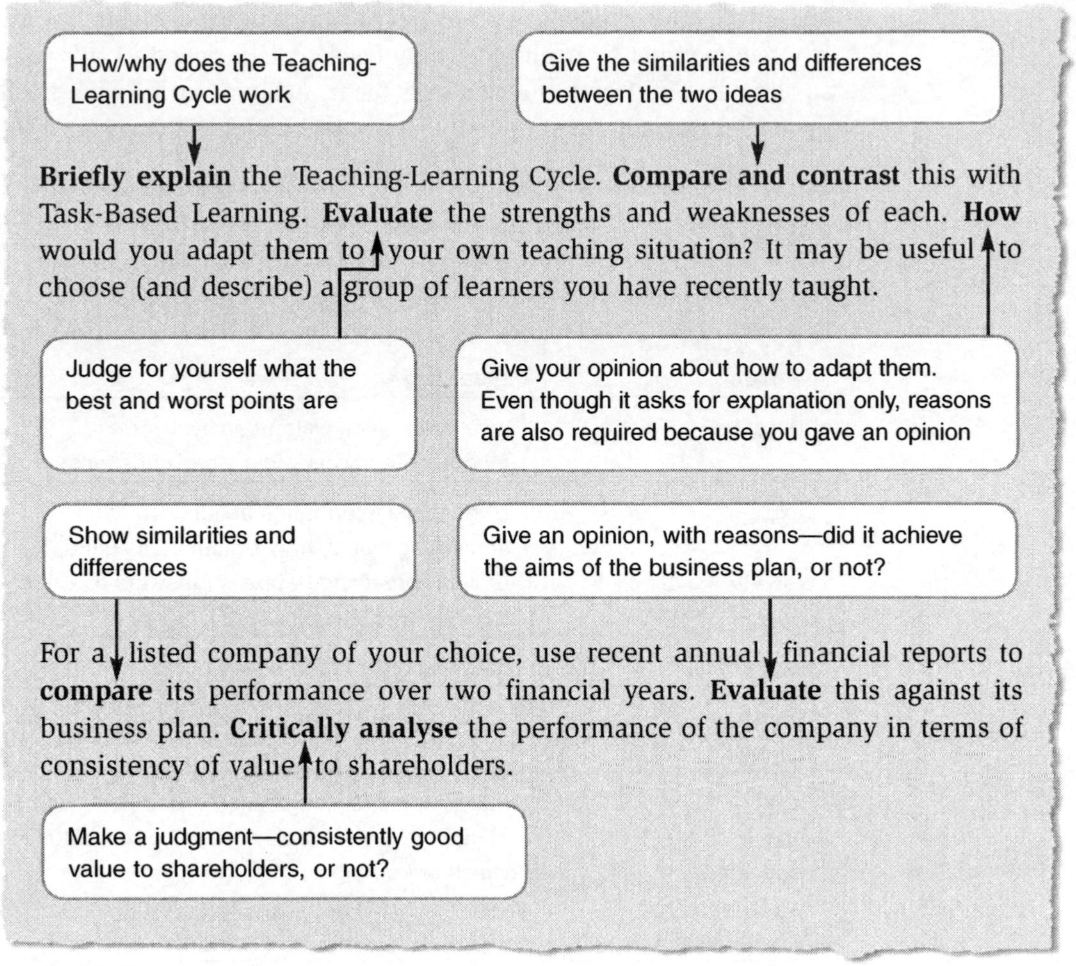
How/why does the Teaching-Learning Cycle work
Give the similarities and differences between the two ideas
**Briefly explain** the Teaching-Learning Cycle. **Compare and contrast** this with Task-Based Learning. **Evaluate** the strengths and weaknesses of each. **How** would you adapt them to your own teaching situation? It may be useful to choose (and describe) a group of learners you have recently taught.
Judge for yourself what the best and worst points are
Give your opinion about how to adapt them. Even though it asks for explanation only, reasons are also required because you gave an opinion
Show similarities and differences
Give an opinion, with reasons—did it achieve the aims of the business plan, or not?
For a listed company of your choice, use recent annual financial reports to **compare** its performance over two financial years. **Evaluate** this against its business plan. **Critically analyse** the performance of the company in terms of consistency of value to shareholders.
Make a judgment—consistently good value to shareholders, or not?

# Expositions revisited and expanded

The *purpose* of this section is for students to:

- examine an essay written from a multi-part question, which contains elements from different genres;
- practise writing an essay from a multi-part question.

## Task A: Orientation discussion

SB P.212

This task gets students thinking about the topic of the sample essay provided, and facilitates prediction of its content.

## Task B: Review of essay structure

SB P.212

This activity reviews the ideas about essay staging covered in the Students' Book Units 2 and 3 (pages 43 and 61), by asking questions that require students to apply this knowledge.

## Answers

1

**TITLE The road to diversity: The economic benefits of universal second language education from primary school**

General statement → Due to the increasingly globalised business environment, companies are more than ever before finding it necessary to communicate with people and organisations from other countries. Traditionally, people in English-speaking countries have relied on English as a language of communication, but the advantages of knowing other languages are rapidly becoming better known.

Thesis statement → It is now extremely important that companies employ people with high level language skills, and that improvements are made in the education system of the country to supply people with the right skills for this.

Preview/scope → This essay will elaborate some ways in which language ability is directly and indirectly useful to business, and then put forward a long-term and a short-term suggestion for how the education system can be improved in order to provide the skills needed.

2 Yes. The General statement leads into the first part of the question, culminating in the strongly stated thesis: 'It is now extremely important that companies employ people with high level language skills'. The Thesis also addresses the second and third parts at the same time: 'It is now extremely important ... that improvements are made in the education system'.

3 From the Preview/scope, it can be seen that the ideas in the body, in order, are:

- direct uses of language ability;
- indirect uses;
- a long-term suggestion for improving the education system;
- a short-term solution.

The first two of these points address the first instruction in the question, as well as supporting the Thesis. The final two points above both address the middle and last point of the question.

4 Just after half way through—but students would skim by reading topic sentences to locate the best paragraph. This question is designed to reinforce the idea of thinking about how to achieve the particular purpose you want before beginning to read and then choosing an appropriate reading technique, instead of starting at the beginning and working your way through, which is what many people instinctively do.

5 Answers will vary!

6 The topic sentences of the body paragraphs are as follows:

- lines 12–14: 'International trade depends on an ability to negotiate deals, and clearly this is much easier if a company's negotiators speak the language of the people they are doing business with'.
- lines 27–29: 'Language learning also leads to greater understanding of other cultures, that is, the cultures of a company's suppliers and customers, thus providing further competitive advantage'.
- lines 38–40: 'Linked to the argument above is the idea of flexibility of thinking and being open to ideas which are different from your own or from the people and culture around you'.
- lines 51–52: 'But perhaps the reason for this is that languages are often not taught seriously until very late, that is, after finishing primary school'.
- lines 58–59: 'However, for this to be successful, primary schools need to be sufficiently resourced. This includes the training of teachers'.

- lines 66–67: 'What is needed in the short-term is an increase in the prestige and perceived benefits of learning languages'.

7 Summary and recommendation (see Students' Book Unit 2, page 43).

8–9 Answers will vary. As Question 9 suggests, a sample conclusion is given in Appendix B together with the references list.

## Task C: Essay and paragraph development—further features

SB P.214

The *purpose* of this task is for students to discover (if they don't know already) that:

- each paragraph must answer part of the question;
- changes in direction in an essay are marked by transition sentences;
- genres should be followed flexibly, to achieve whatever purpose is required;
- every sentence in an essay has a purpose.

It is also to provide further practice of analysing writing for purpose.

### Answers

1 Yes, every paragraph answers part of the question.

2 a] First part of question: first three body paragraphs.

b] Second and third parts of question: last three body paragraphs.

3 a] The first sentence of para 5 is the transition sentence which separates the two parts of the essay.

b] If it was missed out, it would be more difficult to see the section or purpose of the sections of the essay, so it would be more difficult to read.

c] The transition sentence is very important because of the point raised in 3b].

4 **Important note:** Emphasise in these questions that the point is not to learn the structure, but to notice, understand and see an example of how genres are adapted to different situations. Essay questions of several parts often require this. See the following box.

Paragraph 6

| Stage/purpose | Wording |
|---|---|
| link to previous paragraph | However, |
| opinion | for this to be successful, primary schools need to be sufficiently resourced. |
| preview/scope | This includes the training of teachers. |
| problem (2nd part of question) | Presently, most primary school teachers are generalists, … But … fluent in the language. |
| solution (3rd part of question) | and the best way to provide this is to train primary school language specialists … spoken. |
| acknowledgment that problems exist | While this would entail considerable investment, |
| conclusion | it is essential in order to … linguistic competence across the nation. |

5 Paragraph 7

| Stage/purpose | Wording |
|---|---|
| link to previous paragraph | This is, however, a long-term solution. |
| opinion (suggestion: 3rd part of question) | What is needed in the short-term is … benefits of learning languages. |
| support (argument) | This would increase the number and quality of students in language courses. |
| explanation I: how? | One way forward with this is … business success. |
| explanation II: how? | Another is to … full of annoying exceptions. |

### Task D: Answering a multi-stage question

SB P.216

As usual, it is recommended that the students begin their writing in class, to give them the opportunity to consult with the teacher if they have any problems, and so that the teacher can tell whether all students are on track. It should be finished for homework.

**Suggested approaches**

a] Suggest two ways that English could be taught from early in primary school in your country, and give advantages and disadvantages of each. Decide which to implement, and give your reasons.

b] Give thesis: speakers of different languages (do?/don't?) think in different ways. Choose three grammatical features that you know well. One by one, show similarities and differences, and also use them to provide evidence for your thesis.

# Reading

## Finding implied meaning

### Task A: Finding implied meaning

SB P.216

The *purpose* of this section is for students to develop their ability to identify implied meaning.

**Note:** If students find it difficult to find the answers, remind them about skimming and scanning for key words or ideas from the question. Lower level students may need to be directed to the appropriate paragraphs for each question.

**Answers**

1 **Yes**. The arguments in para 5 would only work if this was the case.

2 **No**. Paragraph 5 states that 'Native speakers of English traditionally complain that they are not good at learning languages', but there is **no** evidence the author believes that this is true.

3 **Probably yes**: Paragraph 5 says 'languages are often not taught seriously until very late, that is, after finishing primary school'. It appears that languages are taught in primary schools, but not 'seriously'.

4 **No**. See answer to Question 3.

5 **Probably no**: Paragraph 6 states 'this would entail considerable investment'. The focus of the essay is on what governments can do, not individuals, so the implication is that governments pay to expand language education for potential primary teachers.

6 **No**. In paragraph 7, the speaker states 'What is needed in the short-term is an increase in the prestige … of learning languages'.

# Listening

## Listening skills: interview with a student

The *purpose* of this section is:

- to provide practice in listening for main ideas, and listening and note taking;
- if necessary, to develop students' confidence that their English, like that of the speaker on the recording, will be understood in academic contexts outside the language classroom, even if mistakes in grammar and vocabulary are made;
- to expose students to ideas about listening that will stimulate a discussion about how listening can be practised.

### Task A: Orientation discussion—listening

SB P.217

This task prepares students for the later tasks by getting them to choose their own answers to the questions they are going to hear.

It also give students a chance to think about these issues without being influenced by what they hear on the recording. Their answers are used in Task D of this section.

14

### Task B: Listening for main ideas

SB P.218

These questions elicit the main ideas that Keiko gives (and a few others) and **must** be read by the students before they begin listening. For lower level classes, it may help to pause the recording after groups of answers. It may also help to point out to students that Question 3 is inadvertently answered while answering Question 2.

The answers act as a springboard for discussion in Task A in the next section, *Listening outside class*.

14

**RECORDING NUMBER 14, INTERVIEW WITH A STUDENT ABOUT LISTENING SKILLS (7 MINUTES, 49 SECONDS)**

The original script for the conversation contained only the questions in Task A. Because these appear in the Students' Book, they aren't reproduced here.

**Comment**: The questions are divided into three categories, originally compiled by Rubin (1994), which are text characteristics (1–3), interlocutor characteristics (4) and listener characteristics (5). These were originally part of a larger set of questions used for research into listening by one of the authors, and were adapted here to allow students an insight into the experiences of a fellow learner.

**Answers**

| Questions in Students' Book | Answers |
|---|---|
| 1 a] Does Keiko believe that pauses in speech are normal? | yes, they're natural |
| b] What are pauses in speaking used for? | thinking, making explanations clearer |
| 2 a] Does she notice individual syllables, all the words or just key words when listening? | key words ('not conscious about syllables', 'can't catch all the words', 'can catch key words') |
| b] What else does she feel is important? | intonation, rhythm and accent |
| 3 a] How do rhythm and intonation help her to understand? | help to indicate the key words |
| 4 a] What isn't important? | place |
| b] What situations are easiest for Keiko? | 'face-to-face and one-to-one' |
| c] How many people are in her preferred listening situation? | two or three |
| d] What's the problem with more than this number? | can't anticipate/predict ('expect', 'imagine') |
| e] What's more important than background noise level? | ability to concentrate, which depends on interest level of the situation/topic |
| 5 a] Does having background knowledge make it easier for Keiko? | yes |
| b] Why is it difficult for her when she doesn't know the terminology used? | can't imagine what they're talking about/saying |
| 6 What advice does she give about: | |
| a] how to listen | carefully |
| b] a technique | shadowing |
| c] who to practise with | native speakers |
| d] what else to do | go out |
| e] what kind of situation is best. | 'unexpectable', ie with an unpredictable element |

14 **Alternative (listening and note taking):** If you have high level students, they may find Task B a little easy. An alternative is to write the table below on the board, for the students to copy into their notebooks large enough to take plenty of notes. Explain that the numbers correspond to the questions in Task A. It may help to point out to students that Question 3 is inadvertently answered while answering Question 2. Students listen to the interview and fill in the table.

| Question | Main points in answer |
|---|---|
| 1 | |
| 2 | |
| 3 | |
| 4 | |
| 5 | |
| 6 | |

14 **Task C: Listening and note taking** SB P.219

**Suggested answer**

- *repeat what you hear*
- *natural speed*
- *try to pronounce same as you hear*
- *important: get used to the sound, rhythm & intonation*

14 **Task D: Finishing long answers** SB P.219

At the end of her answers to questions 2, 3 and 5, Keiko gives a summary of her main points—a good technique to use.

The next section builds on the work done in the previous section. It is recommended that these sections are done together.

# Learner independence & study skills

✓ *Listening outside class*
✓ *Poster session about language learning experiences*

## Listening outside class

The *purpose* of this section is:

- to encourage students to reflect critically on their previous experience of listening practice;
- for students to produce a list of strategies that would be appropriate for them and also for lower level students and;
- for students to produce posters giving successful strategies for improving their English, which can be seen by other students.

**Task A: Ideas for listening outside class** SB P.219

This task should be proceeded by the previous section (*Listening skills: interview with a student*).

**Variation:** Before they answer the questions in the Students' Book, ask students to write comments or reactions to the opinions expressed on the recording while you play it again.

**Activity as per book:** Groups of three are ideal for this task.

There are two sets of questions: (1) and (2) focus on things that can be done within any listening situation; (3) to (5) encourage students to think about actual out-of-class listening situations, and to think critically about the usefulness of these for their learning. Question (6) encourages students to put their ideas into action. Setting aside a future lesson segment, perhaps the week after, to conduct feedback, will provide motivation to follow the plan.

It should be reinforced here that the learner independence sections of this book show students that their language learning should continue after their English course finishes, and that they themselves have to take responsibility for making this happen.

**Suggested answers**

1–3 Answers depend on students.

4 It's probably true, but many other factors are also important.

5 & 6:

- The library has tapes, DVDs and videos, with listening and watching facilities.
- Listening to the radio or TV can help, though choice of program will be important—those who need to improve their ability in casual conversation could choose soap operas and dramas, while those who need academic English can concentrate on documentaries.
- Many of the situations given in Unit 7, *Learner independence & study skills* (Students' Book, page 175; Teacher 's Book, page 156) also provide listening practice.

## Poster session about language learning experiences

### Task A: Poster session about language learning experiences

SB P.220

This task brings together work from various *Learner independence and study skills* sections of this book (Students' Book, Unit 2, page 56; Unit 6, page 141; Unit 7, page 175). Students will also reflect on their own language learning experiences, and hopefully distil some of the best points from them.

Students will also gain experience at producing work for a poster session, which is used as a form of assessment in some tertiary courses. Organising a poster session would provide a good opportunity for students from other classes to learn from your students. As the Students' Book explains, in a poster session, students in small groups (or individually) make posters, which are then displayed together. The authors answer questions from people invited to the poster session—these are often students and staff from the same institution. Poster sessions also sometimes take place at conferences.

# Speaking 2

## Explaining grammar features of languages other than English

The *purpose* of this section is:

- to increase students' awareness of grammar by comparing some grammatical features of their own language with English. By noticing differences, some of the features of English may be made more memorable and perhaps clearer;

- for students to gain practice in giving and listening to some quite complex explanations around a topic which is relevant and which for many will be interesting.

Depending on the emphasis given by the teacher, the oral presentation skills from the Students' Book, Units 5 (page 108), 6 (page 145) and 7 (page 159) can also be reviewed and practised here.

The length of time to be spent on this section should depend on the needs of the class. If the priority is practising oral presentation skills, or giving well staged, complex explanations, then this could be quite a lengthy section, and could be spread over different days, with the preparation section to be completed outside class and supported by additional class work, for example. Alternatively, if building speaking confidence and fluency is a greater priority, the preparation could be de-emphasised and greater priority given to the performance.

**Variation for a single nationality class**: Although the student instructions specify mixed nationality groups, this task can be done with single nationality classes, and should provoke some interesting discussion. Just ensure that each group chooses a different grammar point. However, some students in the class may know other languages, and could use these instead.

## Task A: Discussion—orientation to the field

SB P.221

Students often enjoy comparing their experiences of this topic, but it's important that the discussion doesn't get too detailed—the students will need to have plenty to talk about for Task B. So, give a time limit of around 10 minutes at the beginning of this task.

## Task B: Preparing a short presentation

SB P.221

You may want to vary this list according to the needs and current proficiencies of your students.

## Task C: Giving and listening to explanations

SB P.221

Before they begin this task, it's important that the students' attention is drawn to what they need to do after each presentation, so that they have a focus while listening.

The emphasis given to note taking or preparing questions should, again, vary according to the needs of the students.

## Task D: Critical thinking—should English be simplified?

SB P.222

This is an optional and interesting follow-up activity. It could be extended in many ways, for example, by asking students to write an essay on the topic (see list of suggested essay titles at the end of the unit in the Students' Book).

**Suggested answers**

1 Answers will vary depending on first language and other factors, but could include removing the continuous and perfect aspects, reducing the number and variety of dependent prepositions, making rules for article use more consistent (eg never use 'the' for place names) or maybe removing articles completely, or simplifying the system of suffixes and prefixes.

2 *Advantages:* Less time would be needed to learn English, so the investment in time and money could be directed elsewhere. Communication in English could become easier.

*Disadvantages:* Native speakers of English may be reluctant to use the new language, so it may be difficult for conversations to take place between native English speakers and people who've learnt the 'new English'. It may become more difficult to communicate nuance. Existing texts in the language will become less accessible to learners, as will texts produced by native English speakers for other native English speakers.

# Writing 2

## Short answer questions

### Task A: Applying guidelines for short answer questions

SB P.222

The *purpose* of this section is to increase students' awareness of, and to give students practice in, answering short answer questions.

After students have finished writing the answers, you could give a mark out of five for each of the areas listed in the preamble to the task, ie:

- being concise and accurate;
- answering the question fully;
- use of full sentences where appropriate;
- avoidance of personal pronouns;
- lexical choice;
- appropriate nominalisation.

# Writing and Speaking

## Discussion and essay questions

SB P.223

These can be used in any appropriate way to provide further writing and/or speaking practice. Remember to refer to previous sections of this and other Units that may be relevant.

unit 10

# a global connection: cross-cultural communication

THE ARTS OF THE NATIONS

The art of the Egyptians is in the occult.
The art of the Chaldeans is in calculation.
The art of the Greeks is in proportion.
The art of the Romans is in echo.
The art of the Chinese is in etiquette.
The art of the Hindus is in the weighing of good and evil.
The art of the Jews is in the sense of doom.
The art of the Arabs is in reminiscence and exaggeration.
The art of the Persians is in fastidiousness.
The art of the French is in finesse.
The art of the English is in analysis and self-righteousness.
The art of the Spaniards is in fanaticism.
The art of the Italians is in beauty.
The art of the Germans is in ambition.
The art of the Russians is in sadness.

KAHLIL GIBRAN

## Skills focus: In this Unit, students will learn and use the following skills:


**Writing:** genre overview 208

**Grammar:** reviewing academic writing—register; nominalisation; referencing; modality 210

**Speaking:** cross-cultural discussion of common beliefs and practices 215

**Listening:** note taking from a lecture—cross cultural communication 216

**Critical thinking:** critical cultural consciousness—political protest 223

**Reading:** peer review of extended essays 224

**Reading and Writing:** precis, abstracts and introductions; extended introductions, conclusions and summaries 225

**Writing and Reading:** interpreting and describing information from charts and graphs 230

**English for the Internet Age:** how does and will the Internet affect you, as a student? 233

**Learner independence and study skills:** end of course—friendship, compliments! 233

If you are using this book and teaching an EAP course, then it is probably a safe assumption that you are aware of some of the more important issues surrounding cross-cultural communication (CCC). In the Listening section of this Unit, there is a lecture around CCC which explores the process of acquiring the skills and abilities that make one competent in CCC.

The Unit reviews major concepts throughout the course, including an essay genre overview (in grid form) of the main essay types and the features of academic writing such as register, nominalisation, referencing and modality. It provides learning tasks around, and models of, explanations, precis, abstracts and extended introductions and asks students to critically consider the concept of political protest in a cross-cultural way. You are encouraged to have a class celebration with the students, and an activity in which friends write comments to one another is provided.

# Writing

## Genre overview

The *purpose* of this section is for students to review the structure of explanation, argument and discussion essays as well as find key words in questions which signal which genre is appropriate.

### Task A: essay analysis—explanations, arguments and discussions

SB P.226

**1** Students are to review previously studied essay genres by selecting an essay of their choice (or, if preferred, one that the teacher selects and provides) and analyse it using the overview. There are many texts in this course book from which students could select. They might be guided to find one that represents each of the genres in the table and analyse them using the table.

**2** Students write the name of each stage of their selected essay next to the appropriate stage within the introduction, body and conclusion of either an explanation, argument or discussion (or all three, depending upon time constraints —this could be set as homework after an initial one is completed).

**3** Identify within their analysis whether the text they have selected is an explanation, an argument or a discussion (argument and discussion can also be included in exposition genre).

**4** To do this students need to match the various stages within the 'Essay genre overview' sheet to the stages found in their selected text.

## An Essay genre overview

| Question<br>Topic<br>Aspect<br>Limitation | Explanation | Argument<br>(Exposition) | Discussion |
|---|---|---|---|
| **Introduction** | Introductory statement<br>Purpose: rewording of essay topic<br>Definition (optional)<br>Preview: points that will be in the body paragraphs | General statement<br>Definition (optional)<br>Position (thesis)<br>Preview reasons or arguments that will be in the body paragraphs | General statement<br>Definition (optional)<br>Issue<br>Statement/position<br>Preview: points for both sides that will be in the body paragraphs) |
| **Body** | Topic sentence (from points in preview)<br>Elaboration (supporting sentences with: facts and examples optional concluding sentence (summary of paragraph) | Topic sentence (from reasons or arguments in preview)<br>Elaboration | Point 1—topic sentence—side 1<br>side 2<br>Point 2—topic sentence—side 1<br>side 2<br>Point 3—topic sentence—side 1<br>side 2<br>OR<br>Side 1—Point 1<br>Point 2<br>Point 3<br>Side 2—Point 1<br>Point 2<br>Point 3<br>(points from preview) |
| **Conclusion** | Restatement of preview<br>Summary<br>May contain recommendation, may not (optional in explanations) | Restatement/ reiteration of position<br>Summary of body paragraphs<br>Recommendation/ prediction | Restatement of issue<br>Summary of body paragraphs<br>Position<br>Recommendation |
| **Question words** | Outline<br>How?<br>What?<br>Describe how/why<br>Explain<br>Account for<br>Give reasons for | Should ...?<br>Why?<br>Give reasons for the statement that<br>Do you agree?<br>Is this realistic?<br>Account for<br>Explain the reasons for<br>Evaluate<br>Do you think? | Discuss<br>Analyse<br>Evaluate<br>Do you think?<br>NB There is an overlap between exposition and discussion genres |

# Grammar

## Reviewing academic writing

✓ *Register*
✓ *Nominalisation*
✓ *Referencing*
✓ *Modality*

The *purpose* of this section and indeed, the Unit, is to examine texts globally and on a sentence level using what students have learned throughout the course. It should be review for them. Should you be using this Unit independently of others, that is also possible. It stands alone as each task is explained.

In the fourth part of this section, the concept of modality, or hedging, is introduced.

## Register

### Task A: What makes a text academic?

SB P.227

SB▷

Examine Text 1 and 2 on page 28 and answer the questions below.

1 What is the theme or main topic or topics of the text?

2 Are there any quotes?

3 Are sources within it reliable?

4 Does it contain more nominalised forms or more verb forms?

5 Does it contain referencing?

6 Does it read like an academic text? Why or why not?

**Text 1**

Releasing butterflies at weddings and christenings has created a wonderful business for Jody Kissle and her partner Mark. As local lepidopterists, they decided to use their knowledge of butterflies and are now quite happy about their success. 'We make around $400 each wedding and we are beginning to do some christenings as well!', said Jody. Mark added that the idea occurred to them when they were watching people throw rice and confetti over a bride and groom. He said they thought '... it was wasteful and not good for the environment'.

**Text 2**

The cecropia moth, like most moth species, is a destructive pest in terms of crops. Very few butterfly species, however, attack what is referred to in this study as 'important' plants. The consideration of these plants has been aided by a group of amateurs to whom I am indebted. 'Amateur lepidopterists have produced a large body of biological and distributional information for a century or more and this has contributed to ecological and evolutionary research' (Bertomi, 2003: 265).

- Students are asked to examine the table and make comparisons by compiling the relevant information under the categories.
- Ask the students to find and list all the nouns and noun groups in each text and then count them. (Note that Text 1 which contains 90 words has only 14 nouns, whereas Text 2 with 77 words contains 17 nouns.) The more academic text has more nouns even though it is a shorter text.
- The opposite applies with verbs.
- Text 1 quotes from ordinary people, whereas Text 2 quotes ideas from academics, with references.

**Answers**

| | **Text 1** | **Text 2** |
|---|---|---|
| Theme/topic/s | *Using butterflies in a business* | *A study about butterflies and plants* |
| Nominalisations/noun groups | – Releasing butterflies at weddings and christenings<br>– A wonderful business<br>– Jody Kissle and her partner Mark<br>– local lepidopterists<br>– their knowledge of butterflies<br>– their success<br>– each wedding<br>– some christenings<br>– the idea<br>– people<br>– rice and confetti<br>– a bride and groom<br>– the environment | – the cecropia moth<br>– most moth species<br>– crops<br>– a destructive pest in terms of crops<br>– very few butterfly species<br>– this study<br>– 'important' plants<br>– the consideration of these plants<br>– a group of amateurs<br>– amateur lepidopterists<br>– a large body of biological and distributional information<br>– a century or more<br>– ecological and evolutionary research |
| Verbs/verb groups | – has created<br>– decided<br>– are<br>– make<br>– are beginning to do<br>– added<br>– occurred<br>– were watching<br>– throw<br>– said<br>– thought<br>– was | – is<br>– attack<br>– is referred<br>– has been aided<br>– am indebted<br>– have produced<br>– has contributed |

| | | |
|---|---|---|
| Quotes | We make around $400 each wedding and we are beginning to do some christenings as well. (Jody)<br>It was wasteful and not good for the environment (Mark) | Amateur lepidopterists have produced a large body of biological and distributional information for a century or more and this has contributed to ecological and evolutionary research (Bertomi, 2003: 265) |
| Who is being quoted? | People from the article | A researcher |
| References | none | Bertomi, 2003:265 |

### Task B: Differences between academic and non-academic texts

SB P.229

**Suggested answers**

1 Text 1 is an informal recount, reporting information about a couple who run a business. It uses a lot of verbs (or processes) and contains short clauses without as many nouns as Text 2.

2 Text 2 is more formal and is an example of academic writing. It contains only a few verbs (or processes) and it uses long clauses containing many nouns and noun groups. It has nominalisations and it quotes an authority who is referenced correctly with the name, date of publication and page number.

## Nominalisation

A review for students to construct and deconstruct some nominalisations is provided. You could also return to the two texts just studied and examine the nominalisations in Text 2. Also, see Unit 8: Students' Book, page 186; Teacher 's Book, page 169.

*A large body of biological and distributional information* and *ecological and evolutionary research* certainly comprise two good examples of nominalisation in scientific academic writing.

### Task A: Constructing nominalisations

SB P.229

SB▷

Construct nominalisations for the following concepts and statements following the two examples.

For instance 'a student understands something and is familiar with it'. So the nominalisation would be **student familiarity.**

'A group of people who have come to and settled in another country from different parts of the world are called migrants. They have formed a group and become associated legally'. So the nominalisation would be a **migrant association**.

**Answers**

1 In a forest all the trees have been cut down. This is a process that people made happen over time and where that forest was, now there is nothing. The nominalisation would be **deforestation.**

2 A government wishes to make changes in the tax system of a country. They consider these changes a type of reform. The nominalisation would be **taxation reform.**

3 Women in many countries, but particularly in the West, believed they should have completely equal rights with men. They were labelled 'feminist' as opposed to 'masculist'. Their activities became known as a movement. The nominalisation would be **the feminist movement.**

4 This refers to the custom of respecting your elders, in particular, your parents. A person should not place their own values over those of their parents. They should be obedient and act piously. Filial refers to the children who must act in a pious and obedient manner. The nominalisation would be **filial piety.**

### Task B: Deconstructing nominalisations

SB P.230

Students are asked to examine the following paragraph and locate each nominalisation and noun groups which need 'deconstruction' or 'unpacking' to make their meaning clear.

#### Answers

**Lack of familiarity** with a country's customs, especially those around showing respect, may lead to **cultural misunderstanding**. For example, in the case of Chinese students, 'Teachers need to remember that learners are likely to use **relative age and status** as **a primary determinant** of **the level of politeness** to be used and this may result in **socially inappropriate speech**' (Brick, 1999).

**Suggested unpacking or deconstruction of the noun groups from Text 1**

1 Lack of familiarity—a person is not familiar with and therefore may not understand.

2 Cultural misunderstanding—all countries have culture. Cultures are understood by those people who live within them. When a person does not understand the culture or something within that culture then they have misunderstood something based on culture which is not their own.

3 A primary determinant—when something is the most important it is considered a first thing or a primary thing. If this important or primary thing determines or helps to decide something else, then it is a first determiner or primary determinant.

4 The level of politeness—to be polite has stages or levels. The level refers to the degree or the amount of politeness being discussed.

5 Socially inappropriate speech—speech or talking usually takes place in social settings. People try to speak to one another so that they all understand each other and so that what they say is appropriate to a given situation. If, when they speak, they say something that is not acceptable, it is inappropriate.

## Referencing

### Task A: Listing references

SB P.230

Students are asked to review the texts they have read thus far in this Unit and to list all the references.

**1** Bertomi, 2003: 265.

**2** Brick, 1999.

## Modality

The *purpose* of this part of the section is:

- to introduce the concept of modality;
- for students to practise adding modality to language.

## Task A: Expressing degrees of certainty in writing and speaking ▶ SB P.231

Students should be made aware that definite statements are easy to prove wrong just by finding one example. Using modality can reduce this danger.

Look at the following examples of statements from A to H:

A Most angels have wings.

B That angel could have wings.

C Angels may have wings

D That angel might have wings.

E An angel has wings.

F Angels have wings.

G It's possible that angels have wings.

H Perhaps angels have wings.

Students write the probability (degree of certainty) on the line below of A to H from definite to not so definite. F is first—it is a definite 'yes' statement. The writer is certain that all angels have wings!

**Answer**

| | | | | | | | |
|---|---|---|---|---|---|---|---|
| | ( similar | ) | | | ( | similar | ) |
| F | E | A | G | H | B | D | C |
| Definite | | | | | | | Unsure |

## Task B: Using modality in your writing ▶ SB P.231

Opinion: *should, must, may*

Recommendation: *should, must*

Argument: *possibly, perhaps, most, might, would, could, some, most, many, usually, often, slightly, almost all*

SB▷ Using the guide words above and your own knowledge, re-write the following essay by adding modal words. A discussion must allow the reader a space to argue or discuss what is written. This essay expresses too much certainty, even though it is a good discussion. There is not enough modality. Words that are too certain are underlined. You must remove underlined words and replace them with others. Add changes where the ^ symbol appears. You may have to change the word order in places.

**Suggested answers**

**ESSAY QUESTION: Although each religion is different, religions around the world share many commonalities. Discuss.**

**This is an example of what could be a re written essay using more modality. Changes are italicized.**

There are thousands of belief systems around the world. *Some examples* are animism, shamanism, monotheism and polytheism. *Most have* different images, rituals, festivals and architectural styles in their places of worship. However, when we examine the basic beliefs and moral systems of these religions, they are *often quite similar. Some of the more* important feature/s of religions are their moral codes. They are stated directly, such as in the Ten Commandments of Christianity and in Islam.

2 *Often*, interlinked with the setting of moral codes is the guidance of social relationships. This guidance is stronger in some religions, such as those in the Judeo-Christian-Islamic tradition, and weaker in others such as Shinto in Japan.

3 *Some (or many or most)* religions teach respect for elders. *For example*, in Confucianism, respect is a part of the basic tenets. Australian Aboriginal cultures also emphasize respect for older people. *Possibly*, this promotes social harmony and reduces conflict.

4 In *almost* all cases religions include rituals to mark the special events of life. It's very rare to find traditional societies that do not have a religious focus to ceremonies for special events such as the naming of new babies, marriage and funeral ceremonies.

5 Thus, religions are *quite similar in many cases.*

6 It is clear therefore that, although religions appear very different on the surface, they are *(delete in fact)* fairly uniform in that they emphasize positive relations and tolerance between people and that this is facilitated through systems of ethics and rituals and ceremonies.

# Speaking

- Students discuss the questions concerning their differing cultural knowledge and a 'note taker' or 'recorder' writes down the points. As throughout this book, it is intended that the teacher uses the students as cultural informants.
- Students could present their findings in groups to other groups (and to you) at the end of an hour.

## Cross-cultural discussion of common beliefs and practices

SB▷

**Students:** Since you are learning another language, you are working in a cross-cultural way. You use your own native language and you possess your own cultural knowledge, beliefs and practices. The 'target' language (English, in this case) also contains cultural knowledge and its users have varying beliefs and practices transmitted through their own native language (English).

### Task A: Discussion—considering your own culture

▶ SB P.232

In every language and in every culture, there are ways to do the things listed below. With a partner or in your groups, explain just how your language would deal with them. Use the bullet points to help you in your discussion.

- How do you do this in English?
- How do you do this in your own language?
- Bring into your explanation the differences you can think of between your own language and carrying out the communications in English:

1 Introduce someone to someone else in a casual social situation.
2 Greet someone you know very well.
3 Greet a relative.
4 Greet someone you have never met and who is superior to you in the situation.
5 Apologise to someone who is 'above' you.
6 Apologise to someone who is 'below' you.
7 Farewell someone who is a loved one.
8 Farewell someone who is a business associate.
9 Enter into a business contract.
10 Write a letter of complaint.
11 Write an essay for an academic situation.
12 Write a letter of friendship talking about your current situation.

# Listening

The *purpose* of this section is for students to:

- gain experience of listening to a longer (15-minute) lecture;
- practise note taking skills;
- to gain feedback on their listening and note taking skills by taking a test.

## Note taking from a lecture: cross-cultural communication

15

### Task A: Note taking

SB P.233

Students take notes while listening to the lecture (Recording number 15) on cross-cultural communication. This is a shortened version of an actual conference presentation (Cox, 2000).

### Task B: Test

SB P.233

You may wish students to use the test provided on the next page and use it as an assessment within the course. Students could use their notes to assist them in answering the questions.

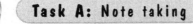

# TEST BASED UPON THE LECTURE ON CROSS-CULTURAL COMMUNICATION

**1** What do the three Cs stand for?

**a]** ____________________

**b]** ____________________

**c]** ____________________

**d]** ____________________

Answer *True* or *False* to the following questions.

**2** Cross-cultural communication is a process.

**3** One definition of CCC is 'to understand differently and act accordingly'.

**4** CCC is an easy skill to learn and one that can be done without frustration or emotion.

**5** The aims for CCC are economic and social.

**6** What are the four processes that Buttjes and Byram listed in their research from 1990?

**a]** ____________________

**b]** ____________________

**c]** ____________________

**d]** ____________________

**7** List two of the human and social aims that Byram proposed:

**a]** ____________________

**b]** ____________________

**8** What is a transformation?

____________________

____________________

____________________

____________________

**9** State one reason for gaining ability in cross-cultural communication.

____________________

____________________

____________________

____________________

**10** Which of the following attributes does not apply to CCC?

**a]** You have to learn to live with doubt.

**b]** You require perseverence.

**c]** You need confidence.

**d]** You must be empathetic.

**e]** You need courage.

**f]** You must convince others of your own opinions.

**g]** You must be prepared to see things another way.

## Answers

*(Test based upon the lecture on cross-cultural communication: Recording number 15)*

1 What do the three Cs stand for?

a] cross-cultural communication

b] communicative cultural competence

c] critical cultural consciousness

d] culture creed colour.

2 Cross cultural communication is a process. *True.*

3 One definition of CCC is – 'to understand differently and act accordingly'. *True.*

4 CCC is an easy skill to learn and one that can be done without frustration or emotion. *False*

5 The aims for CCC are economic and social. *True.*

6 What are the four processes that Buttjes and Byram listed in their research from 1990?

a] There is a process of reflection.

b] There is a process of self-criticism and thinking.

c] There is a time when your own prejudices must be thought about.

d] You must make judgments and perhaps re-think those judgments.

7 List two of the human and social aims that Byram proposed (there are six to choose from), including:

a] to increase social competence

b] to foster positive attitudes towards other countries ... and to counter prejudice

c] to enable learners to meet foreigners and to travel abroad

d] to awaken an interest in foreign cultures and life styles

e] to develop a capacity for understanding and accepting the unfamiliar

f] to encourage tolerance and willingness to work together.

8 What is a transformation?

A transformation is a change. It simply means to change and become something or someone else. In terms of CCC, to expand and to know and understand more.

9 State one reason for gaining ability in cross-cultural communication, (any number of answers here will be correct). Mine is ... that a person can become a better person.

10 Which of the following attributes does not apply to CCC? f].

a] You have to learn to live with doubt.

b] You require perseverence.

c] You need confidence.

d] You must be empathetic.

e] You need courage.

f] You must convince others of your own opinions.

g] You must be prepared to see things another way.

## Recording script

(15) RECORDING NUMBER 15 (15 MINUTES, 32 SECONDS)

**TITLE: Lecture on cross-cultural communication**

*Lecturer: Cross-cultural Communication—creed, colour, culture. Communicative cultural competence. Critical cultural consciousness: the three Cs of life in and out of the classroom.*

1 Good morning students, I'd like to begin today's lecture concerning what you will come to know as the three Cs with a story.

2 A young Australian/Lebanese man whose family own and operate the local fruit and vegetable store near my home, told me this story about travelling ...

3 In Amsterdam, he enjoyed standing on bridges and viewing the water from there. He's not a drug user of any kind and could not comprehend the fact that he was approached daily several times with offers to purchase whatever he wanted. Someone would come up to him and say, 'Would you like to buy some grass, no? How about speed? Heroin then?' He finally gathered the courage to ask someone why he was constantly being approached and asked to buy these things. And they answered 'But of course, because you are standing on a bridge. This always means that you wish to make a deal. If you cross over the bridge, or if you like, continue walking slowly, then it means you are not looking.' This was a cultural norm for that part of Amsterdam and the way my friend discovered it was to gather the courage to inquire.

4 Most travellers, including yourselves, I am sure, would have a tale or two about cultural misunderstandings or miscommunications. These incidents may be humorous, entertaining or frustrating, but they can also be far worse. Misunderstanding between cultures can give rise to 'otherness' which continues the evils of prejudice, racism, and ultimately war. In today's world of mass communication, it would be wonderful to facilitate for all humans intercultural communicative competence. This goal would encompass a desire to promote understanding across continents and seas, nations and, perhaps soon, even galaxies.

5 As I said before, today's lecture concerns what I like to refer to as the three Cs. Whether we call cross-cultural communication just that, or we refer to communicative cultural competence, or we discuss the concepts of creed, colour and culture in relation to language, or we refer to critical cultural consciousness where we question and become aware of other cultures, we still come up with three Cs. Did you notice? Let me repeat those key concepts for you—cross-cultural communication; communicative cultural competence; creed, colour and culture; and critical cultural consciousness.

6 Well, what is cross-cultural communication? Mostly, research around the area defines it in terms of a process rather than as a thing in itself. Yes, a process—the idea is ... that it takes effort and conscious work to really be successful at communication with anyone, and particularly when you are speaking, working

or studying with people who speak different languages. They may have a different religion (or no religion at all), different values and different customs. They most probably will view certain aspects of life differently from you, and as well have more obvious things such as different food or clothing, hair styles, and perhaps skin colour.

7 Now, why should you bother gaining an understanding of people different from yourself? Why should you attempt to communicate with people different from yourself? I believe most people listening today would already know the answer to that—in that you travel and wish to make new friends, you wish to further your education, you wish to do business, you wish to speak more than one language.

8 Given that you may know why CCC is important, the next question is how to achieve it and what difficulties and further benefits may occur as a result of striving to achieve it.

9 Let's begin with some definitions of what this 'it' is before we address the other issues of difficulties and benefits. My own very short definition of CCC is to 'understand differently and to act accordingly'; yes ... to 'understand differently and to act accordingly'. I don't think it is too dramatic to state that if you become competent and expert in cross-cultural communication you will find yourself in a process which leads to transformation of yourself and to new ways of understanding. A transformation simply means a big change. You will change when you learn how to be culturally competent, when you learn about other cultures and actually understand how to engage in cross-cultural communication. It is my belief that this is a big change for the better.

10 I said before that CCC has been defined in terms of being a 'process', thus it is an evolving thing, rather than a static thing. Definitions by Paige in 1993 and also by Buttjes and Byram (in the 90's) both look at CCC in terms of the qualities and skills that people must possess in order to become competent in cross-cultural communication and intercultural understanding.

11 Here's a statement from Paige:

> *The process of adapting to a new culture requires the learner to be emotionally resilient in responding to the challenges and frustrations of cultural immersion. Intercultural education ... must help learners develop culture-learning skills and enable them to manage their emotional responses (1993:1).*

12 So, here we see that the learner, that is, you—is going to feel some strong emotions and be challenged and frustrated. Also, looks like you're going to need help in managing your emotions. Doesn't sound like very much fun, does it?

13 Well, the truth is, it's not very much fun for some time. I'll give you a list in a moment which gives an explanation of the process of CCC. You will note that discomfort or just plain feeling bad does seem to be a part of it. It would

appear that humans are the starting point for culture and for one human to understand another is not easy.

14 Here's a short list based on Buttjes and Byram 1990's research, umm, this research is about the processes that you will go through to gain CCC: first, there's a process of reflection; second, there's a process of self-criticism and thinking; third, there is a time when your own prejudices must be thought about; fourth, you must make judgments and perhaps re-think those judgments.

15 Again, why should you bother? What real benefits may come overall?

16 In 1990, Byram and others proposed that there are human and social benefits. Here is a list of aims written by them which explains the human and social side of CCC:

The human and social aims are:

- to increase social competence by promoting an awareness of and sensitivity to differences in social customs and behaviour;
- to foster positive attitudes towards other countries and those who live in them and to counter prejudice;
- to enable learners to meet foreigners in any country and to travel abroad with confidence, enjoyment, interest and advantage;
- to awaken, that's awaken, to awaken an interest in foreign cultures and life styles and to foster a willingness to see one's own culture in a broader context;
- to develop a capacity for understanding and accepting the unfamiliar;
- to encourage tolerance and a willingness to work together (Byram, Esarte-Sarries,Taylor, 1990: 103–105).

17 Ah, yes, these are all very noble aims and perhaps you understand them and have the desire to realise them. What will you go through to get there?

18 A friend of mine who works with indigenous peoples within her own country says this:

- You must be prepared to not fully understand many things.
- You have to learn to live with doubt.
- You require perseverance. I remember she said to me one time 'I picked myself up and I went back many times'.
- You need confidence,
- and you must be empathetic.

19 A professor friend, this is another friend of mine, who's set up an independent research station in Cape Tribulation, Australia, tracks flying foxes, which are fruit bats and keeps a bat house. He's an active advocate for the total preservation of the world heritage areas around the world as well as particularly the Daintree Rainforest. Over the past 12 years, hundreds and hundreds of

scientists and other researchers from every imaginable part of the globe have stayed as volunteer workers at the bat house in the Daintree. My friend believes that 'generosity' is a main, overriding concern within CCC. He also said to me 'The visitors to the Daintree are as diverse as the rainforest itself' (Spencer 2000 personal communication).

20 So, now you must add 'generosity' to your list.

21 I mention these personal friends' comments in order to help you understand what is meant by cross-cultural communication because they are very competent communicators in terms of CCC.

22 Let me tell you now about some students and their writing. Now, these students wrote a story based on a series of pictures. This particular series is a story about two friends from differing cultures. One girl invites her friend to her house for dinner. Upon arrival, the guest is given chopsticks which she cannot use. She pretends that she's not hungry and refuses the food, but the perceptive mother provides her with a spoon and she eats happily. Listen, now, while I read part of the differing students' comments about the story that the pictures tell. I think the answers show an awareness of cross-cultural communication, even though that isn't asked for in the task.

> *Then Nancy was becoming untalkative. But she began to eat when Aki's mother gave her a spoon. Aki's mother could understand why she didn't eat, that is, Nancy just worried about her clumsy hands.*
>
> *After that, they could spend a good time. It is quite difficult for foreigners to understand the other country's customs. But we could help each other if someone wants to help.*

23 Now it seems to me that this student is aware from their statement, you know it's 'difficult for foreigners to understand another country's customs' but the student says we can help each other if 'someone wants to help', in other words, if we are willing to help. Here's another student's comments:

> *I mean, it is a problem about mind of challenge when we are facing a new something. So if I were Suji, I recommend her using chopstick because it is able to help understand each other and they can make a deep relationship.*

24 This student recognises the difficulty and states that it is a 'problem' and it is a 'challenge' to face something new, yet she 'recommends her using chopstick(s)' in other words she thinks that 'Suji' should take a risk and try being culturally sensitive because the reward may well be a deeper understanding of each other.

25 In a different essay, a student wrote the following:

> *If I could choose this, to stay here (in a country) ... because I am learning about different cultures, their thinkings, foods, idioms, and this had changed my mind. I think that this beautiful experience here will be my best experience after my university ...*

26 Well this student's been going through the process where his mind has been changed or his mind has grown and expanded to understand new things about the country where he is. He considers it a 'beautiful experience'.

27 Well, in conclusion, students, I hope that your understanding of the concepts around CCC, and you will remember, cross-cultural communication; cultural communicative competence; creed, culture and colour; and critical cultural consciousness has increased today. These key concepts concerned the fact that when a person makes the decision to consciously become more culturally competent in a country and a culture and a language outside their own, they will undergo a transformation. They will change. And in the process of this change, they will experience discomfort. As well as that, their own beliefs and knowledge of the world may be challenged. They may have to change their thinking and open their minds. They will grow.

28 You may remember being a teenager or perhaps you still are one now. There's a time when you grow very rapidly and you experience aches and pains. Becoming expert in CCC is rather like that. You grow rapidly and painfully, but the result is maturity. And this maturity, I believe, has the power to change the world. I truly believe that ... gaining understanding between people and entering into harmonious communication between diverse cultures will create a world where people may work together and create their own world view. They can work together to decide how the world should be organised—socially, economically and environmentally. With cross-cultural communication, people do not believe in a world view based upon prejudice, racism and the belief that we are all too different to get along with one another. With critical cultural consciousness, you have the power to become yourself, one among a complex multiplicity woven together in interdependence and mutual respect.

Thankyou.

# Critical thinking

## Critical cultural consciousness: political protest

The *purpose* of this section is for students to:

- critically consider when and whether political protest is ever appropriate;
- consider what form that protest may take, if it is ever appropriate.

In this section, students and teachers will continue to be cultural informants. Each individual will be asked to form an opinion, discuss this opinion and ultimately come to a class consensus concerning it. It will take thinking and negotiation.

### Task A: Cross-cultural comparison around political protest

SB P.233

SB

In this section, you will consider political protest. You need to think about what it is, where it occurs, the sorts of issues that give rise to it, what type of people carry it out and whether or not, in your culture, it is ever an appropriate response to governments and their policies.

Your teacher will lead your discussion and set up the tasks around this important concept.

**Teaching preparation**

You, the teacher, should bring to class, an article or recent news clipping about a protest, photocopied for students.

Below are some steps that you might consider following to present this task.

**Step 1**: Using elicitation and open-ended questioning, ask students if they know of any political protests that have occurred in their own countries. Ask them if they think these protests were at all justified. What were the reasons for the protest? Did the media make it clear why people were protesting? Who protested? How did they carry out the protest? What happened in the particular protest individual students are considering?

**Step 2**: Students go into their groups. In groups, they discuss the above questions again and examine the protests mentioned for similarities and differences. (A recorder should be appointed to write the main points of the discussion.)

**Step 3**: The recorder or another appointed leader reports back to the class and summarises their discussion. Questions and answers could be allowed.

**Step 4**: The teacher shows the class an article concerning a protest that has occurred in the host country.

**Step 5**: Students return to their groups and compare the political protests they discussed with the one the teacher has provided. They record their comparisons.

**Step 6**: Leaders again report back. This time they discuss the cross-cultural perspectives they have worked out concerning the political protests under discussion.

**Step 7**: The teacher could bring into the discussion any knowledge they have of different types of protest—peaceful and non-violent as compared to violent or spontaneous.

**Step 8**: The teacher completes the discussion around political protest, using whatever knowledge has come forward from the students and tries to create a harmonious consensus around the concept of political protest, its merits and otherwise.

# Reading

## Peer review of extended essays

The *purpose* of this section is for students to:

- have the opportunity to gain ideas and expand their developing understanding of features of extended essays through exposure to each others' work;
- be aware of how other students in the group have been approaching the task;
- practise providing, receiving and reacting to oral constructive criticism.

By now, students should be at the end of the extended essay project started in Unit 7. (Students' Book, page 175)

It goes without saying that activities of this kind need to be handled with sensitivity. The section in Unit 7 (Students' Book, page 168) about giving constructive feedback could be usefully reviewed.

Throughout this section, teacher monitoring is particularly important, as is ensuring the students know that you are a resource they can draw upon for resolution of contentious points. It often builds students' confidence in this kind of activity if the teacher as well as the students provide feedback, especially if the students are new to the concept of peer checking.

If time allows, it's useful to do the peer review a few days before you take in the essays, thus giving students the opportunity to revise them in the light of the peer review. This may be a strong motivation for the students to undertake this activity, and will also ensure a higher standard of essays returned to you.

### Task A: Checking essays against criteria

SB P.234

This refers to the same check list from Appendix C that the students should have been using since the beginning of the project.

### Task B: Discussing extended essays

SB P.234

This stage can be skipped if there is little time or if the students are not comfortable with the concept of peer review.

### Task C: Giving feedback to the writer

SB P.234

Techniques for giving feedback were discussed in Unit 7, page 168 of the Students' Book.

# Reading and Writing

- ✓ *Precis, abstracts and introductions: reading to discover the usefulness of texts for assignments*
- ✓ *Extended introductions*
- ✓ *Conclusions and summaries*

## Precis, abstracts and introductions: reading to discover the usefulness of texts for assignments

SB P.233

The *purpose* of this section is for students to:

- understand what precis and abstracts are;
- use introductions to determine whether a text is useful for an assignment;

- review the stages of introductions.

There is an example of an abstract in Students' Book at the beginning of the research report on page 138.

SB▷

Both precis and abstracts are a type of summary. They are used to summarise research and essays. You might write an abstract or a precis of your own work (a long essay, for example) or someone else's work in order to recall what you have read. Both types of summaries are a kind of paraphrasing. This means you must re-write what has been written. You must make it much shorter.

### Precis?

What must be included in a precis?

- Your own wording of the author's writing;
- the main ideas;
- the main arguments;
- the main conclusions.

### Abstract?

An abstract must include:

- the author's wording—the author's exact words;
- the main ideas—in the author's exact words;
- the main conclusions—in the author's exact words;
- don't forget to reference those exact words.

### Further features

Note that you may link the two together by using transitions and connectors/ discourse markers.

- A **precis** can summarise an **abstract**. It is a summary of a summary!
- An **abstract** pulls out (extracts) the main concepts using quotes from the original.
- A **precis** has to be written by you, in your own words, incorporating the main concepts.

When researching by using journals that are written by specialists within your own field, you will find a format that will assist you to understand what you are reading. All articles within journals begin with an abstract or an introduction which will outline exactly what the article will be about.

By reading the abstract/introduction alone, you should be able to discover whether or not the research or the theory put forward in that particular article will be useful to you.

## Task A: Reading to discover usefulness of texts for assignments

SB P.235

Students are to read Text 1 and Text 2 and decide whether they would be useful to them if their assignment was to *Discuss various learning style theories.*

SB▷

### Text 1

When attempting to learn anything new, it is advantageous to maximise your understanding of your own learning. All individuals have learning styles and there are differences. You can discover which learning style you feel most comfortable with (concrete, reflective, abstract or active) and explore different learning opportunities for yourself. The following test was devised to analyse individual abilities.

### Text 2

A great deal of research has been carried out around learning styles of individuals. All individuals have learning styles and there are differences. Four major styles which have been in the literature for a number of years are concrete, reflective, abstract and active. In this paper, in addition to a thorough examination of these categories, the concept of multiple intelligences is explored.

### Answers

The answer for Text 1 is 'no', it would not necessarily be useful because it is a test, as stated in the final stage of the introduction. The next text (Text 2) would be useful because it deals with the theories directly, again, as stated in the final two sentences of the Abstract/Introduction).

SB▷

### More review!

In English, texts make themselves known in the introduction. They explain what they will be about in the final stage of the introduction.

## Task B: Staging

SB P.236

Staging in introductions and throughout whole texts has been a feature of this course book (see especially Unit 2, page 43 and Unit 3, page 61 of the Students' Book). Students should be able to locate the three introductory stages quickly and easily. The *main purpose* of this exercise is:

- to focus attention on the final stage of introductions which should set out what the text that follows will really cover.

The three stages of an introduction or abstract;

- general statement which orients the reader to the topic;
- definition of terms, explanation or viewpoint of the author;
- preview, scope (what the text will actually be about).

**Answers**

**Text 1**

| | |
|---|---|
| General statement | When attempting to learn anything new, it is advantageous to maximise your understanding of your own learning. |
| Explanation/ viewpoint | All individuals have learning styles and there are differences. You can discover which learning style you feel most comfortable with (concrete, reflective, abstract or active) and explore different learning opportunities for yourself. |
| Preview-scope | The following test was devised to analyse individual abilities. |

**Text 2**

| | |
|---|---|
| General statement | A great deal of research has been carried out around learning styles of individuals. |
| Explanation/ viewpoint | All individuals have learning styles and there are differences. Four major styles which have been in the literature for a number of years are concrete, reflective, abstract and active. |
| Preview/scope | In this paper, in addition to a thorough examination of these categories, the concept of multiple intelligences is explored. |

# Extended introductions

The *purpose* of this section is for students to:

- read an example of an extended introduction;
- discover that an extended essay introduction is similar to a normal essay introduction.

Students need to know the following:

SB▷

In an extended introduction, each stage is far longer than in the introductions covered elsewhere in this book. The principle, however, remains the same, that is, there are three main stages that must be included. You can write more background information and include longer and more thorough definitions. You can include some historical background in the second stage which orients the reader to your point of view.

## Task A: Recognising an extended introduction/model

▶ SB P.237

Photocopy the first page of the recording script for Recording number 15 on page 219 and distribute to your students. The script is not reproduced in the Students' Book in order to avoid the possibility of students reading ahead before doing the listening test (Students' Book, page 233).

**Answers**

The extended definition from the listening tapescript on cross-cultural communication ends at the bottom of paragraph 5.

## Task B: Writing an extended introduction

▶ SB P.237

Opportunity is now given for students to write the introductions to their extended essay, an ongoing project since Unit 7 (page 175). Alternatively, students could practise writing a longer introduction, based upon previous work they have accomplished. Individual essays could be re-written with a view to extending each stage of the introduction to include more information than previously.

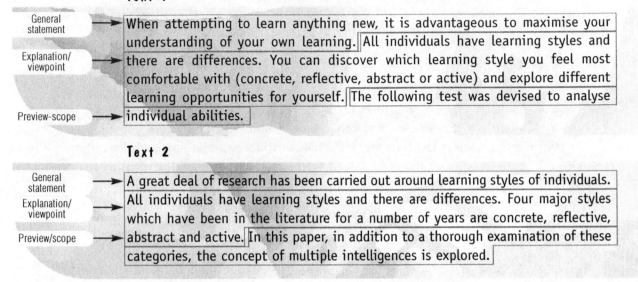

# Conclusions and summaries

The *purpose* of this section is for students to:

- review discourse markers which can be used to introduce conclusions;
- review stages in conclusions;
- practise writing conclusions.

## Task A: Concluding discourse markers

SB P.237

### Answers

The discourse signals that might indicate are conclusion are 3 and 8.

Answer 5 ('finally') usually indicates the last of a sequence of points or arguments. It is rarely used to introduce conclusions.

## Task B: What makes a conclusion a conclusion?

SB P.237

### Answers

1 It is, as expected, a conclusion.

2 It is a conclusion because it begins with a summary statement—'It is clear therefore that …' which could be used within a body, yet the statements are full of summary of what went before.

## Task C: Writing conclusions

SB P.238

- Students write conclusions to texts provided.

Student answers will vary according to their own paraphrasing and summary abilities. However, as a general guide, the following could be used to demonstrate possibilities:

### Answers

#### Text 1: Bangkok ferries

Thus, in the interest of the public, the environment and public transport, the new Bangkok ferries' scheme of closing the river to private use during certain hours and increasing the availability of ferry boats to the public, will reduce pollution, promote tourism and provide an economical way for people to access important areas of the city.

#### Text 2: Capital punishment: right or wrong?

In conclusion, capital punishment has a long history across many different cultures. The moral question of whether it is right or wrong also has a long history. Death for crimes was painful and often brutal. But the questions that require answering in today's world centre around whether this method of punishment is relevant to faiths and societies which like to consider themselves as humane and civilised.

# Writing and Reading

## Interpreting and describing information from charts and graphs

The *purpose* of this section is for students to:

- learn language to assist them in writing about charts and graphs;
- understand how to read a written description of numerical information;
- identify language useful for such a description;
- write a description of numerical information.

### Task A: Interpreting numerical information

SB P.240

#### Answers and comments

1 a] Pie chart: Figures 10.2a, b and c.

b] Line graph (graph): Figure 10.3.

c] Bar chart: Figure 10.1.

2 **Comment:** The purpose of this question is for students to realise that the title of a graph or chart contains very important information. It is the macro-theme, the overview and the reason for the chart or graph.

**Answer:** When writing captions for graphical information, the convention is to give enough information for the graph to be understood even out of the context of the article/report/book in which it appears. As a guideline, place and time are given as well as a nominalisation of what is represented (To look back at nominalisation, see Students' Book, Unit 8, page 186; Teacher's Book, page 169.

3 a] **Example answer** for Figure 10.2: These pie charts show the proportions of Govinda's adult residents who spoke one language only, two languages, three languages or four or more languages, in 1982, 1992 and 2002, together with forecasts for 2007.

**Example answer** for Figure 10.3: The line graph shows the number of immigrants to Govindia between 1982 and 2002, from each of four regions of the world. It also projects what is expected to happen from 2002 to 2007.

b] This should provoke some good discussion about the construction of accurate meanings. **Answers** will vary.

### Task B: Features of written descriptions of numerical information

SB P.241

**Note:** It may be necessary to point out to students before they begin to read this passage that many countries allow people with origins in another country to take out citizenship. To students from some countries, this may be an unusual concept.

The text is similar to IELTS Writing Task 1, and contains language that will be very useful for this task. However, there are differences, due to the fact that, in reality, academic descriptions are more likely to use graphical information to illustrate points they make, rather than to describe graphical information they are given. Also, the writing will occur in a context, though by necessity a fictional context has been used here. Also, good IELTS Task 1 answers are not so likely to have conclusions.

## Answers and comments

1 By asking students this question (which features of written descriptions they can identify), we are showing them that we have confidence in their abilities to identify this kind of feature by themselves. Showing this kind of confidence in them will help them become more independent learners. The questions after the passage provide the support that almost all students will eventually need and also ensure that all students have the same information.

2 a] para 2: migrants from Africa
para 3: migrants from Asia
para 4: migrants from Europe and 'other' regions
para 5: conclusion

Each paragraph represents one region, throughout the period.

b] The most significant paragraphs were put first (in English, the theme comes first. The most important information is first).

c]
- to describe the actual chart, not the data on it (line 3): present simple
- to describe the data in the bars representing 1982, 1992 and 2002: past simple
- to describe the data in the bars representing 2007: present simple passive with verbs such as *forecast, predicted, expected and anticipated*

To review the last point, students can look at Students' Book, page 154, Task A.

d]

| | verbs | nouns |
|---|---|---|
| go up | *(rise)/rose/(risen)* | *an increase, a(n) ... upward trend* |
| go down | — | *a ... fall, a drop, decrease* |
| no change | *was ... (constant)* | — |

e]

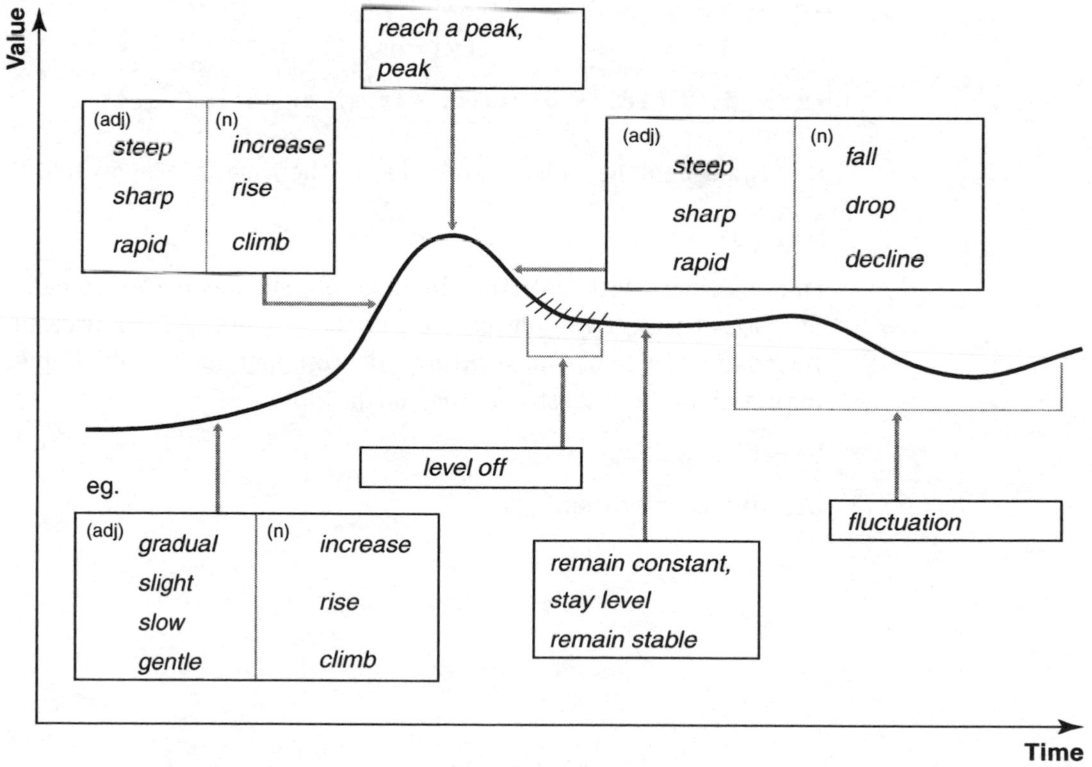


Other language that can be quite useful here is that of comparing and contrasting (see Students' Book, Unit 2, page 48; Unit 3, pages 66–69 and Unit 8, page 178).

## Task C: Common mistakes to avoid

SB P.244

These are so common that it is worthwhile covering them before writing. They are typical mistakes of meaning.

### Answers and comments

1 'Fell down' is also often used in this way. However, only physical objects, people, animals etc, can fall down or drop down; numbers and percentages can't.

2 Though the percentage increased in this time, we have no information about the actual number. If the total population of the country increased significantly in this time, there may have been fewer people of European origin in 2002 than 1982, even with an increase in proportion. It is extremely important not to get mixed up between straight numbers and percentages or proportions.

3 Though it's easy to infer the meaning here, this does create a strange impression ... did the Govindians from Africa get fatter? Did they take the growing potion from *Alice in Wonderland*? It's important that students are able to differentiate in their writing between nominal groups representing people (eg 'Australians', 'migrants from Europe') and nominal groups representing numbers (eg 'the number of people with dyed hair') and percentages or proportions (eg 'the proportion of Govindians from Africa').

## Task D: Writing to describe numerical information

SB P.244

When peer review, as in Questions 2 to 4, is done, it's particularly important that the teacher is on hand to give reassurance where necessary.

This task could be done after Task E. This would enable students to incorporate language they found while doing Task E into their own writing.

## Task E: Reading descriptions of numerical data

SB P.244

This could be done as homework, due to the time it takes to find this information.

### Extension:

**1** Find a website with statistical information, such as the Australian Bureau of Statistics (http://www.abs.gov.au), or the University of Pennsylvania's Center for International Comparisons (http://ptt.econ.upenn.edu), which gives statistical information about most countries of the world.

**2** Select some data.

**3** Describe it in writing.

# English for the Internet Age

## How does and will the Internet affect you, as a student?

The *purpose* of this section is for students to:

- discover an old way to research for assignments and compare/contrast with modern ways;
- review the writing of explanations;
- discuss the effect of the internet on their future field of study.

### Task A: Comparing a student from the past with the present

SB P.244

Students read the text which is an explanation of how a student in the early 1900s might have researched, prepared, written and submitted his assignment at University.

### Task B: Write an explanation of you as a modern day student

SB P.245

Students use the fields they focused on in Task A (research, preparation, writing and submission of assignments) to write their own explanation.

### Task C: Discussion around your future field of study

SB P.246

Students may discuss the possible use of the Internet using the questions in the Students' Book.

# Learner independence & study skills

## End of course: friendship, compliments!

### Task A: Compliments activity

SB P.246

**Teacher:** You and your students might have an end of course friendship party. They can use the grid for making comments about one another, as explained in the Students' Book. If your institution allows, you might have everyone make a contribution and order food to be delivered to your classroom, or you might suggest that the students bring a plate and share food. Put some music on and enjoy each other's company after all the hard work put into preparing for tertiary study in English. Alternatively, you may want to hold the activity outside the college, for instance, in a park or a coffee shop.

SB▷

1 Write your name in the box at the top of the diagram. Write the other students' names in the other boxes.

2 Pass it around the class. Each time you receive another book, write against your name, comments about the book's owner, such as:

- A compliment for that person. This can be anything, for example 'You had a great sense of humour,'; 'I was impressed by your determination.'
- What you learned from that person during the course, for example, 'I learned from you that determination is very important'; 'You demonstrated that a sense of humour makes academic study more fun and motivating.'

3 When you receive your book back, you can keep the grid and comments as a memento of your classmates—your fellow travellers on the EAP journey you have just completed.

This activity can be very helpful in cementing relationships developed during the course. However, it won't work with every class – if your instinct says it will just cause embarrassment, follow your instinct!! Instead, see the *Alternative activities* section below.

If you do decide to use this activity, and the class has more than, or significantly less than, sixteen students, it may be better to draw a more appropriately-sized grid on the board, and ask students to copy it onto a piece of paper. Alternatively, a circle divided into one less sector than there are students, with a circle in the middle for the name of the student drawing the diagram, also works well.

### Alternative activities

1 Students write comments about the class and their experiences in it on a large piece of paper, which is then photocopied and distributed to all students.

2 Divide the class into groups. Each group has the task of deciding awards for students in another group—for example, 'the chef's award for person who brought the best lunches'. When all groups are ready, the results are given to the class. This can be done as ceremonially as imagination and circumstances allow.

# Appendix A—Correction codes

| Symbol | Kind of error | Example | Correct sentence |
|---|---|---|---|
| c | capitalisation | c<br>I went to england, once. | I went to England, once. |
| P | punctuation | P<br>She said, yes, that's right. | She said, 'yes, that's right'. |
| // | new paragraph | // (start a new paragraph) | |
| S | spelling | S<br>My freind is here. | My friend is here. |
| PS | word form (part of speech) | PS<br>She was hope. | She was hopeful. |
| o | plural/singular mistake | I have three sister° | I have three sisters. |
| # | subject-verb agreement | #<br>She like swimming. | She likes swimming. |
| T | verb tense mistake | T<br>Last week I <u>have</u> a great party. | Last week I had a great party. |
| [ ] | delete (erase) | I'm going [to] shopping tonight | I'm going shopping tonight. |
| ↑ | add a word | They are my house.<br>↑ | They are (coming to) (going to visit) my house. |
| W | wrong word | W<br>Turn write at the corner. | Turn right at the corner. |
| A | wrong or omitted article | A<br>We're studying good book. | We're studying a good book. |
|  | reverse word order | That was a movie long. | That was a long movie. |
|  | word order mistake | I <u>you</u> <u>see will</u>. | I will see you. |
| / | separate these words (new sentence) | They'll eat dinner/ they'll go home. | They'll eat dinner. Then they'll go home. |
|  | should be one word (combine sentences) | There was rubbish every where | There was rubbish everywhere. |
|  | rewrite (meaning unclear) | I very often trying new. | I often try new things. |

# Appendix B—Information gap activities

This appendix is reproduced here from the Students' Book for the teacher's convenience.

## Unit 3: Graph I—Retention versus time without review

This is how much is remembered as time passes after a lesson if no reviewing is done. To see what happens if reviewing is carried out regularly, see Graph II on page 237.

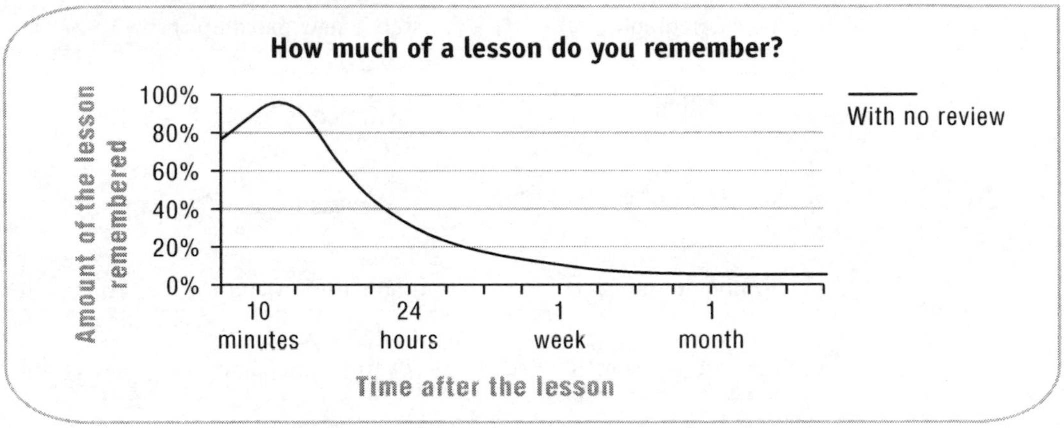


*Source:* Adapted from Tony Buzan (1995) *Use Your Head*, 4th ed, BBC Books, London, p. 65.

## Unit 7: Role play

### Student A's parts (Lecturers)

The following are the prompts for the student-lecturer role play

**7.1** (Lecturer role) **How to apply for a further degree?**
→ Must obtain a distinction or high distinction in current studies.
→ Must have reference from your tutor to say your work is of sufficient academic standard—I'll be happy to give you one!
→ Fill in Further Studies Application Form.
→ Submit to department office. Deadline: 23 December.

**7.2** (Lecturer role) **Advice—problems at home, worried about assignment deadlines**
→ Fill in 'Genuine Reason for Extension of Deadline' form.
→ Explain problem to counselling service—someone will sign the form for you.
→ Give a copy to each of your lecturers.

---

**7.3** (Student role)
You feel you are falling behind in your studies. Other students have finished their first assignment of the term, but you've hardly started. Ask for advice from your lecturer.

**7.4** (Student role)
You need a particular piece of equipment to carry out your research. You have heard that if you get your lecturer's permission, you can buy it and the university will pay. Ask for permission from your lecturer.

## Unit 9: Conclusion to essay

8 In conclusion, it is clear that there would be great economic benefit for English speaking countries if they improved the ability of their population to speak other languages. It is also clear that this has to be done from the earliest levels of primary school, and that this requires significant investment. Investment is also needed in campaigns to promote and increase the prestige and intrinsic interest of language learning. It would be beneficial therefore if these changes were set into motion as soon as possible.

**References**

Crystal, D (1997) *English as a Global Language.* Cambridge: Cambridge University Press.

Kramsch, C (1998) *Language and Culture.* Oxford: Oxford University Press.

Saunders, G (1988) *Bilingual Children: Guidance for the Family.* Clevedon: Multilingual Matters.

## Unit 3: Graph II — Retention versus time when reviewing

This graph shows what happens when review is carried out at regular intervals.

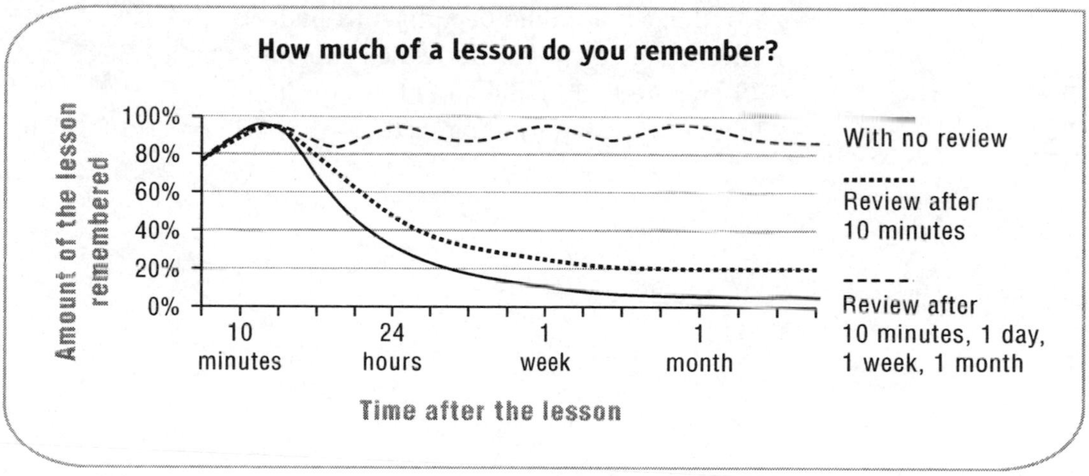


*Source:* Adapted from Tony Buzan (1995) *Use Your Head*, 4th ed, BBC Books, London, p. 65.

## Unit 7: Student B's parts (Students)

The following are prompts for the student–lecturer role play.

**7.1** (Student role)
You want to apply for a further degree in the department you're studying in now. Find out from your lecturer how to do this.

**7.2** (Student role)
You have urgent family problems in your own country and dealing with them will make your assignments very late. Find out from your lecturer what you can do.

---

**7.3** (Lecturer role) **Advice—study problems**

→ I understand the problem—it affects many first year students.
→ Thank you for letting me know before it's too late.
→ The academic advice service can provide excellent advice and help.
→ It's on the third floor of the Collingwood building, which is on South Road, on the left about ten minutes' walk past the university library.
→ There's also an English language support service available if you want to make use of that.

**7.4** (Lecturer role) **Permission for equipment purchase**

→ Yes, that's within the department's budget.
→ I need to give you a letter which explains why it is necessary.
→ I'll prepare that by the end of the week.
→ Take it to the requisitions section—they will order it for you.

# Appendix C—Assessment sheets: Oral presentation and essay

## Oral presentation observation sheet 1: content

Write notes, not sentences!

**Introduction**

**Background**

**Definitions**

**Thesis/discussion point**

**Main points to be covered (preview/scope)**

**Body**

**Main point 1**
Support

**Main point 2**
Support

M
o
r
e

s
u
p
p
o
r
t
e
d

i
d
e
a
s

Continued ...

**Conclusion**

**Summary**

**Recommendation**

**Question time**

**Question 1**

**Answer**

**Question 2**

**Answer**

More questions

After the presentation:

- Were the main ideas in the preview/scope, body and summary the same?

  ______________________________

- Comment on the strength of support for the opinions expressed.

  ______________________________

- Were there sufficient references?

  ______________________________

- Did the talk sound well researched?

  ______________________________

- Were ideas from the literature questioned and analysed (critical analysis)?

  ______________________________

- Write down the most interesting things you leaned about the topic of this presentation.

  ______________________________

  ______________________________

# Oral presentation observation sheet 2: techniques

## Signposting

| Stage | Function | **Signposting expressions used** (X = none used) |
|---|---|---|
| **Definitions** | To define | |
| **Thesis/ discussion point** | To give opinion(s) | |
| **Preview/ scope** | To introduce preview/scope | |
| **Body** | To move on to new main idea | |
| | To move on to a new supporting idea | |
| **Conclusion** | To summarise | |
| | To recommend | |
| | To give sources | |

## Presentation techniques

Start time: ______________________ Finish time: ______________________

| Technique | Notes |
|---|---|
| Use of visual aids | What used?<br><br>Comments |
| Gestures, eye contact etc | Eye contact with all sections of the audience?<br>Other paralinguistic features used?<br><br>Comments |
| Involvement of audience | How?<br><br>Comments |
| Voice and clarity of expression | Comments |
| Timing | Comments |

After the presentation:

- What techniques did the presenter use most effectively?

_______________________________________________

_______________________________________________

- With which techniques is there room for improvement?

_______________________________________________

_______________________________________________

## Oral presentation observation sheet 3: outcomes

| Outcome/competency | Achieved? (Yes or No) |
|---|---|
| Can provide appropriate background and context | |
| Can define technical terms used | |
| Can clearly give thesis/discussion point | |
| Can give preview and scope of talk near beginning | |
| Can clearly state main points of the talk | |
| Can provide adequate support | |
| Can summarise the talk | |
| Can give recommendations based on ideas mentioned | |
| Can deal adequately with audience's questions | |
| Can ensure overall coherence to the talk | |
| Can argue logically | |
| Can sustain an argument throughout the talk | |
| Can critically analyse the issue | |
| Can research a topic using library resources | |
| Can provide clear signposting throughout | |
| Can use a visual aid effectively | |
| Can use appropriate paralinguistic features, such as gestures and eye contact | |
| Can involve the audience, eg by asking questions | |
| Can express ideas clearly and audibly | |
| Can present within a time limit | |

# Extended essay assignment cover sheet

## Assignment Cover Sheet

**Student's name** Family .................................... Given ....................................

**Assignment title**

Class/course ....................................................................

Date due .................................................................... Date submitted ..............................

I hereby declare that:

i] this work is entirely my own.

ii] all sources used in the preparation of this assignment are fully referenced.

iii] no part of this work has been submitted for assessment in any other course of study.

Date: ______________________________ Signature: ______________________________

**ASSESSMENT:**

| AREA | GRADE |
|---|---|
| Clear argument | |
| Strong support | |
| Appropriate staging throughout | |
| Key concepts and terms defined | |
| Evidence of extensive library research | |
| Critical analysis | |
| Full and appropriate in-text referencing | |
| Full reference list | |
| Vocabulary (use, register and variety) | |
| Sentence structure (accuracy and variety) | |

**General comments** (continue on other side if necessary):

______________________________________________________________________

______________________________________________________________________

**Final grade** **Teacher's signature:** ______________________________

# Appendix D—IELTS Grid: Preparation tasks for IELTS Academic module: Answers and Explanations

## What is IELTS?

IELTS is the acronym for International English Language Testing System. There are two types of IELTS tests, the General and the Academic. This book deals with the Academic. IELTS is a measure of English language proficiency in the four skills of Reading, Writing, Speaking and Listening. The total test time is 2 hours and 45 minutes. It is divided as follows:

Reading—three sections (three reading passages) with 40 questions over 60 minutes.

Writing—two tasks, one of 150 words and one of 250 words over 60 minutes.

Speaking—three sections. The whole takes 12 to 15 minutes. You speak one on one with the examiner.

Listening—four sections with 40 questions over 30 minutes (+ 10 minutes for transferring answers to an answer sheet).

## Rationale

The IELTS practice exercises have been designed for students to utilise the existing work within units in *EAP Now!* using a progressive approach. Within this approach, students are often asked to construct questions based on work they have read or thought about. Students are expected to move backwards and forwards within texts and activities constructing understanding of texts through a process of deconstruction. The pedagogy here is one of access for the students—access to the question types they will encounter, and access to the thinking behind the creation of those questions. The experience of formulating the test themselves wherever possible, based upon the provided texts or tasks, under the direction and guidance of their teacher should empower students to gain a real understanding of what they must do within the genre. Further, the IELTS test itself *is* a genre—an examination genre. It also serves as a gate keeping test. Students must gain a certain mark in order to study at many higher learning institutions where the medium of instruction is English. This mark is determined by the institution, and varies.

## Quick reference table

Below the table, in unit order, are instructions on how to use activities in the book as preparation for the IELTS test, together with explanations and answers.

| Part of IELTS test | Location in the Students' Book |
|---|---|
| Listening | Unit 7, page 156, Tasks A and B<br>Unit 9, page 204, Task B |
| Reading | Unit 1, page 28, Task A<br>Unit 3, page 62, Task B<br>Unit 5, page 117<br>Unit 6, page 152, Task A and B |

| Part of IELTS test | Where it is practised in the Students' Book |
|---|---|
| Writing Task 1 | Task 1, Unit 4, page 102, Task A<br>Unit 10, page 240, Tasks A to D |
| Writing Task 2 | Unit 2, page 46, Task E<br>Unit 3, page 75, Tasks A and B |
| Speaking: all parts | Unit 8, page 178, Tasks A–D |
| Speaking part 2 | Unit 1, page 2, Task A |
| Speaking part 3 | Unit 2, page 36, Task A |

# Answers and Explanations in Unit order

## Unit 1, page 2 (SB), Task A: Speaking/Discussion—Exploration of previous education system

## Unit 1, page 2 (TB)

## Time: 2 minutes plus 1 minute preparation

Students work in pairs and time one another during an unsupported speaking task. One student must speak on the topic for two minutes without any dialogue between the two. In this section of the speaking test the examiner may be busy writing down things or flipping pages or simply not making much eye contact with the candidate. The examiner is not allowed to speak in this section so the student needs to become accustomed to delivering a monologue which answers the question before her/him.

## Unit 1, page 28 (SB), Task A: English for the Internet Age/Identifying stages in an explanation essay and skimming—further practice

## Unit 1, pages 23–24 (TB)

## Time: 10 minutes

Students follow the instructions in the IELTS grid, skimming for main ideas and matching main ideas to paragraphs. Direct students to read the questions prior to reading the text, read the first (short) paragraph to get an idea of the main point of the text, and then read mainly topic sentences to achieve their aim. They should only read paragraphs in detail in cases where they have identified two or more possible topics for one paragraph. The time allowed should be 10 minutes.

**Answers:**

1. iv 2. iii 3. vi 4. i 5. v 6. ii

## Unit 2, page 36 (SB), Task A: Speaking/Orientation discussion

## Unit 2, page 30 (TB)

### Time: 5 minutes

Students work in pairs and time one another. This is similar to the final stage of the speaking test. The examiner and the candidate speak together a little. The examiner still asks the questions, however. So students may practice asking each other the questions from the sheet. They should think about the future and speculate on future events. They should make comparisons.

## Unit 2, page 46 (SB), Task E: Writing and Reading/Writing an argument essay

## Unit 2, page 40 (TB)

### Time: 40 minutes

The work in *EAP Now!* focuses upon the introductory and concluding stages of an argument essay. IELTS Writing Task 2 can be an argument essay. Students should complete tasks A through D before attempting this essay. As a reference for teacher or peer checking and marking of essays – use 'An essay genre overview' from (Teacher's Book, page 209 or Student's Book, page 226) and the 'Extended essay assignment cover sheet' (Appendix C) on (Teacher's Book, page 244 or Student's Book, page 257) (eliminating referencing and library research which do not apply to IELTS).

## Unit 3, page 62 (SB), Task B: Reading/example discussion essay

## Unit 3, page 60 (TB)

### Time: 40 minutes (20 minutes to create questions—20 minutes for answering questions)

There are two parts to this task. In the first, students work from inside the text to create 12 questions which require no more than three words in the answers. This is a common constraint within IELTS in both the reading and listening sections. Second, they draw a box and insert the words from the grid. Then, they complete the summary from the same model essay, 'Genetically modified foods'. Once students have written their questions, give them 20 minutes to complete both tasks.

## Unit 3, page 75 (SB), Tasks A–B: Writing 3/Analysing questions—which genre?

## Unit 3, page 70 (TB)

### Time: 40 minutes

The primary purpose of this essay writing practice which pertains to Academic Writing Task 2 in the IELTS examination is for students to address the question according to the instructions within whichever question they select. In other words, they must explain, argue or discuss depending upon their choice of question. Using the key words within each question from Task A: 'Analysing questions – which genre', refer to the table (page 209, Teacher's Book) which provides 'An essay genre overview' in order to mark or check their essays.

### Unit 4, page 102 (SB), Task A: Learner Independence and Study Skills/Time management—Examining your use of time

### Unit 4, page 89 (TB)

### Time: 20 minutes

Students truthfully design their own timetable based upon a real week in their lives. Writing an explanation and description of what that timetable contains will give them practice in comparisons and writing in the third person. This is useful for both writing tasks in IELTS, but the genre for this task corresponds most closely to Writing Task 1. Ask them to refer to themselves as 'the student in this table' in their written description of the information contained within the table.

### Unit 5, page 117 (SB), Grammar/Tense Review: Perfect tenses Text 1: Narrative of the most extraordinary and distressing shipwreck of the whaleship Essex by Captain Owen Chase, 1821

### Unit 5, page 100 (TB), reading text in SB only

### Time: 10 minutes

#### Answers:

1. G 2. F 3. C 4. D 5. B 6. B 7. A 8. E

Locating information within a certain paragraph is a feature of the IELTS reading test. Information may be similar between paragraphs, so reading each statement of information carefully and matching it to the correct paragraph is a skill to be practised. You might devise many more exercises based on this type of question from readings that you and/or the class choose. The format of numbering down the page and matching the correct letter from a paragraph to the number on a separate answer sheet should be followed.

### Unit 6, page 152 (SB), Task B: Reading/Title: Waste disposal in Asia

### Unit 6, page 132 (TB) reading text in SB only

### Time: 60 minutes (30 minutes to formulate questions—30 minutes to answer questions)

This task will assist students to understand differing question types used within the reading section of IELTS. True and False questions will be familiar to them. Answers such as: *Information given, not given, yes or no* (in terms of whether a statement agrees with the author's opinion or not) may be new to them.

Students must work from inside to outside and forwards and backwards within the text in order to understand meaning and to create question types. They must use inductive reasoning based on their experience of the text to create the statements which are used as a distinct question type.

## Unit 7, page 156 (SB), Tasks A–B: Listening and Speaking 1/ Academic requests and replies 2—Recording number 10

## Unit 7, pages 137 (TB)

## Time: 12 minutes

Students follow instructions as per Tasks A and B. They then answer the three questions within the grid.

**Answers:**

1. B 2. A 3. C

## Unit 8, page 178 (SB), Tasks A–D: Reading and Writing/ Title: Economics and Governments: who calls the shots?

## Unit 8, page 160 (TB)

## Time: 60 minutes

This is a speaking task based upon the reading above. The goals are accuracy and fluency. Students work in pairs asking and answering the questions provided. While answering the questions, the students practise for all parts of the speaking test, but Part 3 is more likely than the others to focus on this relatively abstract topic. The teacher's role is one of facilitator and monitor. Monitor the students' ability in using the following skills in their speaking: paraphrasing; expressing comparison and contrast; grammatical accuracy and pronunciation. By circulating around the room and tuning into different student pairs, you can work with individual students to make corrections. If trust has been established in the classroom, students may also monitor and correct each other.

## Unit 9, page 204 (SB), Task B: Listening, Speaking and Critical Thinking/Listening for main ideas: Recording number 13

## Unit 9, page 187 (TB)

## Time: 8 minutes

Give students 30 seconds to read the instructions in Task B on pages 204 and 205 in the Students' Book. Students listen to Recording 13 (6 minutes, 6 seconds), marking the main ideas while they listen. The skill practised here is to learn to listen for and read main ideas simultaneously. After the end of the recording, give students 30 seconds to check their answers. Check answers without playing the recording a second time.

**Answers:**

1. A 2. D 3. G 4. E (any order is acceptable)

## Unit 10, page 240 (SB), Tasks A-D: Writing and Reading: Interpreting and describing information from charts and graphs (Fig. 10.1)

## Unit 10, page 230 (TB)

## Time: 20 minutes

Students must describe the information from a bar chart. They need to write 150 words. There are 3 models below, marked between 0 to 9 to give an approximate indication of band scores. All answers are the required length. Note that if a student does not write the full 150 words, they will be penalised. Task 1 is worth less than Task 2 as this text type is considered less linguistically demanding. Answers must include statistical data (both year and country) and students have to demonstrate that they can manage the grammar that describes the picture, graph, chart or other diagrammatic information. Note that approximate scores in the example answers below are authors' opinions only. They are to assist you to find a band range for your students' answers and are based upon Fig. 10.1, Students' Book, page 240.

*Question: The chart shows the percentage of citizens of Govindia by region of birth from 1982 to 2002, as well as projections for 2007. Describe the information found in the chart. Write for a university lecturer. You must write a minimum of 150 words.*

**Model 1—Approximate band score – IELTS equivalent – 7**

*The bar chart is about the region of birth of Govindian citizens, at ten year intervals from 1982 to 2002, and also projections for 2007.*

*The place where the biggest proportion of Govindians came from during the whole of the period was Africa. Overall, the proportion increased steadily, from just over 7% in 1982 to just over 8% in 2002 with a forecast of 9% in 2007. However, there was a dip in 1992 to nearly 6%.*

*The most significant change was in the percentage of Govindians from Asia. In 1982, they represented less than 3.5% of the population, but this rose throughout the period to around 6.5% in 2002. An increase to 7% is expected by 2007, which indicates it has doubled in 25 years.*

*The proportion from Europe stayed relatively constant during the period. In 1982, just over 3% of Govindians were born in Europe, and this figure rose every year, was still expected to end the period at less that 3.5%.*

*The proportion of Govindians born in other regions of the world fluctuated between 2.5% and 3.5%. The others projection for 2007 are expected to make up 9%. The second largest group is Asia for each year shown. Europe was the third largest group in 1992 and 2002 but made up only 3% in 1982.*

**Model 2—Approximate band score – IELTS equivalent – 6**

The information in the bar chart shows the region by birth of Govindia's citizens from 1982 to 2002 and projection for 2007.

According to the chart, most of Govindians come from Africa. Next is Asia and then Europe. However, most importantly citizens from Asian in 1982 were around 7% then in 1992 they dropped down to about 6% whereas in 2002 it equalled 8% and the projection was 9% for 2007. The percentage of citizens from Asia is second after Africa.

During the period of 1982–2003 Europe percentages were similar. In 1982 the percentage of Europe's citizens by region of birth in Govindia was a little bit more than 3%. This increase a little each year but for 2007 it was projected at 3.5%. This is still only a small percentage.

The Others – people from other regions not Africa, Asia or Europe changed each year. It grew from 2.5% to 3.5% and in 2007 it is actually 9%.

Africa increased each year except for 1992 when it fell down to almost 6% from being 7% in 1982 and 8% in 2002.

**Model 3—Approximate band score – IELTS equivalent – 5 (under length script)**

(do not count the first sentence as it repeats the words from the question)

The bar chart shows citizen of Govindia by region of birth, 1982–2002 and projection for 2007.

In 1982 Europe was 3.1%, Africa 7½%, Asia higher 4% and other, including the Americas, Oceania and the Pacific was around 3½%.

Then in 1992 Europe is a little up, around 3.2% but Africa is less with 5.8% citizen.

Africa is the most percent every year and other is smallest except 1982. In this year it was Europe. Projected is Europe 3.2%, Africa 9%, Asia 7%, others 2½% in 2007.

The region of birth in 1992 and 2002 are different because of Africa and Asia. But Europe and others are almost same.

Europe 3.1% and 3.2% and others equalled 3% in 2002 a little more than 1992 was about 2.9%. But Europe was almost same all the time.

*While these are estimates based upon our experience of teaching students who have taken the IELTS test, they do not represent any official IELTS scores and serve as approximate equivalents only.*

# References


BBC (2001) Secondary Schools, BBC News. http://news.bbc.co.uk/hi/english/education/uk_systems/newsid_115000/115872.stm (6 May 2002).

Billington R & Stanford P (1988) *Child Workers Around the World.* London: Fount.

Brown, K (1999) *Developing Critical Literacy.* Sydney: Macquarie University (NCELTR).

Burns, RB (1994) *Introduction to Research Methods.* Melbourne: Longman Cheshire, p 2.

Butt, D, Fahey, R, Feez, S, Spinks S, & Yallop, C (2000) *Using Functional Grammar: An Explorer's Guide* (2nd ed). Sydney: Macquarie University (NCELTR).

Buzan, T (1995) *Use your head* (4th Ed). London: BBC Books.

Campbell, C (1997) *The coming oil crisis.* Brentwood, Essex: Multi-science Publishing.

Columbia University Press (1998) Basic CGOS Style *About the Columbia Guide to Online Style.* http://www.columbia.edu/cu/cup/cgos/idx_basic.html

Commonwealth of Australia (2002) Australian way of studying, *Study in Australia.* http://studyinaustralia.gov.au/Contents/WhatToStudy/AustStudy.html (21 April 2002).

Cox, K (1994) 'Tertiary Level Writing by Magic—Presto! Nominalisation'. *EA Journal* 12/1, Autumn 1994.

Cox, K & Eyre, J (1999) 'A Question of Correction'. *English Teaching Professional* 12.

Cox, K (2000) *Changing Cultures, Changing English.* Paper presented at the 13th EA Educational Conference, Fremantle.

Crystal, D (1997) *English as a Global Language.* Cambridge: Cambridge University Press.

Crystal, D (2000) *Language Death.* Cambridge: Cambridge University Press.

Derewianka, B (1990) *Exploring How Texts Work.* Sydney: Primary English Teaching Association.

DETYA (2000) Australia Country Education Profile, 3rd Edition On-line. Canberra: DETYA. http://www.detya.gov.au/noosr/cep/australia/index.htm (21 April 2002).

Fairclough, N (1992) *Discourse and Social Change.* Cambridge: Polity Press.

Feez, S (1998) *Text Based Syllabus Design.* Sydney: Macquarie University (NCELTR).

Fischer, S (2001) Asia and the IMF: Remarks at the Institute of Policy Studies. *IMF News.* http://www.imf.org/external/np/speeches/2001/060101.htm

Fulbright Commission (2001) *School Education in the USA.* http://www.fullbright.com.uk/eas/school/school.htm (12 May 2002).

George, S. (1990) *A Fate Worse than Debt.* London: Penguin.

Ghuma, K (2001) 'It's Not Just Watcha Say'. *IATEFL Issues* 161: 11–12.

Gibran, K (1990) *Spiritual Sayings of Kahlil Gibran.* A Ferris (ed and translator), New York: Carol.

Halliday, MAK & Hasan R (1989) *Language, Context and Text: Aspects of Language in a Social-Semiotic Perspective.* Melbourne: Deakin University Press.

Halliday, MAK (1985) *An Introduction to Systemic Functional Grammar*. London: Edward Arnold.

Harmer, J (1991) *The Practice of English Language Teaching* (2nd ed). Essex: Longman.

Haycraft, J (1986) *An Introduction to English Language Teaching* (revised impression ed.). Harlow: Longman.

Hoey, M (1997) *How Can Text Analysis Help Us Teach Reading?* Paper presented at the IATEFL conference, Brighton, England April 1997.

Janks, H (1993) *Language, Identity and Power.* Johannesburg: Hodder & Stoughton.

Kaplan, RB (1966) 'Cultural Thought Patterns in Inter-Cultural Education'. *Language Learning* 16: 1–20.

Kaplan, RB (1993) 'TESOL and applied linguistics in North America'. In S Silberstein (ed) *State of the art TESOL essays*. Alexandria, VA: TESOL Inc.

Kenworthy, J (1987) *Teaching English Pronunciation*. Essex: Longman.

King, S (2000) *On Writing, A Memoir of the Craft*. London: Hodder and Stoughton.

Kramsch, C (1998) *Language and Culture*. Oxford: Oxford University Press.

Kress, G. (1993) Genre as social process in The powers of Literacy (eds) Cope, B and Kalantzis, M. Falmer Press, London p 36.

Lambert, T & Barreto, L (2001) *UTS Students' Association Postgraduate Handbook 2001*. Sydney: UTS Students' Association.

Larsen-Freeman, D (2000) *Techniques and Principles in Language Teaching*. Oxford: Oxford University Press.

Lewis, M (1993) *The Lexical Approach: The State of ELT and a Way Forward*. Hove: Language Teaching Publications.

Lewis, M (1997) *Implementing the Lexical Approach: Putting Theory into Practice*. Hove: Language Teaching Publications.

McCarthy, M (1990) *Vocabulary*. Oxford: Oxford University Press.

*Macquarie Dictionary* 2nd ed. (1991) Macquarie Library.

Malouf, D (2002). 'A great escape'. *The Age*, 31 August.

Martin, JR (1991) 'Nominalisation in science and humanities: Distilling knowledge and scaffolding text'. In Ventola E (ed), *Functional and systematic linguistics: approaches and uses*. Berlin; New York: Mouton de Gruyter.

Modjeska, D (2002) 'The fictional present', *The Age*, 31 August.

Moore, M (2001) *Stupid White Men ... and other sorry excuses for the state of the nation*. New York: Harper Collins, p 204.

Nunan, D (1991) 'An Empirically Based Methodology for the Nineties'. In Arivan, S (ed) *Language Teaching Methodology for the Nineties*. RELC, p 78.

Nunan, D (1992) *Research Methods in Language Learning*. Cambridge: Cambridge University Press.

Oshima, A & Hogue A (1991) *Writing Academic English* (2nd ed). California: Addison-Wesley.

Oxford University Press (2000) *Oxford Advanced Learner's Dictionary* (6th ed). Oxford: Oxford University Press.

Phillipson, R (1992) Lingustic Imperialisation. Oxford: Oxford University Press.

Pilger, J (1989) *A Secret Country.* London: Vintage Press.

Powers, J (1997) *Ancient Greek Marriage.* MA thesis, Tufts University. http://www.pogodesigns.com/JP/weddings/greekwed.html (25th November 2002)

Rubin, J (1994) 'Review of Second Language Listening Comprehension Research', *The Modern Language Journal 78*/ii: 199–221.

Saunders, G (1988) *Bilingual Children: Guidance for the Family.* Clevedon: Multilingual Matters.

Schlosser, E (2001) *Fast Food Nation: What the All-American Meal is Doing to the World.* London: Penguin.

SIL International (2001) Languages of Vanuatu. *Ethnologue: Languages of the World (14th ed).* http://www.ethnologue.com/show_country.asp?name=Vanuatu (11 August 2002).

*South Asian Voice* (2000) Unrestricted globalisation—boon or hazard? *South Asian Voice: Views from South Asia.* http://members.tripod.com/~India_Resource/globalization.html (17 September, 2002)

Superville, D (2001) Many world languages on brink of extinction, UN says. Global Policy. www.globalpolicy.org/globaliz/cultural/2001/0619language.htm (11 August 2002).

Swan, M & Smith B (eds). (2001) *Learner English: A Teacher's Guide to Interference and Other Problems* (2nd ed). Cambridge: Cambridge University Press.

The US-UK Fulbright Commission (1999) School Education in the US. *The US-UK Fulbright Commission.* http://www.fulbright.co.uk/eas/school/school.html (12 May 2002).

Underhill, A (1994) *Sound Foundations.* Oxford: Heinemann.

UNEP (2000) *Global Environmental Outlook 2000: UNEP's Millennium Report on the Environment.* London: Earthscan Publications.

UTS Equity & Diversity Unit (no date given) Preventing discrimination and harassment. *UTS Equity & Diversity Unit.* http://www.uts.edu.au/div/eounit/unit/discrim.html (25 August 2002).

Weller, C Scott RE & Hersh A (2001) The unremarkable record of liberalised trade after 20 years of global economic deregulation, poverty and inequality are as pervasive as ever. *EPI Briefing Paper* (October 2001) http://epinet.org/briefingpapers/sept01inequality.html

Wolpert, E. (1984). *Understanding Research in Education - an introductory guide to critical reading.* USA: Kendall/Hunt, p 113.

# index


- 'a' (indefinite article) 192–193
- abstracts 225–226
- academic requests 2, 137–142
- academic writing 169–174
- addition discourse markers 42–43, 63, 64
- agriculture, mechanisation 60–62
- 'an' (indefinite article) 192–193
- *Aqua Blue Surfgear International* 168
- argument essays 7, 37–40, 208–209
  - differentiating between main and supporting ideas 43
  - differentiating between weak and strong evidence 44–45
  - predicting content 37
  - providing supporting evidence 45
  - stages 37
- art, Korean 50
- articles
  - definite 51–52, 192–193
  - indefinite 192–193
- assignment research skills 114

- *Bangkok ferries* 229
- bias, identifying 110
- bibliographies, compiling 97–99, 114
- books, taking notes from 81–82
- brainstorming 40
- business and environment, tutorial 121–125

- campus vocabulary 136–137
- *Capital punishment* 229
- cause and effect 75–76, 165
- certainty, expressing 213–215
- charts 230–232
- cohesion, writing 19–20, 42, 62–63, 73
- collocation 55–56
- colloquialisms 4
- compare and contrast essays 160
- compliments activity 233
- computer presentations 127–129
- conclusions 229, 237
- conditionals (verbs) 155–156
- constructive criticism 148–149
- contrast discourse markers 42–43, 63, 64
- correction codes 53, 235
- cosmology 50
- creative writing 74–75
- criticism, constructive 148–149
- cross-cultural communication 215–223
- cross references 28
- cues *See* discourse markers

- deduction discourse markers 63, 65
- disability, requesting dispensation for 138
- discourse markers 21
  - addition 42–43, 63, 64
  - cause and effect 75–76
  - contrast 42–43, 63, 64
  - deduction 63, 65
  - example 63, 65
  - function 63
  - grammar of 63–64
  - identifying 63
  - oral presentations 95–96
  - summation 63, 64
  - time 11, 19
  - turn-taking 88
  - using 65–66
- discrimination 145–147
- discussion essays 60, 68, 208–209
- discussions
  - accepting ideas 67–68
  - interrupting 67–68
  - rejecting ideas 67–68
  - suggesting ideas 67–68

- *Earth Summit 2002* 183
- *Economics—a global connection* 178–182
- *Economics and governments: who calls the shots?* 160–164
- editorials, newspaper 109–110
- education
  - issues in 158
  - purpose 150
- *Effects of global economics* 175, 178–182
- ellipsis 76–77
- essays
  - analysing essay questions 194–196
  - argument *See* argument essays
  - choosing genre 69–70, 208–209
  - compare and contrast 160
  - conclusion 39–40, 229
  - definition 8
  - discussions *See* discussion essays
  - explanation *See* explanation essays
  - exposition *See* exposition essays
  - extended *See* extended essays
  - introduction 11, 39–40
  - key phrases 9
  - outline 10
  - planning 7–10, 40–41, 43
  - types 9, 70
  - useful expressions 39–40
- example discourse markers 63, 65
- explanation essays 7, 8, 10, 12, 208–209
- exposition essays 7, 166–167, 196–199
- extended essays 157–158, 224–225, 244
- extension of time, requesting 2

- fact, distinguishing from opinion 105–108, 130–131
- faculty handbook, using 184
- families 30–31, 38–39
- *Families* 49–50
- *Fast food around the world* 105–107
- formal speech 4
- forms, asking for 139
- friendship activity 233
- *Funding for Education* (tutorial discussion) 152–153

- *Genetically modified food* 58–59
- genre, choosing 69–70
- global trade 174
- *Goin' down fighting* 83–87
- grammar, languages other than English 203–205
- graphs 230–232
- group projects 118–120

- harassment 145–147
- hypotheses 119
- hypothesising (verbs) 154–155

- IELTS 245–251
- implied meaning 199
- informal vocabulary 4
- informal writing 26
- injury, requesting dispensation for 138
- International English Language Testing System 245–251
- Internet 23–26
  - directories 193–194
  - evaluating information on 90–91
  - library catalogues, searching 126
  - referencing 99, 144
  - research project 113, 183
  - scanning for information 36
  - search engines 66
  - use to students 233
- interrupting discussions 67–68
- introductions
  - essays 11, 39–40
  - texts 227–228
- issue, defining 109

- judgment
  - definition 9
  - using text to make 145, 146

- key phrases, in essay questions 9

- language
  - persuasive 187–191
  - as power 112–113
- languages quiz 186
- learner independence 27
- learning, in home country 2
- learning styles 3
- leave of absence, requesting 138
- lectures
  - focus, identifying 46, 48
  - supporting ideas 47–48
- lexis (vocabulary) 114
- library catalogues, searching on Internet 126
- library orientation talk 21–23
- listening
  - interview with student 200–202
  - for main focus 121–122, 174–175, 200–202
  - for non-linguistic clues 82, 86–87
  - outside class 202–203
  - for pleasure 82
  - for reasons 57–59

- marking codes 53, 235
- meaning
  - implied 199
  - unpacking 172–174
  - using context 33–35
- *Mechanisation of agriculture* 60–62
- memory 69, 236, 237
- metaphors 166
- modality 213–215

- narratives
  - first person 102
  - third person 102
- *The New Student* 3–5
- news story 104
- newspaper editorials 109–110
- nominalisation 169–174, 176, 212–213
- note taking 46, 147
  - from book 81–82
  - from lecture 175, 216
- notes, reviewing 69, 236, 237
- noun groups 64
- numerical information 230–232

- opinion
  - choosing language to express 111–112
  - distinguishing from fact 105–108, 130–131
- opinions, editorial 109–110
- oral presentations 94–97
  - cover sheet 239–240
  - observation sheet 239–243
  - observing 149–150
  - peer marking 149–150
  - skills 142–143
  - visual aids 127–129
- *Our world is one place* 130
- overhead transparencies 127–129

- paragraphs
  - elements 12–16
  - formatting 12–16, 72–74
  - methods of development 73–74
- paraphrasing 131
- participant tracking 99–100, 103
- peer review 224–225
- personals, removing from writing 171–172

persuasion
cultural aspects 191
techniques 187–191
phrases, key, in essay questions 9
pilot surveys 119
poetry 74
political protest 223–224
poster session 203
precis 225–226
prediction 37
presentations *See* oral presentations
*Prime Minister supports higher university fees* 104
processes *See* verbs
projects
group 118–120
research 118–120
pronominal referencing 99–100

questionnaires 119
questions, asking, in tutorials 125

radio talk back program 105–107
re-mark, requesting 139
reading, outside class 120–121
reason and result 165–166
reasons, listening for 57–59
Reassessment Request Form 139
references, cross 28
references (bibliographies) 97–99, 114
referencing
from Internet 144
pronominal 99–100
refugees (Internet research project) 113
register (tone of language) 3, 26
academic 5, 210–212
news story 104
spoken 5–7
remembering notes 69, 236, 237
repetition of words, avoiding 62
reports
language features 118
research 116–118
requests, of academics 2, 137–142
research projects 118–120
research reports 116–118
research skills, assignment 114
result and reason 165–166
reviewing notes 69, 236, 237
rheme (concluding sentence) 13, 14
*'The road to diversity'* 197
role play 236, 238

*Saving languages* 187–190
scanning 31–33, 132, 176, 182
Internet 36
science, vocabulary 56–57
scientist, interview 58–59
search engines 66
sentence markers 19
sentences, support 13, 14
sequence markers 19
short answer questions 205
signals 21
similes 166
skimming 17, 23, 31–32, 132, 182
slides 127–129
*Social benefits of extended families* 38–39
speaking
different to writing 3, 5–7
in front of others 89
outside class 156
speculating (verbs) 154–155
speech
formal 4
informal 4
subject planning 139–140
substitution, word 76–77, 99–100
summaries 229
summation discourse markers 63, 64
support sentences 13, 14
surveys 119–120
synonyms 62

table of contents 27
taking notes 46, 81–82, 147, 175, 216
talk back radio program 105–107
technology
analysis of positive and negative aspects 68
vocabulary 56–57
temporal sequencers 19
tenses
for future predictions 133–134
past simple 118
perfect 100–103
present perfect 118
present simple 118
tests (IELTS) 245–251
texts
analysing cultural content 147
examining for differing viewpoints 145
types 78–80
'the' (definite article) 51–52, 192–193
theme 13, 14, 72
developing 74–75
identifying 17
thesis statement 7
time discourse markers 11, 19
time management 89–90
timetables 89–90
topic sentences 16–17, 72
tracking participants 99–100, 103
turn-taking language 88
tutorials 11–12
asking questions in 125
discussion techniques 151–154
turn-taking 88–89

university handbook, using 184
university word lists 114
unpacking meaning 172–174

verbs
changing to nouns 169–174
choosing tense 101
conditionals 155–156
to express future 133–134
hypothesising 154–155
reporting 131
speculating 154–155
visual aids 127–129
vocabulary
campus 136–137
informal 4
science 56–57
university word lists 114

*Whaleship Essex* 103
word lists, university 114
word repetition, avoiding 62
word substitution 76–77, 99–100
World Wide Web *See* Internet
writing
academic 169–174
creative 74–75
informal 26
purpose 110–111
styles 87
writers talk about 77